THE NEW MI

BONNIE WHEELER, *Series*

The New Middle Ages is a series dedicated to pluridisciplinary studies of medieval cultures, with particular emphasis on recuperating women's history and on feminist and gender analyses. This peer-reviewed series includes both scholarly monographs and essay collections.

PUBLISHED BY PALGRAVE:

Women in the Medieval Islamic World: Power, Patronage, and Piety
edited by Gavin R. G. Hambly

The Ethics of Nature in the Middle Ages: On Boccaccio's Poetaphysics
by Gregory B. Stone

Presence and Presentation: Women in the Chinese Literati Tradition
edited by Sherry J. Mou

The Lost Love Letters of Heloise and Abelard: Perceptions of Dialogue in Twelfth-Century France
by Constant J. Mews

Understanding Scholastic Thought with Foucault
by Philipp W. Rosemann

For Her Good Estate: The Life of Elizabeth de Burgh
by Frances A. Underhill

Constructions of Widowhood and Virginity in the Middle Ages
edited by Cindy L. Carlson and Angela Jane Weisl

Motherhood and Mothering in Anglo-Saxon England
by Mary Dockray-Miller

Listening to Heloise: The Voice of a Twelfth-Century Woman
edited by Bonnie Wheeler

The Postcolonial Middle Ages
edited by Jeffrey Jerome Cohen

Chaucer's Pardoner and Gender Theory: Bodies of Discourse
by Robert S. Sturges

Crossing the Bridge: Comparative Essays on Medieval European and Heian Japanese Women Writers
edited by Barbara Stevenson and Cynthia Ho

Engaging Words: The Culture of Reading in the Later Middle Ages
by Laurel Amtower

Robes and Honor: The Medieval World of Investiture
edited by Stewart Gordon

Representing Rape in Medieval and Early Modern Literature
edited by Elizabeth Robertson and Christine M. Rose

Same Sex Love and Desire among Women in the Middle Ages
edited by Francesca Canadé Sautman and Pamela Sheingorn

Sight and Embodiment in the Middle Ages: Ocular Desires
by Suzannah Biernoff

Listen, Daughter: The Speculum Virginum and the Formation of Religious Women in the Middle Ages
edited by Constant J. Mews

Science, the Singular, and the Question of Theology
by Richard A. Lee, Jr.

Gender in Debate from the Early Middle Ages to the Renaissance
edited by Thelma S. Fenster and Clare A. Lees

GEOFFREY CHAUCER HATH A BLOG

MEDIEVAL STUDIES AND NEW MEDIA

Brantley L. Bryant

with contributions by
Geoffrey "LeVostreGC" Chaucer,
Jeffrey Jerome Cohen,
John Gower,
Robert W. Hanning, and
Bonnie Wheeler

GEOFFREY CHAUCER HATH A BLOG
Copyright © Brantley L. Bryant, 2010.

First published in 2010 by
PALGRAVE MACMILLAN®
in the United States—a division of St. Martin's Press LLC,
175 Fifth Avenue, New York, NY 10010.

Where this book is distributed in the UK, Europe and the rest of the
world, this is by Palgrave Macmillan, a division of Macmillan Publishers
Limited, registered in England, company number 785998, of Houndmills,
Basingstoke, Hampshire RG21 6XS.

Palgrave Macmillan is the global academic imprint of the above companies
and has companies and representatives throughout the world.

Palgrave® and Macmillan® are registered trademarks in the United States,
the United Kingdom, Europe and other countries.

ISBN: 978-0-230-10507-2 (paperback)
ISBN: 978-0-230-10506-5 (hardcover)

Library of Congress Cataloging-in-Publication Data

Geoffrey Chaucer hath a blog : medieval studies and new media /
Brantley L. Bryant [editor].
    p. cm.—(The new Middle Ages)
Includes the key 2006–2009 postings from "Geoffrey Chaucer Hath a
Blog," a humor blog written in the voice of Chaucer in an
approximation of Middle English.
Includes bibliographical references.
ISBN 978-0-230-10507-2 (pbk. : alk. paper)—
ISBN 978-0-230-10506-5 (paper over boards : alk. paper)
1. Chaucer, Geoffrey, d. 1400—Criticism and interpretation—Blogs.
2. Geoffrey Chaucer hath a blog (Online) 3. Civilization, Medieval—
Study and teaching—Blogs. I. Bryant, Brantley L., 1977– II. Geoffrey
Chaucer hath a blog (Online) III. Series: New Middle Ages (Palgrave
Macmillan (Firm))

PR1924.G365 2010
821'.1—dc22   2010003249

A catalogue record of the book is available from the British Library.

Design by Newgen Imaging Systems (P) Ltd., Chennai, India.

First edition: May 2010

D 10 9 8 7 6 5 4 3 2

Printed in the United States of America.

For Sakina and Mateo

CONTENTS

ACKNOWLEDGMENTS

This unusual project could not have come about without a vast amount of good will, good humor, and support from many people near and far, known and unknown. For the congeniality and good spirits that went into the blog's original posts, I thank my friends and colleagues throughout graduate school and my first years as junior faculty, though not many of them are aware of how I spent my time online. Jon K. Williams was a crucial early interlocutor, as were the online and real-world friends and colleagues who combined to form *In The Middle*: Jeffrey Jerome Cohen, Eileen Joy, Mary Kate Hurley, and Karl Steel. Thanks also to the Columbia Medieval Guild and the members of the inefficient but hilarious Medieval Latin Reading Group (who will pardon the paucity of Liutprand of Cremona references in this volume). Thanks to my colleagues in the Sonoma State University English department for their warm welcome, support, and friendship.

A bigger, wider, and unlimited thanks goes to all who have read, enjoyed, and commented on the Chaucer blog. Thank you especially to Patrick and Teresa Nielsen Hayden, whose early and frequent links to the blog on their *Making Light* (http://nielsenhayden.com/makinglight/) helped LeVostreGC reach a wider audience (though we have never met or communicated personally about it). Thank you to all of the medieval bloggers who have provided a wonderful sense of community and support over the years. I am honored to have your voices and experiences shape part of this book. And thanks to medievalists, kalamazoologists, and philologists of all kinds. Keep on dancing.

As for this volume itself, I am deeply grateful to Jeffrey Jerome Cohen for supporting the idea, Bonnie Wheeler for taking it up, and Brigitte Shull, Lee Norton, and the rest of the team at Palgrave for seeing it through. Thank you to my friends and family for support and understanding.

For permission to print Chaucer's "Compleynt on the Deth of Sir William," previously published in the eighty-fifth anniversary issue of *Weird Tales* 63.2 (2008): 17, I thank Stephen H. Segal and Wildside Press. I also thank Baba Brinkman, Chaucer rapper extraordinaire (www.babasword. com) for his permission to include his online exchange with LeVostreGC.

PART I

MEDIEVALISM, BLOGGING, AND POPULAR
CULTURE

CHAPTER 1

WHY YE SHOLDE NAT REDE THIS BOOKE

John Gower

Malus bloggus de Chaucer in librum nefandum commutatur;
Chaucer peior quam Lolcats, qui sepe me VVankerum vocat;
Si tu es bonus, cave; hic bloggus est bogus.

In proverb men seye, withouten doute:
"Garbage in and garbage oute."
Thus redeth nat thys book of lyes
Lest garbage enter in your eyes
And towardes foulness turn your hertes
That ye may nat from synne asterte:
Beware, ye shal nat L O L
The while that ye burne in helle.
Geoffrey Chaucer, poet fals,
(Wolde he were honge by the hals!)
Hath in his pryde composed a booke
In which let only harlotes looke.
Within he hath hys poostes collected
Ful of filth and synne infected
Devoyd of sentence and solaas,
Yet fulle of lore of Sathanas.
No thing of lust, and noon of lore,
Ye shal fynde in thys book, therfore.
Seriousli, saveth yower money:
This book maketh plague looke funnye.
No man kan whyne and whinge the waye
That Chaucer kan aboute hys daye.
And basicallye what is hys beefe?
He hath two sones, and eek a wyf,

And decent jobbes for the King
(who nevir listneth whan I sing).
Wherfor sholde Chaucer thus complayne?
I am half blynde. I suffir payne
From fingres soore, but at no hour
Do ye heare wamentynge from Gower.
And worse than Chauceres lame kvetching
Ys whanne he thinketh he acteth fetching
And talketh of japes and poyntless thinges
(the while I wryte advyce for kinges).
What care I of thes video games?
Or of the Gawain-Poetes shame?
Or of abbreviaciouns?
Lo swich abhominaciouns
Doth Chaucer wryte, that if I hadde
A doghter that were half as badde
As Chaucer ys, I wolde spank her:
He even cleped me a wanker.
Wers still, he wrote thes things *en blog,*
Which is a maner kind of fog
Composid of electronic words
And ment to fill the myndes of nerds;
O wofull daye! What shal betide
If blogges wyth books be dignified?
A book requireth furrowed brows
And also several sheep or cows
Whos skin bycometh many pages
Hoolding trouthe for futur ages.
Nedeth a book precisioun
And topical divisioun
And wordes from auctoritees:
Nat just witty repartee
Created on the internet.
We have nat fallen so far yet!
Yet Geoffrey getteth all the breakes;
Mene while, moral Gower aches.
"Poor ol'" Gower, I shold saye,
For Chaucer ay shal win the daye.
Everyoon saith, "what could be neater
Than hys iambic pentameter?"
Thei think nat of the subtle magic
I fashion wyth octosyllabics.
This wrecchid Chaucer, I shal nat lye,
Folk call "Fathir of poesy"—
Yet for Gower? Noon shal prayse me;
I fare lyk to an uncle crazye.

Yet ther is comfort, heere I chortle:
Geoff ys a man, and men are mortal:
Oon daye he shal go to hys reste;
He shal be nayled in a cheste;
Hys soule shal go to Styxes bog,
And then he shal nat have a blog.

CHAPTER 2

INTRODUCTION

GO LITEL BLOG, GO LITEL THYS COMEDYE!

Bonnie Wheeler

Do medievalists have more fun than other academics? Sure. Not surprisingly, Chaucerians are more likely to LOL (laugh out loud) than, say, scholars of Gratian or Columbanus. Perhaps papyrologists also chortle, but not in such numbers. Academic comedy has an ancient tradition and a presence as continuous as schools themselves. Academic graffiti is found in stone carvings and under antique seats—and now it has exploded on the WWW (World Wide Web). Readers of and participants in *Geoffrey Chaucer Hath a Blog* are a particularly gleeful international bunch, mixing it up in Middle English, trading compliments, complaints, and kankedorts with equal verve. They uphold a long tradition.

Medievalists at Work and Play, or How to Lose Jobs

We medievalists have such an ingrained habit of playing together that we've created a genuine professional dilemma for ourselves. Our mega-organizations, like the Modern Language Association (MLA) and the American Historical Association (AHA), meet annually and provide formal occasions for the world to keep its eye on the ups and downs of the academic marketplace and "hot" academic fields. Each year one notices the paltry proportion of medieval sessions at these annual conferences. As a consequence, some of our colleagues who are committed to compulsory modernism presume that the study of the Middle Ages is in decline. They are wrong. They clearly don't understand that May follows April ("with his shoures soote") and that in May, "foweles maken melodye / That

slepen al the nyght with open ye." But these fools are not to be found in
New York, San Francisco, or even Cambridge, MA.

When Medievalists Play in Person

We medieval foweles/fools are found in Kalamazoo, Michigan.

You might think that, by choice, medievalists would meet in places
that had culturally vibrant Middle Ages. Perhaps Paris, London, Istanbul,
Kyoto, Rome, Florence—or even Santa Fe or Canterbury? But no: we
rush each May from all corners of the globe to the concrete-block dorms
of Kalamazoo's Western Michigan University (WMU), where medievalists of all disciplines and nations mix the secular and the sacred, talk
shop, exchange ideas, give hundreds upon hundreds of papers on subjects
that span the thousand-year period that we (strangely) call the Middle
Ages. Scholars from other periods long ago figured out how to join our
fun: Spencer scholars glom on, and the billowing cadre of contemporary
"medievalism" scholars who write and study texts based on medieval
themes or movies about medieval topics, or Harry Potter or Tolkien's
hobbits, are welcomed as well. That open welcome makes the annual
International Congress of Medieval Studies at Kalamazoo a worldwide
marvel. I've met more scholars from Africa and Japan in Kalamazoo than
in any other single place. There we are the United Nations of medieval history, literature, law, numismatics, religious studies, philosophy,
art history, musicology, and all the other arts and sciences. Of course,
we have smaller focused conferences around the world and even regular meetings elsewhere of the New Chaucer Society, but as medievalists
our pluridisciplinary range is wide, and every field is full of new lore at
Kalamazoo.

As the conference workday temporarily winds down, conferees swoop
down on the book exhibits, relax at the loosely described "Wine Hour"
(a form of swill, it nevertheless disappears in a thirty-five-minute "hour")
and often eat in the student cafeterias. This wouldn't seem very unusual
for conferees in any profession except for the fact that more than 3,000
of us currently gather in this fashion each May—that's a lot of scholars,
many of them with tenure—as job candidates contemplating potential
crashes in those puddle-jumping planes gravely, perhaps sometimes too
gravely, note.

With a history that started in the expansive 1960s, this conference has
developed some peculiarities that provide renewed delight. First of all, it
started as a counter conference, "a fledgling rival to the lofty Medieval
Academy," as Joel Rosenthal noted.[1] It was the democratic openness of
WMU's John Sommerfeldt that started the ball rolling in 1962, and the

Congress came to its full amplitude under the directorship of historian/ institution builder Otto Gründler. One of the funniest moments I will forever remember took place at a recent meeting of the council of the Medieval Academy. One councillor urged us to move the Academy's annual meeting to the fall in order to avoid the inevitable competition with the irresistible Kalamazoo conference. The ball doth turn.

By the mid-1970s, participants in the Kalamazoo conference developed their own carnivalesque routines. This is not the place to discuss the origins of the Saturday Night Dance,[2] but it is worth noting that before David Lodge wrote his comic novels about the ticks of academic frolicking, we had already kicked it up a notch in Kalamazoo.

Medieval Word Play, Old Style

On Saturday evening at Kalamazoo, erudite academics risk their reputations by becoming temporary stand-up comics who play to a demanding audience in the Pseudo Society (a.k.a. Societas fontibus historiae Medii Aevi inveniendis, vulgo dicta) presentations. Several conferees miss dinner altogether to grab good seats before the crowd overwhelms the largest auditorium on campus and latecomers block the aisles. It is always Standing Room Only (SRO). And woe to speakers if the timing isn't good, or the joke goes flat, since the exceedingly well informed audience then grumbles and hisses. One must know a lot to catch the drift: Exactly at what point, for example, does the presentation veer from the plausible to the impossible? Were you hearing a really funny true translation or was it sheer invention? Were you seeing a weird but accurate image or (even before Photoshop) was it elaborately faked? It renews your faith in scholarship to see it "in drag." Every pomposity is paraded, prodded, exposed, and exploded. Every paper depends upon the "spin" by which the speaker adds invented sources to real ones, revives dead causes, and plucks droll delight from the dead and the dull. If ever there was an example of the ephemeral joy of erudition—no one is paid, no papers counted for tenure—it is celebrated at meetings of the Pseudo Society.

It all began in 1974 when the Medieval Academy met for the first time in conjunction with the Western Michigan Medieval Institute at Kalamazoo: it was very much a Mountain-coming-to-Mohammed event. The Medieval Academy dinner prompted the usual writing of collaborative comic sonnets from the irreverent, but after the Saturday "banquet," Penelope Doob and Bonnie Wheeler left the Valley III cafeteria to chat in the closest empty classroom. A few friends—including Jeremy Adams, Judson Allen, John Leyerle, and Larry Benson—dropped by and seated themselves as if they had come to hear another round of papers. During the day we had been shocked and amused by papers on such topics as the exact extant number of Holy Foreskins, the plethora of reliquary heads of John the Baptist, and "Medieval Mules: A Study in Asinine Sexual Behavior," but it was Penelope's recounting of bizarre stories from Irish penitentials that inspired what followed. People kept gathering and waiting for a real scholarly session to unfold. It was irresistible, so we duly called to order a postprandial scholarly fantasy session, entitled the 823rd Meeting of the Holy Foreskins Society. By now the group included, among others, such literary luminaries as Maureen Fries, John Pope, and B.J. Whiting, as well as historians John Benton, Dennis Cashman, David Herlihy, and Stefan Kuttner. Harvard's great wit Whiting, ever eager to interject a paper of his own, was restricted instead to commenting on each pseudopresentation in turn. Rarely have the creative efforts of frustration been better or more hilariously demonstrated. Surely any society with women members that named its academic journal *Speculum* deserves the occasional parody. Extemporaneous papers by Adams, Leyerle, Doob and Wheeler concluded with calls for "encore," and Dennis Cashman followed up in 1976 with a return engagement under the protection of the "American Society for Jutish Studies" (a group that was invented for the occasion and expired with it) with the Old Stones Society and International Porlock Society also adding their bit. These mock-serious traditions are now institutionalized annually in the Pseudo Society under the grand circus-masters Richard Ring and Richard Kay. Some other groups now imitate the Pseudo Society and some Pseudo Society members have tried to export it, mostly to the general befuddlement of more staid organizations. Many of the early presentations are lost, but several were found and edited by Ring and Kay.[3] Read them aloud with your friends. Potential participants shouldn't miss "Inventing the Past: The Methodology of Pseudo History" by James A. Brundage.[4]

Word Play: For the Nonce All

I don't know to what music "Virgile, Ovide, Omer, Lucan, and Stace" were high-stepping, but medievalists can't seem to listen to a dinner lecture without collaborating on subversive ditties. The Medieval Academy dinner was always the best place for rhymes, usually on paper napkins. Talbot Donaldson would sometimes act as collective taskmaster correcting rhyme-royal gangplays. Almost everyone could be counted upon to add a line to a surreptitious banquet sonnet or late-hour limerick. The rule? No one was allowed to hog the paper and contribute more than one line. One limerick sequence of several years' duration began "There was a director named Otto" and ended where all limericks do—in some hole-in-the-wall, but often with reference to an Otto Grotto.

> There was a director named Otto
> Whose banquets left us all blotto
> The next day our crapula
> Was cured by a scapular
> Now "Repent and Reform" is our motto!

Or,

> There was a director named Otto
> Who played with his texts in a grotto
> He collected his variants
> While he was… [remainder suppressed for fear of offending
> youthful ears,
> but the last line ends with "Chicago"].

As a retirement gift to Otto, a grateful group funded what WMU administrators promised would be an *Otto Grotto* behind the WMU Medieval Institute Building. Designs were produced; expenses estimated; money provided. Years passed and the project languished, but under duress a plaque and some plants were erected elsewhere at WMU. This Otto Grotto still reminds us of the long durée of old friendships and silly poems (and the short durée of administrative commitments). For a few years, "haggis" was a required word in every Kalamazoo poem and a flurry of "haggis"-ridden postcards ensued. None of these exuberances begins to equal the poetic parodies written by Bob Hanning, medievalist *extraordinaire*, that are included in this volume. Hanning's keen wit and deep erudition mark his scholarship as well as his teaching. He sustained generations of students at Columbia University through some otherwise humorless years. His suggestions here for Chaucerian bumper stickers might fund the Web maintenance of *Geoffrey Chaucer Hath a Blog* for some time. Buy 'em now!

Pixel Play

Chaucer never goes out of style and is easily brought to mind, as we all know. He is loved for his high seriousness and accused of lack of high seriousness. Joan Acocella's review essay in *The New Yorker* (December 21 and 28, 2009, pp. 140–145) rejects Peter Ackroyd's recent "retelling" of the *Canterbury Tales* although she herself adds some kinky new interpretations of Chaucer's rambunctious *Miller's Tale*—a "Tee Hee" to her, though I laugh lightly since I am so happy that Chaucer still gets "play" from Wide World Writers.[5] Now we can crawl, tweet, and blog Chaucer as well as read about him in print. If the Kalamazoo (or even the slightly dourer Leeds) medieval conferences provide us with pub-crawl games, the WWW ups the ante. You can have an academic pub-crawl in your own room, on your own time. The scholarly group blog is even more capacious than the Great Bed of Ware at London's V&A: we have the Great Bed of Wherever. Blogs are standard fare on the Web, and (as Michele Tepper noted in *networker* [2003; 20] "perhaps the first native publishing format for the Web." Some wonder (along with Jeffrey Jerome. Cohen later in this volume) whether blogs have been techno-outdated by Facebook, and so on. It's true that many blogs are significantly omphaloskeptical as they mirror our culture's wild self-absorption. But a blog can also be a "conference-without-walls" with all the wit and joy of real conversation with everyone's best self. One example is Mary Beard's blog begun in 2006 for the *Times Literary Supplement*. She describes herself as a "reluctant blogger" who "had a dim view of the blogosphere (full of dumbed-down journalism and ranting commenters)." She was, however, such "an almost instant convert" to the pleasures of serious blogging that she has now produced her blog in book form, convinced that (even though you lose the hyperlinks in book form) you gain something: "You can flip, and browse more easily. And you can take it to places still largely out of bounds to laptops. I'm thinking of bed—and the loo."[6] From blog to book and back to blog again. Such is our aim here. Should all other forms of data retrievals in the future fail, one can still read here the adventures of Chaucer from 2006 to 2010.

Geoffrey Chaucer Hath a Blog is play pluperfect: it has rules (write Middle Englishy), the Web is its playing field, it incites controversies about Chaucer's foes and contemporary academic or political deadheads and duds (queynte ideas), but, we hope, the blog has no limited duration to its enchantment. Every posting is a winner. Chaucerians delight in word play, in Very Bad Puns, in Great Vowels Unshifted, and in collaboration as much as pseudoflaming. The greatest compliment many Chaucerians receive is that they are thought to be the blog's author. I didn't want to give away the whole game, since I really wanted our brilliant Blog Author to remain Anonymous—but here all is revealed, the Big Tease ends, and you can wallow in its galauntyne. I am delighted to bring Brantley Bryant's blogwork into print, knowing as we do that the blog's Web future is well assured.

And we only hope, along with Chaucer, that wherever this little blog book goes—read ye barefot, read ye shod—you enter its pleasures:

> And for ther is so gret diversite
> In Englissh and in writyng of oure tonge,

So prey I God that non myswrite the,
Ne the mysmetre for defaute of tonge;
And red wherso thow be, or elles songe,
That thow be understonde, God I biseche!

(T&C 5.1793–1798)

Notes

1. Joel Rosenthal, "Recollections of Times Past," *The Book of Forty*, compiled by Patricia Hollahan (Kalamazoo: Medieval Institute, 2005), p. 38.
2. For which see Wheeler, Adams, and Doob in *The Book of Forty*, pp. 43–45.
3. *Proceedings of the Pseudo Society, First Series 1986–93*, ed. Richard R. Ring and Richard Kay (Kalamazoo: Medieval Institute, 2003).
4. *Proceedings of the Pseudo Society*, pp. 33–37.
5. Joan Acocella, "All England: 'The Canterbury Tales' Retold," *The New Yorker* (December 21 and 28, 2009), pp. 140–145.
6. http://timesonline.typepad.com/dons_life. Accessed January 4, 2010.

CHAPTER 3

PLAYING CHAUCER

Brantley L. Bryant

A mong other treats, this book contains the key 2006–2009 postings
from "Geoffrey Chaucer Hath a Blog," a humor blog written in the
voice of Chaucer in an approximation of Middle English. Publishing the
blog has allowed for significant revision of the blog posts (including the
correction of several misfired jokes), and the content that originated on
the blog is presented here in an improved and expanded form. You could
call it pseudoauthoritative. Readers will also find a new, never-before-
published document that expands the blog's fiction, the "Book of the
Feere and Sentence," describing Chaucer and Richard II's road trip to
the United States (an event woefully unremarked in the standard
scholarship).

Partially because of the expectations of print publication, and partially
to take credit for the work that has gone into the blog, I have decided to
publish the blog under my own name. At this point it would be difficult
to maintain the fiction that I was not the author at all, that Chaucer was
merely speaking through me somehow or that the real Chaucer Blogger
is out there still, laughing at the elaborateness of my faux-coming out.
Yet you may believe that if you would like. I certainly did not receive a
large cash reward from the Blogger's agents in order to "take the fall."
No, not me.

I wrote the blog while a graduate student in New York City and then
as a junior faculty member in Northern California. I created all of the
entries published as Chaucer ("LeVostreGC") and his son Litel Lowys,
as well as the material published by Thomas Favent and the Lords
Appellant during Chaucer's absence (and collected here under the head-
ing "A New Order"). Friends and contacts wrote as some of the other

characters on the blog, though to this day I have no idea who wrote the Katherine Swinford entries, since she (?) and I corresponded only in-character as Chaucer and his sister-in-law. Only Chaucer's entries are collected here.

In this essay, I share the circumstances of the blog's creation and comment on it from my perspective as its writer. In doing so, I move quickly through several topics, such as medievalism, Chaucerian reception, and fan fiction, that lie outside of my scholarly specialty. Given that, and also considering how ponderous this piece would be if I tried to analyze my own humorous creation, I do not speak in an academic voice here. Instead, I hope to offer some earnest, informative, very straightforward comments about the blog in order to give some new information about its origins and context. As it is, I am afraid the essay still sounds rather overserious for the topic at hand, and may prove the least fun part of the book; please imagine me in a clown suit if necessary.

Social Networking Chaucer

"Geoffrey Chaucer Hath a Blog" emerged with the growth of online socialization in the 2000s. The Chaucer persona began as a profile for Geoffrey Chaucer on the social networking site Friendster (founded in 2002).[1] Friendster allows users to register for free and create profiles made up of pictures, contact information, and personal details, including favorite movies as well as the catch-all category of "interests." Users then search for and "friend" other users, who appear on each other's profiles as a list of names and pictures. As a Ph.D. candidate in my late twenties in New York City, I was quick to join the site, since it gave me the illusion of being able to keep up with friends from high school and college around the country.

Many Friendster users turned the site's professed mission of factual self-presentation on its head by creating what became known as "fakesters," profiles of dead, famous, or fictional persons (sometimes all three). Users could add Thomas Hardy or Dorothy Parker to their lists of friends.[2] As a graduate student focusing on late fourteenth-century literature and politics, I thought it would be funny to have Chaucer listed as my "friend," so I created a tongue-in-cheek profile in the autumn of 2005. Chaucer's "interests" were listed in the same form in which they now appear on his blog's user profile: "pilgrimage, astrology, allegory, lyric poetry, the potential of the vernacular, drinking, hanging in Southwark, penance, bastard feudalism, surviving political upheaval, my yearly tun of wine." Although some "fakesters" were wildly popular, the Chaucer profile gained only a few friends, mostly personal contacts of mine and medievalists. It seems appropriate that Chaucer makes his entry here as someone created to be added to a list of "friends." The users enjoying the fantasy of adding Chaucer as one of their Friendster friends engaged, through newly minted social media, in the long-standing "nostalgic projection that places Chaucer's modern readers in an intimate relationship with him" traced through centuries of Chaucerian reception by Stephanie Trigg in her book *Congenial Souls*.[3] The relationship was, however, not particularly vibrant; the Chaucer fakester did little more than post a comment or two on friends' profiles in the approximation of Middle English that would become the blog's language.

In the winter of 2006, Friendster began to offer a "blogging" feature that allowed users to post online journals. Although I kept a small personal blog on Livejournal, a site that allowed for privacy locks restricting one's online diary to select friends, I had not thought of starting a public blog until Friendster offered one to Chaucer. In this way, the Chaucer Blog was completely accidental. Logging in to Friendster after dissertation work (probably quite late at night), it seemed fun to accept Friendster's offer of a prefabricated blogging site for Chaucer. The first Chaucer blog entries appeared on Friendster, written on a lark. The "Abbreviaciouns" post (January 27, 2006) attracted a decent bit of attention and reposting, and when the Chaucer persona solicited requests for an advice post, e-mails came in, leading to the "Ask Chaucer" post of February 23, 2006, written, like the comments and the later blog, in a rough approximation of Middle English spelling, vocabulary, and syntax.

Writing as Chaucer was fun, and I committed more time to it as the audience grew. On March 20, the "Ask Chaucer" post was linked to by the popular Web tastemaking site BoingBoing, which called the blog a "hilarious blog maintained by Chaucer, who answers readers' questions."[4] The Chaucer Blog's first truly wide-reaching post was the response to the film version of *Brokeback Mountain* posted on March 16, 2006. Framed as an answer to an advice letter asking whether Chaucer had been "with the *Pearl*-poet in France," the post narrated a young Chaucer's gay love affair with the *Pearl*-poet. The "Mount Dorse-Quassee" post was widely linked to and recopied. Given a sense that there was, improbably, a receptive audience for pop culture parody written in cod-Middle-English by a Chaucerian persona, I responded by putting more energy into the postings, which became longer and more complicated. Like many of the bloggers discussed by Jeffrey Jerome Cohen in his essay here, I most enthusiastically embraced writing the Chaucer Blog during an extended "momen[t] of career uncertainty," namely the finishing of a dissertation and my encounter with the academic job market. Faced with doubts about career prospects, I found it comforting to lead a secret life as "The Chaucer

Blogger," especially as the blog began to gain recognition. In addition, I found that blog writing both complemented and relieved me from work on my heavily historicist dissertation on parliament, economics, and a variety of late-medieval poets (including Chaucer). Writing in the Chaucer Blog, I was imagining the same world and drawing inspiration from the same scholarly works, but I was free to approach the material in an irreverent way that I found refreshing.

In March 2006 I moved the Chaucer Blog from Friendster to Blogger, a free blogging service, and the blog assumed the format it has kept until the printing of this volume. Although my computing skills are limited, I chose an antique-looking layout, added an illuminated page border, put together a list of links to bands, charities, and Chaucerian resources, and began to post much longer and more carefully worked-over pieces. Social technologies continued to affect the blog's circulation, since I used my private Livejournal account to test drafts of the blog entries for an audience of friends and other medievalists whom I had met online (and who have since become colleagues and contacts "in the real world"). A thriving group of medievalist blogs, detailed by Cohen in his essay, provided a larger audience and group of interlocutors for the Chaucer Blog. I was deeply encouraged, and inspired to keep writing, by the various medievalist bloggers who linked to entries, responded (in various characters' voices), and kindly expressed the pleasure they drew from the blog's humor. Early on, speculative fiction editors Teresa and Patrick Nielsen Hayden linked several of the blog posts on their blog *Making Light*, drawing in readers from the Science Fiction parts of the Web (complicatedly linked, of course, with many of the medieval parts of the Web).

Friendster, Blogger, Livejournal, BoingBoing—a constellation of developing technologies for communication and community-building, used by some nice, smart people, made it possible for a humorous, fictional imagination of Chaucer to find an audience.

Congenially Lost in Time

The blog began as a lark and was encouraged by a series of happy accidents, so it would be disingenuous to present it as a high-minded and strategic project. As the blog gathered steam, however, I did decide on two guiding principles: Chaucer should be nice, and the temporality of the blog should be muddy.

Though chosen quickly, the blog's titles and URL helped me point to the spirit of the project. The URL "houseoffame" fit, since that short poem's discussion of the fleeting uncertainty of both communication and literary reputation seemed to foreshadow the absurd possibility of a pseudo-Chaucerian persona coming "alive" on the Internet. "Geoffrey Chaucer Hath a Blog" emphasizes the central conceit of the blog. The present tense in "hath" helps promote the fiction that Chaucer is somehow alive and blogging, while its archaic form is meant to juxtapose humorously with the contemporary neologism in "blog." Many commenters have also pointed out the unintentional resonance with the traditional lyric "Old McDonald Had a Farm."

This Chaucer persona was a "congenial soul," to use Trigg's adapted form of a comment by John Dryden.[5] The blogger username LeVostreGC refers to the signatures of Troilus and Criseyde in Chaucer's poem, but was also intended to imply that this Chaucer was "your" Chaucer, a Chaucer with whom readers could speak. The blog format, in which the persona reacted to comments posted on entries and also commented on other blogs, made LeVostreGC an interactive and sociable figure. LeVostreGC was meant to be consistently "congenial." I tried to keep the humor of the entries kind, if occasionally lascivious. In no way was a post ever meant to look down upon whatever phenomena it discussed or parodied. In this way, LeVostreGC was meant to evoke the traditional interpretation of the narrator of the *General Prologue* as a wide-eyed, nonjudgmental spirit, a good-natured soul low on cynicism. The persona's boundless affection and enthusiasm was a useful mode for blog posts that took up pop cultural concerns. The approach is evident in the "Wondrous Messages from the Internette" post (May 24, 2006), in which Chaucer proudly and enthusiastically discusses a series of spam messages as "the wondirs of myn inboxe."

The Chaucer persona is also overworked and frequently unsure about his poetic potential. LeVostreGC's self-characterization was meant to match the deflating authorial self-portraits in *The House of Fame* and "The Prologue to Sir Thopas." His references to his weight ("for Ich am a rolli-polli man") and his "litel woolen hatte" were intended to establish Chaucer as a modest, unthreatening, and inadvertently ridiculous figure. Although occasional disdain slipped into the posts (such as some of the snarky comments in the versification of the "Cipher of Leonardo"), LeVostreGC was meant to read as a friendly, unpretentious soul—a move meant to make his unmitigated hatred for John Gower, a borrowing from tradition, more pronounced and potentially amusing.[6] In a kind of scholarly full-circle, Stephanie Trigg, whose work on Chaucer helped me think through the blog's approach, remarked in a May 2007 post on her own blog that the LeVostreGC persona stood out as "a kindly presence."[7]

The congenial LeVostreGC was a man rich in family and friends, so the blog's fictionalized Chaucer necessitated the creation of fictionalized

versions of Chaucer's household and contemporaries. The mention of
"Litel Lowys my sone" in the "Treatise on the Astrolabe" inspired a
series of references to Lewis, conceived as an opinionated adolescent
and hip-hop fan, who wrote a few posts of his own. The successful
Thomas Chaucer is a straight arrow in the fiction of the blog, perpetu-
ally away from home on state business. Philippa Chaucer is mentioned
as a beloved but stern companion, implicitly more directive and practical than her husband; a gentler version of Harry Bailey's Goodelief.
LeVostreGC, informed by Paul Strohm's account in *Social Chaucer*,
frequently mentions his coterie, including most notably Thomas Usk,
who serves as Chaucer's link to parliamentary politics. Other bloggers,
without any communication or coordination, joined in the fiction by
commenting on the blog in-character or starting blogs of their own;
for a few brief months in the spring of 2006, someone blogged in the
persona of Henry Scogan, a courtier and addressee of one of Chaucer's
short poems.[8] And of course, the LeVostreGC persona has a friendly
though cagey relationship with Richard II, who appears throughout
the blog entries as, alternately, a power-obsessed psychopath or a figure
of excess and indulgence (the former role is, later, to be taken up by
the blog's version of Henry Bolingbroke). The increased presence of
Richard II was inspired by an early commenter who took on the role
of the king, repeatedly leaving comments approving or disapproving of
LeVostreGC's posts.

The choice of a congenial, well-friended persona for LeVostreGC made
for a pleasant blog but, of course, defanged and dehistoricized Chaucer
in crucial ways. Notably absent from the Blog's otherwise relatively
wide inclusion of Chaucerian biographical details (including Chaucer's
jobs, family, and travel) is any mention of Cecily Chaumpaigne, the real
historical woman whom the real historical Chaucer most likely raped.[9]
When a canny anonymous commenter left a message in her name on
March 30, 2006, a flustered LeVostreGC responded: "Myne mainper-
nours haven advised me nat to make mencioun of anye of the detailles
of the cas yn a public forum." Clearly, some undeniable aspects of the
biographical Chaucer do not make for fun blogging, and a popularization
of a "fun" Chaucer obscures vital historical realities.

Yet if the blog's creation of a friendly, scandal-free Chaucer affirmed
long-standing, even stale, interpretations of Chaucer, another part of the
blog's developing mission aimed at carrying on the more recent projects
of queerer, more irreverent approaches to Chaucer. The blog was meant
to offer a Chaucer without canonical fame, to blend specialist medieval
scholarship with pop culture, and to throw the medieval and the contemporary together in a way that would inextricably mesh them.

The blog's chronology was meant to tell a coherent story but to resist definition as past or present. In one way, the blog matched the pace of Chaucer's life with the progress of present time. Once I realized that the blog would be an extended project and not a few posts, I began to incorporate biographical details so that the events of 2006 would roughly match those of 1386, 2007, 1387 and so on. This works out most explicitly in the posts that riff off of the politics of King Richard II's reign. The posts detailing LeVostreGC's election to and attendance of Parliament (September 30, 2006; October 5, 2006; October 31, 2006) match roughly with the October 1386 beginning of the "Wonderful" Parliament the historical Chaucer attended as a representative for Kent.[10] Similarly, the political drama in which the Lords Appellant took over government from King Richard in 1388–1389 was played out in the narrative of the blog posts of 2008–2009. During this time, the Lords Appellant took control of the blog from LeVostreGC and placed Thomas Favent (in historical reality, a political writer whose *History or Narration Concerning the Manner and Form of the Miraculous Parliament* has often been construed as praise of the Appellants) at the helm of a tackily "rebranded," sadistic, and jingoistic "Geoffrey Chaucer Hath an Extreme Blog! Go England! Yt ys Rad!"[11] Of course, many other events do not map out so well. In the narration of the blog, LeVostreGC becomes Clerk of the King's works in a blog post of May 2007, whereas Chaucer did not take up that office until 1389. Most notably, as several e-mails sent to LeVostreGC have pointed out with confusion, in the current fiction of the blog Philippa Chaucer is alive and well and living in Kent, though the historical Philippa died in 1387.[12]

Besides the internal chronology meant to give the blog a developing plot, the blog's posts do not give a clear sense of where and when it is being written. The blog was not conceived of as a first-hand account of goings-on in the past times of medieval England. Such direct broadcasts from the past exist online: most notably, Phil Gyford's blog version of the diaries of Samuel Pepys, which began publishing Pepys' diaries in sequence in January 2003.[13] The Chaucer blog, however, leaves accuracy behind whenever necessary. Its medieval timeline is muddy in many ways, for example, allowing for the presence of Margery Kempe (who would have been in her teens if the timeline were kept consistent and thus not old enough for an MLA interview).[14] The blog can depart from realism completely, most notably in its depiction of Thomas Usk being saved by a time-traveling Anglo-Saxon (hinted at in the July 24, 2008 "A New Order" post). Not straightforward historical fiction, the blog also refuses to create the fiction that Chaucer is somehow living in the historical present. LeVostreGC did not emerge from a time machine to start posting on the Internet; no stated conceit or context explains the fact that Chaucer is posting on a blog. Instead, the world of the blog is meant to give a muddy sense of time and resist consistency building, allowing the medieval to freely cross-pollinate with contemporary pop culture. In one post, LeVostreGC plays video games, on an archaically named analogue of a home gaming console, but the games themselves refer to medieval concerns (August 5, 2006). A well known open-world game of crime and havoc is rewritten as a simulation of the violent local politics decried in fourteenth-century texts, allowing players to "run arounde and commit various actes of trespass with force and armes, and then use [their] patrones and affinitee groupes to get [them] out of prisone." Readers can judge the effectiveness of the technique, but the implicit goal was to place Chaucerian texts and topics, in all their historical particularity, into contemporary context, and see what kinds of resonances and similarities arise; to put it another way, the blog looked for ways to pun the past and the present for laughs. It also aims to provide a Chaucer open to queer and resistant readings. Despite all of its constructions of a very Chaucerian Chaucer as a middle-class family man, the blog got its first burst of attention from a post imagining a queer Chaucer having a torrid love affair with the *Pearl*-poet. A lover of contemporary pop culture, LeVostreGC was meant as a pleasurable disorientation of the canonical Chaucer.

The burgeoning discussions of the bloggers on *In The Middle* and the BABEL working group underwrote and inspired many of the blog's choices.[15] The BABEL group, in fact, includes LeVostreGC on their list of members. Both *In the Middle* and BABEL, during the time of the blog's writing, were concentrating on rethinking the methods of medieval scholarship and on finding new configurations between the medieval and the modern. In the introduction to the 2007 volume *Cultural Studies of the Modern Middle Ages*, BABEL cofounders Eileen A. Joy and Myra J. Seaman introduce the book's essays, which analyze medieval and contemporary culture in productive relationship with each other, as an attempt to point the way to "a medieval cultural studies where the Middle Ages can disturb and disrupt the present's sense of itself as wholly modern...."[16] In its own jokey way, the blog aimed at the same effect through its simultaneous appropriation, disruption, and estrangement of contemporary concerns and Chaucer's texts (at this point, please remember, however, that we are discussing a joke blog).

Unlike the articles I was trying to shepherd toward publication at the time of the blog's heyday, the blog foregrounded the pleasure and enjoyment of engagement with medieval literature. In doing so, it was reacting to scholarly trends emphasizing a return to aesthetics and enjoyment (which for me most notably surfaced in BABEL's panel for the 2009 International Medieval Congress, "Are We Enjoying Ourselves? The Place of Pleasure in Medieval Scholarship"). The openly sentimental "Make Melody Today" post invites readers to celebrate the first day of April by reading Chaucer's opening lines, and it asks readers unfamiliar with Middle English to approach the language as if it were "an olde relative whom thou lovest verie much," who will "talk back to thee" (April 1, 2006). Forgetting some of the stark realities that can keep readers and Chaucer far apart, the post imagines, for a moment, a transhistorical love-in. In this unabashed appeal to affect, the blog also could be numbered among the ranks of enthusiastic American appropriations of Chaucer discussed comprehensively by Candace Barrington.[17]

Because, of course, the blog began with a fascination with and enthusiasm for Chaucerian texts, with the possibilities they afford for interpretation, play, and self-creation. My attempt to place this all in context here (please remember the clown suit) obscures the fact that writing the blog has been an incredible amount of fun and has, at least as far as I can tell from readers' responses, provided a good bit of fun and enjoyment for others.

Out of the Academy

But while the above might make the Chaucer Blog sound like a refined working-out of scholarly views in a fictional voice, a quick flip to the blog section of the book will remind you that we are dealing with something much more untheorized, comic, and unprofessionally exuberant. In addition to its more recognizable scholarly impulses, the blog took its momentum from a long-unpublicized medievalist penchant for humor and from a variety of contemporary pop cultural preoccupations. The blog's discovery of an audience outside of professional medievalists has been its most rewarding aspect, although it is the most difficult to explain here.

Stephanie Trigg has noted a time-honored predisposition for informal joking and adaptation among Chaucerian critics. The existence and popularity of the Pseudo Society, a session for presenting humorous and parodic pieces at the well-populated Kalamazoo conference, shows that such a predisposition for play characterizes medieval studies in general (a topic taken up by Bonnie Wheeler in her introduction to this book). The Chaucer Blog is, in one way, a public outgrowth of the usually deeply internalized, if not hidden, tendency of medievalists to weave complicated jokes out of their topic. They have a lot to work with, after all: a wealth of gloriously specialized terminology, rich and varied languages in all their stages of growth, the accumulated improbabilites of history, and the medieval period's well-noted combination of alterity and kinship with present concerns. The Chaucer blog tries to capture some of the well-researched punning and virtuoso intertemporal jokes that I have enjoyed from friends and colleagues.

Such good-natured transformation of the pedantic into the humorous, so visible to me throughout my socializing and conference-going as a graduate student and yet, I suspect, so rarely shared with the world outside, inspired the blog's voice and approach. Although readers will quickly identify the "New Media" of this book's title with electronic publishing, I would also suggest that this volume celebrates the "new" medium of the medievalist joke. Trigg has observed that Chaucerians traditionally keep their playful adaptations far from the real work of scholarship; the "academic play" of such creations is only permissible "*outside* the 'real' book" and indeed "serv[es] to point up by contrast the absolute seriousness" of scholarship.[18] Part of the fun of this volume is to see what happens when the playfulness, and the pleasure, of medieval studies is generously awarded the dignity of print publication (though in my comments here I cannot keep from the kind of distancing moves that Trigg observes among Chaucerians at play).[19] To that end, I am deeply grateful that Professor Robert W. Hanning has shared his wealth of medievalist humor to be bound together along with the Chaucer Blog. As a graduate student of Professor Hanning's, I saw the possibilities and potential of medieval humor first hand, not least of all in his unforgettable (and perhaps unforgiveable) pun "Chaucerians Do It with Pronounced E's" (a direct ancestor of some of the slogans on the Chaucer Blog's t-shirts). There have to be many kinds of "real" books out there, and as the humanities continue to find their place we could perhaps do worse than to think about the fun of what we do.

Besides drawing inspiration from scholarship's inside jokes, the blog was informed by contemporary interests outside of academia, most notably the culture of fan fiction. Though personally neither a producer nor a consumer of fan fiction, I was exposed to its trends and tendencies through friends and online acquaintances. Inasmuch as fan fiction is, in the august words of the OED, "fiction...written by a fan rather than a professional author, *esp.* that based on already-existing characters..." a case could be made that there are deep affinities between the long tradition of rewriting and reimagining Chaucerian texts and the contemporary thriving culture of fan fiction.[20] Stephanie Trigg has noted that Chaucer already himself found his way into fan fiction in reimaginings of Brian Helgeland's 2003 Film *A Knight's Tale*.[21] The Chaucer Blog similarly fills in the life of Chaucer as a character. It takes direct inspiration from the

"Very Secret Diaries" created by writer Cassandra Claire.[22] Purporting
to be the diaries of the protagonists of the film version of *The Lord of the
Rings*, the "Very Secret Diaries" explore the amusing tension between the
epic medieval adventure of the films and the petty, day-to-day personal
(and sexual) lives of their characters that the diaries pretend to record. In a
similar way, the Chaucer Blog exploits the potential for humor in the dis-
tance between the image of a canonically authoritative medieval Chaucer
and LeVostreGC who, when composing the fragmentary notes for the
Canterbury Tales, accidentally dips his quill into his cup of ale and mutters
his hatred for his co-workers at the customs house. Other connections to
fan fiction can be seen: the "Ich and the Perle-Poet" post owes an obvious
debt to slash writing (in which characters from the same or different fictional worlds are penned into obvious or improbable romantic and sexual
relationships), while the blog's own homages to Helgeland's film, itself a
work of chronological line-blurring, are also apparent.[23]

For a series of posts written in something close to Middle English
about medieval topics, the Chaucer Blog has reached a large amount
of readers. Running the blog as an amateur and not an online entre-
preneur, I was unable to invest much time or money in tracking the
blog's users and traffic. Unfortunately, a site meter was installed only
after the blog's period of almost weekly posting in 2006. Even so, as
of this writing, the site meter of total visits since the summer of 2007
reads 254,434. This number is microscopic in Internet terms (a single
celebrity "tweet" could easily find quadruple that amount), but a much
vaster audience than I could ever imagine for one of my scholarly articles
(the Web page of the International Medieval Congress, for comparison,
notes that the congress receives over 3,000 yearly attendees).[24] Because
of the demands of the first years of a faculty job and a new family, I have
kept the blog mostly inactive, but even in its dimmest and most inert
months it sees around 250 independent visits a day. A Google search
for the word "Chaucer" produces the blog as its eleventh search result
(behind Wikipedia, e-texts of Chaucer's works, and a score of invaluable
introductory scholarly pages).

Outside of academic medieval studies, the Chaucer Blog has reached
a variety of audiences, each of which seems to see the blog as amusing
and "congenial," despite differences in politics and subculture. In addition to its appearance on BoingBoing, the blog has been linked to on
"The Valve," a literary Web site.[25] Political writer Norman Geras "inter-
viewed" LeVostreGC for his personal blog in June of 2006. Shirley Dent
in an April 2007 post on the "book blog" of the British publication *The
Guardian* cited the Chaucer Blog as an example of delight in linguistic
complexity.[26] In May 2007, the popular "Language Log" blog linked to

Chaucer's LOLCat versions of Canterbury Pilgrims.[27] The blog has been mentioned with enthusiasm on the Web pages of both a writer of science fiction for queer teens and a priest who lists Rush Limbaugh in his blog's "What I'm Listening To." LeVostreGC's video game–related posts drew attention of the popular *Kotaku* video gaming site.[28] This last link is especially indicative of a larger trend. As medievalists have already begun to note, contemporary video games are a key locale for the merging of medieval texts and new media.[29] At the time of this book's writing, video game consumers are eagerly awaiting an action adventure game based on Dante's *Divine Comedy* entitled, in a way that replicates and thus replaces the medieval work, *Dante's Inferno*.[30] Carl Pyrdum, who has been tracking the game's development and progress from a medievalist's perspective on his blog *Got Medieval*, observed that a Google search for "Dante's Inferno" produced the game, not the text, as its number one result.[31] But what do gamers anticipating a reverse-bowdlerized, hi-def *Inferno* have to do with clergy and political theorists? One can only say that all of these audiences have some interest, some investment, in the Middle Ages as a source of traditions to revere or to readapt, some ability to find the blog's Chaucerian voice amusing or enjoyable.

In his address to the New Chaucer Society's 2006 meeting, David Wallace both gently acknowledged the Chaucer Blog ("I bypass the Chaucer blogger") and went on to propose the affinity of Chaucer with "the Web-tracked globalism of our present time" and announce the 2000s as "the epoch of…new Chaucer topographies."[32] In one way or another, it would seem that the Chaucer Blog's humorous recreation of the poet's voice provides one more *topos*, however peripheral and virtual, for Chaucerian redefinition in the twenty-first century. The Chaucer Blog section of this book offers readers the polished and revised products of Chaucer's pseudonymous Web appearances for their continued and expanded enjoyment, and also records the funny moment when Chaucer reception history and new media crossed.

Notes

1. http://www.friendster.com/info/index.php
2. Daniel Terdiman, "Friendster's Fakester Buddies." http://www.wired.com/culture/lifestyle/news/2004/07/64156
3. Stephanie Trigg, *Congenial Souls* (Minneapolis: University of Minnesota Press, 2002), p. 25.
4. http://www.boingboing.net/2006/03/20/geoffrey_chaucer_hat.html
5. Trigg, *Congenial Souls*, p. xix.
6. On the Chaucer/Gower rivalry, see, for example, Carolyn Dinshaw, "Rivalry, Rape and Manhood: Chaucer and Gower," in *Chaucer and*

Gower: Difference, Mutuality, Exchange, ed. R. F. Yeager (Victoria, British Columbia: University of Victoria Press, 1991), pp. 130–152.

7. http://stephanietrigg.blogspot.com/2007/05/voicing-blogging-working-and-recovering.html

8. http://scogan.blogspot.com/

9. For a recent discussion and relevant bibliography, see Ruth Evans, "Chaucer's Life," in *Chaucer: An Oxford Guide*, ed. Steve Ellis (Oxford: Oxford University Press, 2005), pp. 17–19 [9–25].

10. For parliamentary chronology and events, now and during the writing of the blog, I relied especially on the texts and introductions in C. Given-Wilson, Paul Brand, Seymour Phillips, Mark Ormrod, Geoffrey Martin, Anne Curry, and Rosemary Horrox, eds. *The Parliament Rolls of Medieval England* CD-ROM (Leicester: Scholarly Digital Editions, 2005). Also see the bibliography provided after LeVostreGC's "Parliament Journal" entries.

11. For more recent interpretations of Favent, see Clementine Oliver, "A Political Pamphleteer in Late Medieval England: Thomas Fovent, Geoffrey Chaucer, Thomas Usk, and the Merciless Parliament of 1388," *New Medieval Literatures* 6 (2003): 167–198.

12. For Chaucer's biography, I rely on Martin M. Crow and Virginia E. Leland's "Chaucer's Life" essay in the *Riverside Chaucer*, as well as Derek Pearsall, *The Life of Geoffrey Chaucer: A Critical Biography*, Paperback Reprint (Oxford: Blackwell, 1994).

13. http://www.pepysdiary.com/about/

14. Clarissa W. Atkinson, *Mystic and Pilgrim: The Book and the World of Margery Kempe* (Ithaca: Cornell University Press, 1983).

15. www.inthemedievalmiddle.com and www.babelworkinggroup.org

16. Eileen A. Joy and Myra J. Seaman, "Through A Glass Darkly: Medieval Cultural Studies at the End of History," in *Cultural Studies of the Modern Middle Ages*, ed. Eileen A. Joy, Myra J. Seaman, Kimberly K. Bell, and Mary K. Ramsey (New York: Palgrave Macmillan, 2007), p. 6 [1–20].

17. Candace Barrington, *American Chaucers* (New York: Palgrave Macmillan, 2007).

18. Trigg, *Congenial Souls*, 43–44.

19. The Pseudo Society has printed an amazing volume of "Proceedings" masquerading as a serious academic journal, the *editio princeps* of medieval jocular scholarly publishing. Richard R. Ring and Richard Kay, eds. *Proceedings of the Pseudo Society: First Series 1986–1993* (Kalamazoo: Medieval Institute, 2003).

20. OED, "fan, n. 2" Draft Additions August 2004: "fan fiction." On Chaucerian rewritings, see Trigg, *Congenial Souls*, 74–108. There is extensive scholarly work on fan fiction that I have not been able to engage in preparing this essay. See, for example, the bibliography available at http://www.karenhellekson.com/theorize/fanfic-bib.html

21. Trigg, "Reception: Twentieth and Twenty-First Centuries," in *Chaucer: An Oxford Guide*, pp. 541 [528–543].

22. Archived at http://www.ealasaid.com/misc/vsd/
23. For an account of the film's soundtrack as a disorienting blend of past and present, though made as part of a critique of the film's "appropriation of the late twentieth-century American culture," see Barrington p. 146.
24. http://www.wmich.edu/medieval/congress/
25. http://www.thevalve.org/go/valve/article/serpentes_on_a_shippe_spoylerez/
26. http://www.guardian.co.uk/books/booksblog/2007/apr/12/theresroomforspicyaswell
27. http://itre.cis.upenn.edu/~myl/languagelog/archives/004541.html
28. http://kotaku.com/192938/olde-tymey-blogger-geoffrey-chaucer and http://kotaku.com/197261/yea-verily-he-pwneth-noobes
29. http://sites.google.com/site/neomedievalisminpopularculture/bibliography
30. http://www.dantesinferno.com/home.action
31. http://gotmedieval.blogspot.com/2009/12/google-inferno.html
32. David Wallace, "New Chaucer Topographies," *Studies in the Age of Chaucer* 29 (2007): 5, 19 [3–19].

CHAPTER 4

BLOGGING THE MIDDLE AGES

Jeffrey Jerome Cohen

Conversation, teaching, conferences, snail- and e-mail, journals, and edited collections and monographs are the long established technologies for sharing ideas and work in progress and then disseminating a "final" form for future readers. Each medium marks a significant stage in a project's gestation. A typical developmental arc for humanities scholarship in the United States might consist of bringing a thesis or discovery into the world via embodied interaction (from chatting to a colleague over coffee to presenting on a panel), with tentative conclusions refined and solidified through the affirmation and skepticism of interlocutors; teaching a single class or a whole course on the subject to try out a thesis and see how well it works; sharing research in a slightly more formal way by requesting comments from friends or from experts not necessarily well known; submitting portions of the project to a peer-reviewed journal and refining the argument in reaction to criticism; and, if all goes well, ultimate publication of the work as an essay, and then perhaps in its fullest form as a monograph. A blog (short for "Web log," that is, an ongoing record disseminated over the World Wide Web) offers a kind of ceaseless electronic conversation that may work in tandem with or might even take the place of some of these junctures and media.

Blogs are Internet-enabled spaces that accelerate some long-standing academic practices while enabling new scholarly modes. They do not offer the blind peer review that sanctions publication in a prestigious journal or authorizes the imprimatur of a revered press; instead they provide a forum in which research and argument can be honed through swift, trenchant feedback. Unlike conference panels or hallway conversation, the reach of a blog can be vast, its audience not stratified in the ways that the academy (with its persisting love of hierarchy) tends to be. A famous *New Yorker* cartoon by Peter Steiner depicts a dog typing on a computer and announcing to a fellow canine, "On the Internet, nobody knows you're a dog" (69.20 [July 5, 1993]: 61). On a blog, no one necessarily knows or cares about your rank, your institution, your publication history; on a blog, everyone can join the colloquy, and have the chance to speak to scholars who might not be so easily conversed with in everyday life. The discussion is open to strangers who happen upon the material. The risk is occasional trolling (gratuitously negative comments given for little reason other than to stir passions). The potential reward is hastening of processes that can otherwise take months to unfold, the gift of unexpected and early insight into where a project might be taken, and the possibility of combining the personal and the professional in fruitful new ways.

As an entryway into blogging I have focused on scholarship, but blogs are not limited to this single area of medievalist practice: they can be pedagogical tools (a forum for student writing, as in the blogs Michael Wenthe and Sarah Rees Jones incorporated into their classes to extend conversation beyond seat time; a place for exploring best classroom practices, as in the many posts about how best to teach a text, convey a concept, construct a syllabus), a form of public outreach, windows into worlds that might otherwise remain unknown, means of connecting to larger communities. Like all genres, blogs have implicit rules and innate structures. Comments will always be secondary to posts; bloggers will always have a louder voice than conversants; most readers will not be contributors, so impact can be difficult to measure; brevity and wit are valued; some self-revelation and a sense of intimacy are expected. Like many Internet-inspired phenomena, blogs lack formality and rigidity, especially when compared to conventional print. Much of what is disseminated through the medium is serious, sober, professional, and worth preserving. Much is also light-hearted, whimsical, personal, and ephemeral. Blogs are inherently gregarious. Though some are nothing more than public diaries, with minimal or invisible readerships, most embrace their status as public spaces fostering communal, collegial endeavor. For that reason, I blogged this essay at the medieval studies blog. In the Middle (www.inthemedievalmiddle.com) as I composed. The finished product represents a group effort. Though the person whose name appears on the byline takes responsibility for all errors, and assembled the essay from its constituent pieces, "Blogging the Middle Ages" could not have come into being without the convivial gathering a blog facilitates.

I. Early Days on the Electronic Frontier

Scholars who study texts inked onto animal skins eagerly employ electronic databases, HTML and other kinds of coding, digital facsimiles, ultraviolet light, and a plethora of sophisticated machines of varying sizes (scanners and pens and notebooks and cameras). This paradoxical conjoining of the ancient and the electronic is most publicly evident in the e-texts, e-mail discussion lists, blogs, Twitter streams, and Web sites that have become part of the contemporary practice of medieval studies. On the one hand, such love for practical and useful tools is nothing new. Quills and vellum are technology, after all, not markers of its absence. The millennium of Latin crammed into Migne's *Patrologia Latina* could not have been bequeathed to us without machinery that in the nineteenth century was at the cutting edge. Printed on cheap paper, the endeavor would not be so useful to us now were it not for electronic storage, search, and retrieval. Yet even if the discipline of medieval studies was built through and looks back to outmoded instruments, we can still ask: Why do scholars who research a past so distant that its inhabitants could not imagine a virtual space like a blog embrace such technology themselves?

Medievalists are, among many other things, philologists: *philos*, "loving" + *logos* "word." As word-lovers we happily dedicate ourselves to apprehending Latin, Old English, Old Norse, Middle High German, Provençal, alien tongues plundered from history's solitude and revivified for communication. Computers likewise speak in arcane languages that demand translation. Is it any wonder that medievalist logophiles were early participants in conversations about technology? J.R.R. Tolkien studied (albeit briefly) to crack enemy codes during World War II. In 1982, Martin Irvine, trained at Harvard as an Anglo-Saxonist, completed one of the first humanities dissertations composed entirely on a computer—this in the days before Microsoft Word and Google Documents. Irvine and Deb Everhart are the founders of an innovative Web portal, the Labyrinth, the first Web site hosted at Georgetown University (http://labyrinth.georgetown.edu; no longer maintained). With minimal institutional support, the site became a clearing house for the vast amounts of medieval-related material proliferating on the Internet in the 1990s. Among the early major pages offering materials for students and scholars of the Middle Ages were the Internet Medieval Sourcebook (http://www.fordham.edu/halsall/sbook.html), the Online Resource Book for Medieval Studies (http://www.the-orb.net), Netserf (http://www.netserf.org), and the Monastic Matrix (http://monasticmatrix.usc.edu).[1] Most of these sites were the product of astounding, unrecompensed labor by tech-savvy individuals like Paul Halsall and Lisa Spangenberg.

Halsall notes that the Sourcebook was supported by his colleagues, but not taken "seriously in terms of career advancement" and tenure. Several of these archives and portals have proven transitory, ceasing to exist once the person behind them became unwilling or unable to maintain their links and content. Though e-mail now seems a conventional mode of scholarly communication, in the early 1990s few humanists used the medium. Medievalists were among the early adopters. Some, like Marty Shichtman and Laurie Finke, employed electronic interchange to facilitate collaborations that, had they been conducted via telephone or traditional post, would never so swiftly have yielded finished projects (e.g., *Medieval Texts & Contemporary Readers* dates to e-mails beginning in 1985).[2] Such Internet-assisted collaboration likely leads to better integrated multiauthored works, since any participant can work on any part of the text at any time. The late 1980s and early 1990s saw the establishment of a number of electronic mailing lists on increasingly specialized medieval subjects: ANSAX-L, ARTHURNET, CHAUCER, MEDIEV-L, MEDTEXTL, MEDFEM-L, to name a few.[3] The discussions that unfolded through these dedicated groups were often impassioned, especially when the subject was the place of those new approaches to the interpretation of literature and culture grouped under the rubric *theory.* E-mail became another space in which the culture wars endemic to the time raged. The heatedness of discussion could become a deterrent to productive conversation. Out of frustration at this lack of sustained focus was born Interscripta, a series of moderated electronic discussions of limited duration focused upon a single topic (http://www8.georgetown.edu/departments/medieval/labyrinth/e-center/e-center.html). The inaugural foray was Jim Earl's conversation on medieval subjectivity, a discussion that deftly interwove medieval materials with philosophical reflection upon the kinds of identity flux the Internet either enabled or made evident. Later topics included "Augustine and His Influence on the Middle Ages" and "The Everyday." I moderated the concluding colloquium myself, on "Medieval Masculinities." The e-mail interchanges were eventually collated into a hypertext article— and, because electronic publication was still very much a novelty at the time—I arranged for the essay to find its way into conventional print.[4] Meanwhile what it means to be "in print" was being challenged by new journals like *Chronicon* (ed. Damian Bracken, http://www.ucc.ie/chronicon) and *The Heroic Age: A Journal of Early Medieval Northwestern Europe* (http://www.heroicage.net), both founded in the late 1990s and existing wholly online (Jonathan Jarrett, Michelle Ziegler). Add to this burgeoning number of professional sites the vast number of personal Web pages, LiveJournal, Usenet groups, BBS boards, and the creation of e-texts and hypertext editions and the phrase "information overload" seems apt. Yet, as Eileen Joy reminds us,

> There has always been information overload. One of my first published articles was about the efforts of 17th-century bibliographers (Humfrey Wanley, Thomas Smith, George Hickes) to catalogue all of the Saxon MSS extant in English and European libraries and even just to record the contents of Sir Robert Cotton's library ... and this required a certain methodology of notation and abbreviated description that required skimming, reading things only partially but never fully. It was also quite the heroic set of labors, in which early modern bibliographers were always swimming against the tides of too little time and too many manuscripts in too many places, some just plain impossible to get to.

The Internet accelerated preexisting processes and made them more visible, even as it rendered access to the results of such labor more widely available, democratizing the field to at least some extent.[5]

In 1995 several medievalists working in the Washington DC area conspired to mount an ambitious conference on the future of medieval studies, "Cultural Frictions: Medieval Cultural Studies in Post-Modern Contexts" (http://www8.georgetown.edu/departments/medieval/labyrinth/conf/cs95). One of the first humanities conferences with Web participation integrated into its staging, the event seemed to arrive before its time, before an eager electronic audience had come into being. Though papers were posted in advance, few questions were submitted for discussion, and the conference mainly proceeded as an ordinary gathering of scholars. The live portion was intense and productive, yielding a collection of essays for the journal *New Literary History*.[6] Yet the Web enabled the conference organizers to advertise the event widely, and then to archive its work electronically for easy future access. The conference has, therefore, had an enduring afterlife. It is interesting to consider how different *Cultural Frictions* would be if it unfolded today, when blogs and Twitter are an accepted part of our medievalist praxis, when electronic publication and integration are nothing so very new.

II. A Brief History of Some Medieval Blogs

The untapped possibilities of the Cultural Frictions project have been amply activated by medievalist-run blogs, which offer the interactive sites for communication and critique that the conference had been striving to create. Among the earliest of these were Wormtalk and Slugspeak (http://michaeldrout.com) and Scéla (2002, http://www.digitalmedievalist.com/news). Both remain active to this day. By 2005 five pseudonymous medieval blogs also were offering thoughtful posts and lively conversation: Blogenspiel, penned by Julie Hofmann writing as Another Damned Medievalist (http://blogenspiel.blogspot.com); HeoCwaeth (http://heocwaeth.blogspot.com); Ancrene Wiseass (http://ancrenewiseass.blogspot.com; begun 2003 and now defunct); Magistra et Mater (http://magistraetmater.blog.co.uk); and Quod She, the creation of Christina Fitzgerald under the *nom de blog* Dr. Virago (http://quodshe.blogspot.com). Explicitly and inspirationally feminist, these forums were initiated by authors at precarious moments in their careers, suggesting something of what the form offers that mainstream medievalist scholarship does not enable. Julie Hofmann writes:

> [When] my academic career took second place to family things…the connections I made to other academics in several fields [via blogs] helped to re-integrate me into a conversation that I'd really been missing for several years…Blogenspiel serves as a sort of a memorial to who I was, and I think shows who I am and am becoming as an academic and as a medievalist…The blog still has one stable purpose, and that is to continue to connect with a community I respect and appreciate.

Hofmann also observes that blogs trace the liminal area between public and private life: "The *limes* is broad, and like the one following the Rhine and Danube, there is a lot of negotiation and interaction that occurs along it." This possibility of bringing the personal so close to the professional is at once an attraction of the genre, and a reason why so many bloggers remain anonymous. Christina Fitzgerald writes of her early engagement with blogs:

> Over time I found myself equally interested in the stories [bloggers] told and the issues they wrote about, particularly on the personal or mixed personal/professional blogs of other academics. Negotiating my own life as a new assistant professor in a regional university, I started to see myself, or at least lives like mine, in these blogs. … Reading and commenting on these blogs became a kind of substitute for the long conversations my friends and I used to have in the TA offices in graduate school, or the long e-mail exchanges I had with a few select friends both during and after graduate school.

This experience of community inspired her to start a blog of her own. Quod She offers "a record of how often academic professional identities become deeply personal to us, and how intertwined the threads of our complicated lives are." Fitzgerald talks of the pleasure, companionship, and even consolation so many of us bloggers feel through our interactions with our commentators when she describes how, after she posted about her mother's death, the mysterious Chaucer blogger offered condolences in modern day English, a touching departure from maintaining character.

Stephanie Trigg describes how a diagnosis of breast cancer trans-formed Humanities Reasearcher (http://stephanietrigg.blogspot.com) from a grants-oriented professional forum to a space where she could talk about illness and treatment, providing information to those she knew and who worried about her and reassurance to others facing the disease. The blog became a place where she could reflect upon her experience as a patient as well as a professor, "a safe space of mediation between my study at home and the world of public interaction." The genre's invitation to "test the limits of my own privacy," she writes, has been motivating. Trigg's Australian perspective is also a draw, especially because the medi-eval blogosphere is dominated by academics from the United States. Her profoundly moving accounts, for example, of the official apologies to the indigenous people of Australia in February 2008 had little to do with humanities research or the Middle Ages, but in a way had everything to do with both.

With its initial focus upon access to research funds, Trigg's blog came into being with a purposefulness that few other blogs possess at genesis. The wildly popular Got Medieval (http://gotmedieval.blogspot.com), for example, was founded by Carl Pyrdum III in 2004 with some intermit-tent entries: "I posted a few times," Pyrdum writes, "and then promptly forgot I had started a blog for a few months." These desultory posts none-theless quickly found an audience, and a burgeoning readership encour-aged a sharpened sense of mission. Mixing analysis of contemporary medievalism with history and art from the Middle Ages (especially saints and marginalia, what Pyrdum describes as "nifty things"), Got Medieval is, when measured in size of audience, the most successful of the medi-evalist blogs. Scatological, pop culture savvy, and smart, the site has been featured on BoingBoing and was named a Top 100 Blog by *PC Magazine* in 2008. Got Medieval, in other words, has achieved what many academ-ics strive for but few attain: wide popular readership. Like the Chaucer blog, Carl Pyrdum's work is enviably public, engendering connections between specialized medievalist knowledge and a general audience.

Other blogs began with a modest or circumscribed ambit but grew quickly thereafter. Around 2005 two widely read blogs appeared, Richard Scott Nokes's omnibus Unlocked Wordhoard (unlocked-wordhoard.blogspot.com) and the eclectic Muhlberger's Early History (http://www.nipissingu.ca/department/history/MUHLBERGER/blog.htm). Both of these sites tend to be straightforwardly professional in their subject mat-ters, both are offered as much to students at their authors' institutions as to a wider public, but both offer moments of whimsy, humor, and personal revelation. Unlocked Wordhoard, for example, offered multiple links to Katrina relief efforts in the wake of that hurricane. The blog grew over time to specialize in medievalism, and its author notes the institutional support he received in maintaining it (Scott Nokes). Matthew Gabriele's Modern Medieval (http://modernmedieval.blogspot.com) likewise began with an in-house emphasis: Gabriele teaches as Virginia Tech, and initiated the blog in response to the massacre on campus in April 2007. He writes:

> My first substantial post was an expanded version of an op-ed I'd written for the local paper. I got into academia because I liked the research and the teaching but also because I believe that there's a place for public intellectuals in our society. Too often, however, academics lament that no one takes them seriously. I think part of that is our fault. The onus, to a large degree, falls on us academics to put ourselves out there and have something to say about something.

Modern Medieval has proven adept in transforming itself to adapt to changing modes of electronic communication. Larry Swain, founder of The Ruminate (in 2003: http://theruminate.blogspot.com) and a longtime Internet presence, now co-blogs there, and Gabriele himself is one of the more prolific medievalists on Twitter. Another site to tap the synergy of blogging, stable Web pages, Twitter and Facebook is Medievalists.net, the collaborative project of Peter Konieczny and Sandra Alvarez. Dating back to an Internet gathering of information on military history from 2001, the Web site now compiles a vast amount of information relevant to the study of the Middle Ages, with an emphasis on breaking news.

Numerous blogs trace their origins to moments of career uncertainty: HeoCwaeth beginning graduate school under difficult family circumstances, Dr. Virago starting a new job, Another Damned Medievalist transitioning back into teaching, Ancrene Wiseass working on her dissertation in frustrating circumstances.[7] Jonathan Jarrett, one of the few British medievalists with a blog, observes that he initiated A Corner of Tenth-Century Europe (http://tenthmedieval.wordpress.com) in 2006 because the job market was offering few prospects and the glacial pace of academic publication was inhibiting his work from being widely read:

> So the choice came down to waiting forever with a bare-bones CV and a web presence basically confined to undergraduate music obsessions, and not getting a job, or to taking over my own presentation on the web and making sure that I looked like, not just a scholar, but one who was in touch with new media and outreach to the public, something which I believed and believe still is a moral obligation of our profession, especially in the UK where it is so substantially state-funded.

Jarrett admits to ambivalence about blogging. While on the one hand the practice has sharpened his writing, enabled unexpected friendships, made his work well known to strangers, and earned him invitations to speak about his research, on the other, he feels, new media are generally undervalued or even looked upon with suspicion within the British academy. Blogging, in other words, has offered few professional rewards. I founded "In the Middle" (http://www.inthemedievalmiddle.com) in January, 2006. I was on sabbatical, had just finished a book, possessed a semester without classes to teach, and had been reading medieval and nonmedieval blogs for some time. Early posts included dictionary and encyclopedia entries as well as fragments from books: scholarly publications pushed into the world through a novel mechanism, but without a significant change of voice or mode. But then the comments started. Among the first to respond to my posts was my future co-blogger Karl Steel. He mentioned my infant site at Quod She, prompting Christina Fitzgerald to send many readers my way. In the Middle took off from there. Having people respond quickly to what I e-published prompted me to write more, to take more risks with what I was disseminating, to use electronic communication to bring into being new kinds of scholarly community. I was especially interested in fostering an interdisciplinary space where hierarchies (grad student versus professor versus interested member of the public) and other sortings endemic to the profession (institutional prestige, geographic location, rank, number of publications in peer-reviewed journals) were simply beside the point. I was uneasy at first about bringing much that is supposed to be segregated into private life onto In the Middle. To a degree the blog form demands it: scholars do not live in disembodied isolation; my friends and my family are my constant collaborators, whether they know that or not; and for reasons I have a hard time articulating, exploring the relation between scholarly practice and lived experience is simply important to me, and a blog offers the ideal form for such exploration. A month after starting to blog I knew that the form could be a catalyst to productivity, as well as a new mode of doing engaged work.

I have never felt a strong sense of ownership over In the Middle, wanting it simply to offer the kind of convivial, communal space the profession too often lacks. Thus I've had many guest bloggers—including, most infamously, the Chaucer blogger himself (with whom I admit to having a long-time friendship, and an early knowledge of the secret behind the identity). I had been promising that "Chaucer" would decloak and reveal himself on In the Middle, but what he did instead was to offer a brilliant account of his own blog's genesis composed in the voice of Holden Caulfield (http://www.inthemedievalmiddle.com/2007/04/chaucer-speaks.html). Three of my guest writers became permanent co-bloggers: Karl Steel, Eileen Joy, and Mary Kate Hurley (who has also long

maintained the gorgeously written Old English in New York, http://
oldenglishnyc.blogspot.com). Working with these three conspirators and
friends has been one of the best results of founding ITM. Together we
have experimented with what the blog can accomplish: book reviews, a
forum for syllabus exchange, conference reviews, book clubs, ephemera,
manifestoes, rants, raves, obituaries, and preludes to print. ITM's readership has steadily grown. At the moment we have 273 subscribers through
Google Reader alone, 73 fans via Facebook, 434 additional visits to the
blog each day. In the Middle reaches many more people than any book or
essay I could ever compose. I have often stated that much of my preblog
scholarship has been a series a letters written to unknown receivers, a
lonely position from which to write. What I love about In the Middle is
that the blog reminds me every day of the community for whom I compose, a community of which I am proud to be a member.

III. Future Frontiers

*Nobody gets the future right, except in retrospect. Then again, no one seems to get the present
and past right, even when its artifacts are all around you.*

Eileen Joy

Some time ago I asked if Facebook had killed Blogger (http://www.
inthemedievalmiddle.com/2009/10/did-facebook-kill-blogger.html),
by which I meant: have social networking sites diminished the impact
of and necessity for blogs? The question's importance is tied not only
to what the years ahead hold for academic blogs, but for their audience
and outreach as well. Blogs are composed in part for the communities
that form around them. The best posts are those that spur lively and
sustained conversation. Nothing surpasses having an unexpected interlocutor arrive, someone who can bring the discussion in productive new
directions. Blogs also exist as much for their silent readers than their gar-
rulous ones: of the 273 people currently subscribing to In the Middle via
Google Reader, probably no more than 50 have ever actually left a comment. The blog surely has some tangible impact upon its silent readers,
perhaps in the classes they teach, the articles they write, the projects they
pursue. Add in those who peruse the blog just by stopping by, those who
subscribe via another service like Bloglines, those who use Facebook or
some other site to access the RSS feed, and it seems evident that most
people treat a blog like an informal version of a journal: a place for news,
a chuckle, a disapproving cluck of the tongue, a quick morning skim,
and sometimes a place with some material to linger over, think about,
respond to.

I worry about the relocation of much of what used to unfold on blogs to social media because those discussions are inherently closed: limited to the friends one already possesses; never stumbled upon due to a fortuitous Web search; not existing as a semipermanent, easily accessible archive in the way that a blog's thread of comments persist (and because they persist, blog comment threads can be reawakened after long dormancy; such reactivation cannot happen on Facebook). It could be argued that no technology actually supplants another: print books and e-books are not at war, but are coexistent phenomena. By this reasoning Facebook will not replace Blogger; we will have both, and different modes of communication will unfold on each: sustained, in-depth, archived and open access discussion on blogs; quick, superficial, fly-by conversations on Facebook and Twitter. Maybe. Yet few of us are reading microfiche these days. Another possibility is that a cloud metaphor best describes the interconnected electronic future. Twitter and FB can be used to direct readers to blogs via the quick dissemination of links via multiple outlets (personal profiles, blog fan pages, tweets, and old fashioned homepages). Thus Eileen Joy writes:

> I don't see Facebook as draining either content or persons away from weblogs, so much as they serve as yet another portal *to* particular blogs and blog posts, via "News Feed" links and the like … I started a Facebook page for the BABEL Working Group because I thought it would be a good way to disseminate sound-bite-style information regarding conference sessions, journal issues, books-in-progress, and so on, but if I wanted to send a message to the widest possible audience with a certain amount of detailed substance involved, I would still consider this weblog the best and most effective medium for doing that. For the most part, Facebook, as powerful and widely used as it is, is still mainly a medium for very fast & quick communications and networking between real friends and acquaintances and would-be-acquaintances and for sharing personal information in the form, again, of nugget-sized "bits."

I'd mostly agree with this account. Facebook *is* best for quick, terse, multimedia communication. But I and many of my FB friends have been employing the site—as well as Twitter—for interactive and sometimes substantial exchanges about topics that have in the past typically unfolded in the more public forum of In the Middle: pedagogy, bibliographic searches, uses of technology, recommendations for texts, and discussions of books and articles. I think especially about a recent conversation that unfolded around Patricia Ingham's important new essay "Critic Provocateur" (*Literature Compass* 6.6, 2009: 1094–1108). The piece was shared and discussed wholly within Facebook, catalyzed by a status update by Eileen Joy mentioning that she was reading the essay.

I complained through my own status update that Literature Compass is not open access. The essay was then provided to me via multiple sources, I shared the PDF with others, and multiple status updates about the essay appeared posted by various medievalists. Comments were posted at these updates. The essay triggered a conversation that was abbreviated in the way that the genre requires, but the dialogue had enough weightiness to it that (as I participated in it and watched it unfold) I was aware that yes, Facebook really has taken on many of the functions that had been the provenance and domain of blogs.

So what's next? Despite the "information wants to be free" ethos of the early Internet, it seems clear to me that much scholarly work that ought to be available is going to vanish behind the wall of limited social networks (where the unexpected guest cannot be inspired by what she did not expect to find) and corporate sites that reserve their content for research libraries that can afford their extortionate access fees. But not all of it: open access journals are not in decline, and the day will come (I hope) when their cachet equals that of those we pay for-profit publishing corporations to sanction for us. E-books should make access to writing done under the imprimatur of peer review at "good presses" easier to get hold of. Medievalists are a techno-savvy, generous, and adaptive bunch. Their work is not going to vanish from the Internet any time soon.

Meanwhile the next generation of humanities scholars may not be quite as enamored of text as we currently are, leading to more work undertaken within and published as multimedia. I don't have the technological proficiency to create a YouTube channel, but other medievalists will no doubt do so. I am also, I realize, already old fashioned: structuring my courses around writing and analysis that take textuality as central. I don't especially enable my students to collaborate as part of the learning process; I don't yet care if they would rather produce a video response to Marie de France than a paper based upon textual evidence and close reading. I talk frequently about new critical modes but insist that students master the old ones before they attempt them. Some day I may be one of those emaciated figures seen lurking in the moldering remains of some abandoned academic program, muttering about how declines in Latin proficiency have triggered the pedagogical apocalypse. I worry that the shifts in resources undertaken by increasingly corporatized universities will diminish the long-term health of the humanities, and make fostering the next generation of researchers and teachers a dead-end endeavor.

The future of scholarly communication will likely mean that the technologies I have been using (traditional print books, blogs, Twitter, FB) will be superseded. The future will arrive, and may well leave me behind, just like those for whom the be-all and end-all of scholarship was e-texts, CDs, or microfiche. Maybe the university will always be a location where face-to-face encounter within the humanities classroom will be prized. Maybe the Chaucer Blog will always inspire those who have not taken a course in Chaucer to take one, and those are taking such a course to find a new way to enjoy and learn from the materials. But it is also possible that by moving so much scholarly interaction online we make it easy for those who make decisions about educational policy to hire fewer humanists, to argue that the electronic pedagogical frontier is in fact the most viable one. I'd like to think that blogging and its siblings are ways to make a case for the vitality and importance of contemporary humanities education. They enable and preserve conversations about what is at stake in what we do, and they challenge us to think seriously about how we do it, and for what future.

Notes

For the archive of discussions behind this essay see http://www. inthemedievalmiddle.com/search/label/blogging the middle ages. Contributors to the essay include Sandra Alvarez, Bavardess, Holly Dugan, Christina Fitzgerald, Fluidimagings, Matthew Gabriele, Rick Godden, Paul Halsall, Julie Hofmann, Jonathan Jarrett, Eileen Joy, Sarah Rees Jones, Peter Konieczny, Janice Liedl, Magistra, Steve Muhlberger, Richard Nokes, Carl Pyrdum III, RR, Karl Steel, Lisa L. Spangenberg, Larry Swain, Ken Tompkins, Stephanie Trigg, and Michelle Ziegler.

1. Jonathan Jarrett surveys some of these pioneering—and now often outmoded, inaccessible, and unavailable—sites and technologies here: http://tenthmedieval.wordpress.com/2009/05/15/medieval-latin-and-the-internet-twelve-years-on
2. Facebook communication from Marty Shichtman, November 4, 2009. The book was published by Cornell University Press in 1987.
3. Medievalists were not, of course, the first to the Internet, as the lively discussion group "Humanist" (founded 1987, http://www.digitalhumanities. org/humanist) makes clear (Sarah Rees Jones).
4. Hypertext article here: http://www8.georgetown.edu/departments/medieval/labyrinth/e-center/interscripta/mm.html; print version published as "The Armour of an Alienating Identity," *Arthuriana* 6.4 (1996):1–24.
5. "The digitising of original sources means grad students (and even senior undergrads) who are not on the American or European continents can pursue research on material that could previously only be reached after spending thousands on international airfares. At my own university, a glance at the library's catalogue of history dissertations and graduate research exercises shows a clear increase in medieval (and early modern) topics, and I'm

sure this is made possible in part by sites like the Medieval Sourcebook, EEBO and various national archives like Gallica" (Bavardess).

6. "Special Issue: Medieval Studies," *New Literary History* 28.2 (1997).

7. For HeoCwaeth's account of the genesis of her blog see http://heocwaeth. blogspot.com/2009/12/am-i-still-medievalist.html

PART II

MEDIEVAL RECREATIONS

CHAPTER 5

CHAUCERIANS DO IT WITH PRONOUNCED E'S
AND OTHER RISIBLE RELICS OF A CAMPAIGN IN
THE MEDIEVAL TRENCHES

Robert W. Hanning

Author's Note: what follows constitutes a kind of comic diary of my
more than fifty years as a medievalist, first as a graduate student,
subsequently as a faculty member. The entries, spread across several
genres, record via good-natured (I hope) parody my encounters with
texts, ideas, colleagues, and scholarly presentations in classrooms, libraries,
and those overheated, overcrowded (or near-deserted), resonantly named
meeting rooms in conference hotels engaged by medievalist associations
and overrun by their members.

Many of these efforts, and the occasions that generated them, were
shared by like-minded denizens of the back row in those meeting rooms:
friends whose serious dedication to acquiring and transmitting knowledge about the European Middle Ages did not prevent them from finding
humor in the accidents, if not the substance, of medieval studies. I am
happy to single out, with gratitude for their inspiration and collaboration,
my co-conspirators George Economou, Joan Ferrante, and Sandra Prior,
and to dedicate these pages to them.

I. Limericks

There was a wise man of Quebec.
Who kept base impulses in check
With proverbs and saws
That spilled forth from his jaws
With profound soporific effect.

> There was an old prof of great wisdom,
> Who loved it when young women kisdom;
> But his sex life was bleak
> For his sight had grown weak:
> When he tried to embrace 'em, he misdom.

On corruption at the Papal Curia:

> In Rome, at the court you won't win a cent
> If you've not to the judge a good dinner sent,
> And, later or sooner, a
> Few timely *munera*,
> For feasts of the not wholly innocent.

On a lecture explaining that medieval manuscripts are usually arranged with the flesh and hair sides of a parchment page facing each other:

> Said that great scholar, W. P. Ker.
> "This codex excites me, I swear!
> For its parchment leaves mesh
> With flesh placed next to flesh—
> And such textual intercourse is rare."

Observation on the popularity of formalist criticism, inspired by the translation into English of Vladimir Propp's *Morphology of the Folk Tale*. (To be read in an egregiously phony Russian accent.):

> Dye formalist creetic, V. Propp,
> Put dye Rossian folk tale on dye mopp;
> "For it's clear," he said, greenink,
> "Dey begeen at begeenink—
> Ond ven dey are feenished...dey stopp!"

After papers, at the Medieval Academy conference, on the living arrangements in early medieval convents and the obligation imposed on all nuns to confess three times each day:

> 1. The Abbess to her young nuns said,
> "To the world you're not yet, alas, dead."
> "So," added the Cellaress,
> "please don't be too jealerous,
> If we old folk sleep two to a bed."

> 2. Said Abbess to novices, "pray
> That you won't into holiness stray.
> For it's tough, when beginning,
> To do enough sinning
> To fill up three confessions a day!"

More on nuns: in response to a paper on miracles of the Virgin, including one that restores the virginity of a peccant but truly repentant Abbess:

> Said the Abbess, "yes, I had an urgin'
> To indulge in some bodily mergin';
> But then Mary, with grace,
> All my sins did erase;
> Now I'm known as the *unabridged* virgin!"

More on penance—on an early medieval theory that one should not absolve sinners until they are too old to sin [?!]:

> Said the monk to the sinner, "at forty,
> You're lustful and greedy and haughty;
> But keep sinning, please do,
> For I'll not absolve you
> Till you're clearly too old to be naughty."

On reading a dissertation on the *lectio divina* and its influence:

> For *lectio*, if we want passion,
> We tend to prefer *pater* Cassian;
> But for elegance we go
> To *Dominus* Guigo—
> His system is always in fashion.

On the election of Teodolinda Barolini, Dante specialist, as a Fellow of the Medieval Academy:

> The student was clueless and green; he
> Had knowledge of Dante most teeny.
> Of Dantistry painless
> He'd certainly gain less
> From any prof but Barolini.

On the prolific Johan Sebastian:

> That musical motormouth, Bach,
> Inundated his Lutheran flock
> With cantatas and passions,
> So despite changing fashions,
> They only had Bach 'round the clock.

Prof. Prior has graciously permitted me to include the following, written when, as a graduate student, she ate an apple (loudly) during a seminar:

> Ms. Prior's crisp apple—Empire—
> When she bit it, aroused her prof's ire:
> "If in class you must munch,"
> He said, "grapes do not crunch—
> Or try a papaya, Ms. Prior."

Not autobiographical:

> There was a bespectacled klutz,
> Who drove his dear wifey just nutz,
> Till with whip and with boot
> She trained the old coot
> To say "yes, dear"—no ifs, ands, or butz.

Complaint to Chaucer:

> Said the Parson, "Geoff, swing into action!
> We your pilgrims demand satisfaction!
> You've not only ignored us,
> With good women you've bored us—
> Now get with it and write that Retraction!"

> A chauvinist poet called Chaucer
> Took a wife and proceeded to baucer;
> Till one day, beside Bath,
> She struck him in wrath,
> Which gave Chaucer good cause to divaucer.

A medievalist prepares for a trip to Iceland:

> An Icelandic tourguide called Gisli
> Will help you find saga sites isli;
> But there's only one hitch:
> You have got to be rich
> To afford his rates, which aren't misli.

With apologies to a great scholar:

> A philologue padre called Ong
> Wrote essays, both complex and long,
> About Christian morality
> And primary orality,
> So his students could tell write from wrong.

In response to a lecture on frontier crusades in the late Middle Ages, contrasting peaceeful commercial interaction with bellicosity and religiously inspired violence:

> A merchant in Muslim grenada
> With Christians attempted to barter,
> Till crusading Castillians,
> By thousands and millions,
> Soon rendered his plan a non-starter.

On Aquinas as a negotiator of the problems of reconciling Aristotle and Christianity:

> "Aquinas, you're just a chameleon!"
> Said an orthodox Aristotelian;
> "You shift your position,
> Eschewing contrition—
> Your world's not one I can move freely in!"

With apologies to Dante:

> There was an old codger from Crete
> Who was driven to tears by his feet:
> One was iron, one was clay,
> And he'd no dough to pay
> To have shoes made by an exegete.

Anent "We are dwarves standing on the shoulders of giants," popular medieval aphorism:

> A learned but tesy old giant
> Struck a posture we must call defiant
> When he said to the dwarf,
> "From my shoulders get off—
> With your topos I'll not be compliant!"

> The hero of Chrétien's tale, *Lancelot*,
> Fought in battle with Meleagranz a lot,
> Which from hour to hour
> Put him back in the tower,
> And let Chrétien expand his romance a lot.

In response to Prof. Economou's fascination with the Dracula story:

> The good count of old Transylvania
> Said, "Come, maidens, I'll entertania;
> Your fancy I'll please
> With my own *neckspertise*,
> And if you're my blood type, I'll drainia."

> That most fertile hero, Odysseus,
> Had sons to fit most of his wysseus;
> They loved fighting and killing,
> But—alas!—none was willing
> To stay home, clean house, and wash dysseus.

Response to a Medieval Academy paper by Prof. Linda Seidel, on ways of testing impotence claims in legal actions by placing the claimant in a closed room with unclothed young women and observing the result

Said the husband, "in bed I fell short,
So I'm impotent"—that's *his* report;
So by maidens (bare breasted)
His alibi's tested,
To see if it stands up in court.

II. Responses to Learned Arguments

On a paper about the construction of medieval noblefolks' genealogies:

Q: How do you keep the family tree healthy?
A: Easy—use an incesticide!

On receiving an invitation to a " *Genre* party" (i.e., a party sponsored by the journal, *Genre*):

Q: At a *Genre* party, how many people would need to come in the guise of a sonnet?
A: Six—two men called Abraham, with baccalaureates;
    two very poorly dressed people;
    and a male and female little person, who are married.

THAT IS: Abie, BA
          Abie, BA
          Seedy,
          Seedy,
          And a couplet.

III. Commercial Products, Advertisements

Now! New! Be sure, use Saussure (pron. "So Sure"), the semiotic detergent that penetrates to clean deep structures.

  * For use with manual or syntagmatic washers
  * available without meaning in this area

Special South Philadelphia pasta dish: the Ziti of Brotherly Love.

On a Greek-owned fish and chips shop in Oxford:

Is this the plaice that lunched a thousand chips?

Name for a combined Italian coffee bar and Chinese teahouse: Shangri Latte

From a medieval personals column:

Big Dog: I can do it four ways. Interested? Exile

Sign on a back road approaching a rural community:
Warning! Hickly Settled.

A fish and chips shop is a site that brings the sole closer to cod.

The Thomistic push-up bra: adds substance to your accidents.

In town to joust?
Need good lodgings?
The best knights spend their best nights at: *The Tiltin' Hilton*
"Chivalry isn't dead; it's just asleep at the Tiltin' Hilton." (Sir Philip
Sidney, satisfied customer)
All major credit cards accepted; we prefer:
The Anglican Express Card: Don't Leave Rome Without It!

Sign, intended for allergic passers-by, on a factory manufacturing
toxic coloring agents:
"Hail, sneezer; we who are about to dye, pollute you!"

For peripatetic Aristotelians:
Being transferred by your company? Retiring to Florida? Have to move
your household *fast*?

Call: *The First Mover!*
—coast to coast
—reasonable rates
—you got ideas? We got forms!

"Putting you in motion is our *telos*!"

Fantasy examination for a potassium-deprived academic:

Q: what would make a banana wear a disguise?
A: A desire for banananymity

Q: In what style of handwriting did Merovingian bananas draft their
charters?
A: In greater and lesser Bunchials

Q: How would an unscrupulous, litigious banana attempt to slip out of a
law suit filed against it?
A: By a peel to a higher court.

Q: A long, husked, yellow vegetable falls off its stalk while quite young,
and is found and nurtured by a good-hearted but near-sighted long,
skinned, yellow fruit. What would we call such a creature?
A: Corn born but banana bred.

IV. Literary Musings

1. *Suggested Titles for the Next* Beowulf *Movie*

Thane there were none
The best Geats of our lives
Till we mead again
He walks with booty in the night
Busby Berkeley's Border Steppers of 2012
Wiglaf all the way to the barrow
Son of Citizen Cain
I can Heorot now

2. *Embarrassing Questions, Addressed to Readers of Chaucer's* Canterbury Tales *(and with Apologies to Dr. Seuss)*

Would you do it with a Pardoner?
Would you do it with a gardener?
(There's no need for special pleadin':
Any garden, not just Eden.)

Would you do it in the derk?
Would you do it with a clerk?
Would you do it in your elde?
Would you, *could you*, with Griselde?

Would you do it on a perch
Or in a tree (pear, fig, or birch)?

Would you do it with a prof,
Or someone who's let cut 'em off?

Could you do it all-out, whole hog
In the middle of your Prologue?
Would your listeners grow pale
If you did it in your tale?
Could you do it while you swynk,
In your prologue, tale, or link?

Would you do it, Madam, sirs,
While on horseback, wearing spurs?

Could you do it (I'm uncertain)
While not bearing a stiff burden?

Could you do it near a crow,
Or beneath a shotte-window?

Would you do it at the Tabard,
With a rusty sword and scabbard?
Would you do it, you all-riskers,
With someone with houndfish whiskers?

Would you do it with a carter,
Or a holy blissful martyr?
Would your relics please a saint,
If you caught her by the queynt?

Would you do't with pulled-up smok,
Or with a dumb, but learned, cok?

Would you dare go at it busily
While perched atop a blak rok grisly?

Would you, could you (tell the truth!) work
Hard at it while still in Southwark?

Would you do it, when desirous,
With a clergeoun or prioress?

Could you do it in Athens (Greece)
With someone who could "hold his pees"?
Could you do it twice a night

(Once Palamon and once Arcite)?
Would you find making love as easy as
Making war was to Duc Theseus?
Could you, if the Duc insists,
Do your knight-work in the lists?

Tell me truly, just between us,
Could you do it with Justinus?
Would you not find it discouragin'
To do it with that wimp, dumb Dorigen?
Could you respond to Cupid's darts
And then divide it in twelve parts?

Could you do it in a jail,
Or with an old and leek-y tail?

Could you do it with a boarder?
Would you follow Ellesmere order?

Or would you do it (catch my drift?)
According to the Bradshaw shift?

Would you do it (no young heifer, he)
With that popet, sly Daun Geffery?

Would you do it just by chaunce,
Or only with God's purveyaunce?

(July 1983)

3. Wiglaf's Warning (to the Tune of "Fugue for Tinhorns," with Apologies to F. Loesser)

I've got a horde right here,
But let me make it clear
That if you take it, it's gonna cost you dear—
It's true, it's true,
The scop tells me that it's true;
Then stop what you plan to do,
Won't you, won't you?

Cause there's this dragon bloke,
And if he sees he's broke
He's gonna come make your hall go up in smoke—
Will do, will do;
That's just what the wyrm will do;
He won't take an IOU—
Would you, would you?

So though your fame is wide,
You'll have to stow your pride.
And find a barrow that's not so occupied—
Please do, please do
Quit before he "fires" you,
'Cause that's what the wyrm will do— To you, to you.

4. A Sentimental Mead-Hall Song (to the Tune of "Home on the Range")

Oh, give me a home
Where the Grendelcyn roam,
Where the thegns and the peace-weavers play;
Where seldom is heard
A superfluous word,
For the half-lines are mostly Type A.

(refrain)

Joy, joy in the hall,
While the scop sings a popular lay,
Calling heroes to mind
With no *hapax* to grind—
And the half-lines are mostly Type A.

Oh, give me a hoard,
And a ring-giving lord,
And a mead-hall that shines through the land;
If it burns, why, who cares?
Let the thegns make repairs—
And ask Grendel to give them a hand.

(refrain).

5. The Lament of the Would-Be Piers Plowman Scholar (to the Tune of Rodgers and Hartis "I could write a Book")

> If they asked me, I could write a book,
> About Will Langland and the snoozes he took.
> I could write a prologue on fields of folk,
> And on all the nonsense they spoke.
> And the simple secret of the plot
> Is to keep writing and re-writing a lot.
> And the world discovers when my book ends
> Why *Piers Plowman* has so few friends.

6. We're Off to See the MARTYR (to the Tune of "We're off to see the wizard" from The Wizard of Oz)

> We're off to see the martyr,
> The wonderful martyr of Kent.
> In *felaweship* we make the trip,
> And know we'll be glad we went.
> Of *myrthe* and *solaas* we'll have our share
> In Harry Bailly's loving care,
> Because that is all wholly his *entente*;
> And even though *quytyng*'s not what he meant,
> He'll guide us to the martyr,
> The wonderful martyr of Kent.

7. A Musical Precis of Norman History as Described by the Notoriously Inaccurate Dudo of St. Quentin (to the Tune of "Camptown Races"):

> I. The northern races sing this song,
> Dudo, Dudo;
> Their tempers are short and their boats are long,
> Hey, Dudo's Danes.

> (refrain)

> Come and sack Rouen,
> Bring your tribe along!
> It don't much matter what we say or do,
> Dudo'll get it wrong!

> II. The Vikings they sailed up the Seine,
> Dudo, Dudo;
> They saw good fish but no good men,
> Hey, Dudo's Danes.

> (refrain)

III. The Norman Dukes, they did such things,
Dudo, Dudo;
They slaughtered earls and counts and kings,
Hey, Dudo's Danes.

(refrain)

A pendant to the preceding:

> A monk of St. Quentin called Dudo
> Saw that Normans, as fighters, were crude; "Oh
> My goodness," he said,
> "They will all soon be dead
> If they don't learn karate or judo!"

8. Lines Composed to Celebrate Prof. Ferrante's Birthday, Coinciding with a Book Party at a Columbia-Area Bookstore Celebrating the Publication of the Hanning-Ferrante Translation of the Lais of Marie de France, with a (Profoundly Irrelevant) Introduction by the English Novelist (and Marieophile) John Fowles, Inserted at the Publisher's Insistence

> Dear friends, today we celebrate
> A medievalist first-rate;
> Also included in our plans:
> An accolade for Marie de France,
> Who now appears in modern dress—
> Stylish? Perhaps; expensive? Yes!
> So now let's render our homage
> To *deux grandes dames d'un certain age*,
> And lay the praises on with trowels;
> But please! Let's not include John Fowles. (11/13/78)

V. Article Titles

"Pause and Clause: The Rhetorical bottom lion of Chretien's *Yvain*"

VI. Series: Things Are Getting Verse All the Time

1. If vice is nice,
and sin is in,
won't the exercise of virtue
hirtue?

2. If Cleopatra
Got any fatra,
She'd need a barge
Size extra large.

3. Advice to a dieter:
Every ounce
Counce.

4. No place safe from self-involvement:
Wherever we go
We find ego.

5. Advice to women in a competitive business environment:
Even in a dress,
Agress.

6. The confessions of a distraught detergent buyer:
No Tide? I cried.
No Dreft? Bereft.

7. Advice to suitors of an anonymous Japanese beauty:
Don't ask, "who she?"
Just bring sushi.

8. Hard choices for urbanites with fantasies of reliving French history:
Want a Frank at the bank,
Or a Norman doorman?

9. On the infancy of frontier heroes:
Even Wyatt Earp
Had to bearp.

10. On consumerism:
Advertising?
Not surprising;
It's just lying
About buying.

11. Lament of the obstinate heretics:
Recant?
We can't!

12. A query about Arthurian festivities:
Did Lancelot
Dance a lot?

13. Advice to skating instructors:
Don't let klutzes
Attempt lutzes.

VII. Bumper Stickers

[outside medieval studies] pro- and anti-Marcel:

BOOST PROUST
OUST PROUST

Biblical Bumper Stickers

Paul is a basket case
Samson does it with a piece of ass
Sarah does it as infrequently as possible

More Bumper Stickers

Chaucerians do it with pronounced E's
Courtiers do it with *sprezzatura*
Ovidians do it for a change
Judges do it under trying conditions
Lawyers do it just in case
Poet laureates do it occasionally
Big game hunters do it to get a head
Tennis players to it when they have two
Tracers do it to make a good impression
Prisoners do it for release
Astronauts do it without any sense of the gravity of the situation
Self-portraitists do it with mirrors
Gardeners do it in many beds
Bagel and donut-shapers do it to make ends meet
Innkeepers do it, but only with reservations
Apocalypse predicters do it as if there was no tomorrow
Deli owners do it with relish
Court jesters do it with bells on
Joggers do it in many laps
Actors do it on cue
Balloonists do it when they can get one up

Chaucerian Bumper Stickers

Is there life after Sittingbourne (or only Rochester)?
Quyte while you're ahead!
Gipoun bismotered? Take it to Canterbury's only "ride-in" dry
    cleaners
Help stamp out shiten shepherds: support your local Parson
It's 10 pm: do you know where *your* litel clergeoun is?
You've made your tub, now sleep in it!
Getting warmer? You're getting coulter.
Would you trust a God called Walter?
Honk if you know Goddes pryvetee
Inspire a Prioress: beat a little dog
Franks for flanks
To thryve, swyve
Be a *pilour* of your community—ransack a *taas* today
Name your *foyson*

VIII. Where Clichés Go to Die

On learning that the editorial board of a scholarly journal included three truly distinguished scholars: R. Howard Bloch, Brian Stock, and Caroline Bynum: "They've cornered the market on medieval superstars, Bloch, Stock, and Carol."

The husband always agrees with his wife, never argues with her, He knows which side his broad is bettered on.

If you want to find out what's really going on within the Baltic states, leave no Estonian unturned.

Q: Why do stag hunters never get sleepy?
A: Because they take no does.

Q: What do you call it when a snake exaggerates?
A: Viperbole.

Q: What do you get if you take a fillet of skate (a ray-like fish), slice it very thinly, and top it with a mixture of butter, sugar, and cream?
A: Icing on thin skate.

Q: What song would a spiritual advisor sing to ward off the advances of a lustful female recluse?
A: "Anchoress away."

Raging argument between friends because of a card game: troubled waters over bridge.

Did you hear about the atheist teacher who wouldn't give credit on a test to a student who listed the Biblical flood as an historical event?

She wouldn't take Noah for an answer.

Did you hear about the man who purchesd lambs for $20 each, implanted antlers in their foreheads, then sold them for $100 each? It's the old commercial story: buy sheep, sell deer.

IX. Chivalric Nomenclature

Le chevalier de la tempête: the Knight in Gale
Le chevalier de bel repaire: call him if the telephones at the castle are down
Le chevalier des grands projets: Sir Plansalot

X. History Reexplained

After their first fund-raising trip (early twelfth century), the canons of Laon built a shrine for the Virgin. After the second, even more successful fund-raising trip, they built her a tax shelter.

Words to the (only recently awakened) audience of an 8:30 a.m. session at a Modern Language Association convention: "In the immortal words of Chaucer's Knight, "Up roos the sonne, and up roos MLA."

XI. A Uniped Commentary

(Dedicated to the memory of a great and sorely missed scholar, Nicholas Howe, whose paper on the Icelandic saga of Vinland, featuring the encounter of the Icelandic explorers with a ferocious uniped, inspired it.)

First Icelander to second Icelander on landing in Vinland: "We're going to conquer this land, if necessary one foot at a time."

First uniped: "Do you know Louie? He's the biggest klutz I've ever seen!"
Second uniped: "Yeah...he must have one left feet."

First uniped: "See that guy over there (pointing to another uniped)? Why do you think he's got bruises all over his ass?"
Second uniped: "Oh, I know him—that's Tactless Tom. He's always putting his foot in his mouth."

Q: Why is it a pleasure to read uniped scholarship?
A: It has limited footnotes.

Q: What's the condition of a uniped who has trouble walking?
A: Dyslegsia.

Definition of "functional impossibility": A uniped playing the cello.

XII. And Finally

At a scholarly meeting, a noted Italian scholar offered a fascinating and well-researched paper on the wills written by Cardinals of the Roman curia in the late Middle Ages. His English was excellent, but inevitably, given linguistic differences, he pronounced wills "weels" (as in "wheels"), which occasioned the following ruminations:

Q: What does the sign say that hangs over the place where Cardinals take their wheels to be fixed?
A: Service servorum Dei.

Q: What does a rich Italian cardinal leave behind when he dies?
A: A wheel of fortune.

Q: Why do Cardinals need wheels?
A: So they can get around without the papal Fiat.

Q: Why do Cardinals have wheels?
A: To hasten their re-tire-ment.

"Enough; no more! It is not so sweet as it was before."

CHAPTER 6

GEOFFREY CHAUCER HATH A BLOG 2006–2009

Geoffrey "LeVostreGC" Chaucer et al.

GEOFFREY CHAUCER HATH A BLOG 2006–2008
Geoffrey "LeVostreGC" Chaucer

January 27, 2006
Abbreviaciouns

Oh newfanglenesse! Ich have learned the privitees of the manye abbreviaciouns ywritten on the internette.

Par ensaumple: OMG: "oh mine ++DOMINUS++". ROFL: "rollinge on the floore laughinge". IRL: "in reale lyfe." WTF: "whatte the swyve?"

Beinge somethinge of an innovator myselfe, Ich presente to yow, churles and gentils alle, the followynge abbreviaciouns. May they serven yow welle in your internette communicacioun:

GP: Gentil person
WC: Woole customes
XC: Exchequer
BATJG: Biggere arsehole thanne John Gowere
BSL!: By Seinte Loy!
OTPBRB: Offe to parliamente, be ryghte back
SNAPSU—BYXCA: Supposedely nyce annuitie paymente swyvede uppe by the XC againe
KRAMTYABJ: Kynge Richarde II assigned me to yet anothir bureaucratic job

AOMSHJDOTBD: Anothere of my servauntes hath just dyede of the Blacke Death

EISBYMIWATCHDNSTHD: Eftsoon Ich shall be ycleped mad if worke at the customes house doth not settle the helle downe

February 23, 2006

Ask Chaucer

My dog is a retriever, but he won't chase a ball. Every time I throw a toy across the room, he climbs in my lap and licks my face. I know he needs exercise—what do I do?

-Pinned To The Floor

Ma Cher Pinnede to The Floore,

By my feithe, firste Ich oght to praise yow for yower carefulle husbandrie and governance of yower hounde. Ther are sundrie folke who feede ther houndes with rosted flesh or milk and wastel-breed and reken litel of the helthe of the dogges in question. Yower care maketh myne eyes to watre with teeres, so like it is unto my love for litel Lowys my sone.

Actuallye, a tale of litel Lowys shal beare the kernel of myn counsel unto yow. This yuletide, Ich gave hym an astrolabe with instructions written by yowers trulie with muchel care and laboure. But whatte does he opene firste? The Exboxe CCCLX that my Lorde John of Gaunte gave vnto hym. The astrolabe ys styll in its brighte shinye wrappinge papere.

By thys ensample ye might undirstonde that alle thynges taken aftir ther nature, especialie dogges and adolescent boyes. And Plinie the Eldre telleth us in booke VIII of hys Historie Naturale that houndes do chace the enemies and bestes awaie from ther maistres, and eek that the hostes of Garamante and of Castabale didde usen armies of dogges, for they are fierce and bloodie. So yow can see thatte "toyes" are not goinge to do it. Ye nede to fynde some animal or enemy for yower dogge to kille, and thenne he will reallye go at yt.

-LeVostreGC

Sir-

Ich wishe for adyce in the matter of fashion and armes. Ys it verrily a mistake to wear a lily-flour in my helm? (Ich have a shylde of golde.?)

-Thopas

Mon Sire Thopas,

By seinte Jerome, finallye someone who kan spelle! Messire Thopas, ye seem a man fair and gent, and Ich sholde muchel relish for to tellen yower tale. Ich shalle have myne peple calle yower peple. As for the lilye? It dependeth how whethir yow wolde ben "Easte coaste" or "Weste coaste."

-LeVostreGC

> My betrothed, a most wicked man, betrayed me near as bad as Tereus did Procne. His woman of choice commited, though, that villainy which women do best, and tempted him away. Presently it is not legal, where I live, to have either of them killed for this treachery—what shall I do to avenge the wrong they both have done to me, and to my virtue? Their joy at my grief does pain me so.
>
> -Cor Fracta Est

Ma Cher Coeur Brisee,

Thogh Ich love a goode revenge tragedie as much as the nexte guye, Ich muste counsel yow to a bettre path. Ye sholde maken pees and kepe faithe, not wyth thyne betrothede nor wyth this womanlie Diomede, but rathir with yowerselfe. For vengence aperteneth and longeth al only to juges. Remembre yow that pacience is a greet vertu of perfeccioun, and remembre that ther are tymes ordained unto al thynges by the first moevere. Of the oakes, and of the hard stones, and of man and womman seen we also, in youthe as well as age, all shal be dumped, a kyng as shall a page. Som are dumped on dates, som are dumped by telephone, som are dumped in compaignie, and eek are som dumped allone; ther helpeth noght, al goth that ilke weye.

And thus, take two pintes of hajen daghaz dulce de leche, a ful seson of *Buffie the Slayere of Vampyres*, and calle me in the morninge.

-LeVostreGC

By my feith, this pooste of blog hath muchel distractede me from myne woole accountes, and now Ich nedes muste worken late ynto the night.

March 16, 2006

Ich and the Perle-Poet on Mount Dorse-Quassee

Lordynges, by Goddes grace Ich yow biseche that ye forgyven me myn tardinesse yn updatinge myn blogge. In this droughty March, the customes house is unusualie bisy.

Ther ys one of the demaundes for myn advyce column that Ich am looth to lette passen unanswerede, yet also looth to answeren, so hevy are the paynes it driveth thurgh myn herte.

Hey, Geoff,

It's my (in all probability fruitless) ambition in life to discover the identity of one of your contemporaries, the so-called Pearl/Gawain-Poet. I've been casually research-ing identity theories for the past couple years now, but they just seem to go in circles. I recently stumbled across an article, however, entitled "Was the Pearl Poet in Aquitaine with Chaucer?" I eagerly await its arrival via ILL. In the meantime, I thought I'd assuage my curiosity by asking: was the Pearl-Poet in Aquitaine with you? And furthermore, why can't we find out who the talented (no offense to you, of course) bastard is?

Yours truly,

Lost in Transcription

Deere Loste in Transcripcioun,

Indede. The makere of Perle was "wyth" me.

Whenne Ich was but X and VI yeeres, aftir mony a daye of kervinge at table for myn lorde Erle of Ulstere, Ich wente wyth my lorde to werre in Fraunce.

In our compaigyne was anothir younge valet lyke myselfe, who likede all the beste songes by Machaut and Deschamps and evene boughte the importe single of "Ma Fin est Mon Commencement." He hadde a high-arched nose, and narwe face, was possesede of a lene and powirful bodie wel suited for the jouste and the clashe of armes. We did swere ful depe to be brotheres, eche of us til other. And oure bloode was hotte for werre and eek, as eftsoones we lernede, for othir thynges.

Fyghten togeder we dide, this valet and Ich, in Rethel-toune whanne the Frensshe layde waste to yt to letten the Prince Noir from crossinge, and in the melee we were scatterede from the hooste, and we two dide runne like eye makeupe on a televangelistes wyf. We coude spyen no banneres of oure lorde, and yn the welken ronge the trumpours of the Frensshe in their victorie.

Fer from the toune, we cam at dawne to a mountayne ycleped Dorse-quasse. The sootie masse of the montaigne palede slowlie vntil yt was a colore lyke thatte of the smoke from the stille-burnynge towne. We hidde us undir a spreadinge tre. He loughe, and oped a gourde filled with a draught of wyn, and sayde, "Wel, syn we hath scaped togedre, I rekne tis tyme we starte to dryken togedre."

The wyn was prettie nastie, yet *pauperes non possunt electores esse.* Ich tolde hym of myne balades, and he dide recyte severale pieces in the alliterative style. He sayde vnto me, "Thou sholdst endite on Englisshe tonge, for yt ys trewely the waye of the future." "But Ich kan not rum, ram, ruf lyke thou kanst," Ich tolde hym.

Depe did we stepe ourselves in drinke. Thenne—and by the waye Ich assume thou wilt kepe this knowledge from dere Philippa!—we dide thynges that wolde make Alanus of Lille his hede explode. We dide thynges that wolde make Peter Damyan spontaneouslie combuste. We dide thynges that are notte even listede in Burchard of Worms. Rum, ram, ruf!

At morwe-tyde, he sayde to me, "Thou knowst I am not of the scole of Edwarde II."

"Me neithere," quod Ich, " 'Tis nobodies privitee but oures."

Eftsoones, the Frensshe dide fynde us ther, and cleppid us in irones and led vs ech fro othir. Ich was ransoumed back to Engelonde for XVI pounde, which ys about half the pryce of a newe sport utilitee vehicle.

Whan passid hadde foure yeres, and Ich was made esquier, Ich lernede that thys valet now was the stewarde of a manoure in Kent. He had bicom a fayre reeve and a merye. By lettre one lusti Mai he wrot me that he was ycomen Londonwardes for bisiness in the Eschequer.

He pullede up outsyde of Westminstere on a dapple mare wyth gold rims. We sesede eche othir, and sodainely oure mouthes came togethir harde— myn litel woolen hatte fallinge to the floore, and the doore openyng and Katharine Swynforde myn soon-to-be sistere-in-law lookinge out for a fewe secondes at myn straiyninge shoulderes seeinge us and sayinge nothynge unto me until aftirwardes (for she ys a bundel of trouble).

Ich mad a tokne excuse of goinge for to buyen salte-herringe, and the houre of vesperes did fynde the fayre reeve and Ich post-coital yn a geste roome at the Tabard. In the aftirglowe, he dide recyte vnto me a tale of Gawaine and the Grene knighte, of whiche he hadde two fitts ywritten. "Ywis," quod Ich, "Shal Gavvaine swyve the wyf of Bertilak? And yf so, ergo, shal Gawayne paraunter swyve Bertilak?"

"Certes," he sayd, "t'wolde plesen Kynge Richarde!"

"But forto speke of thynges sadde and trewe. Come away with me! Thou knowst, it coude be like this, just like this, for ay."

"Nay," quod he, "Sholde this thynge seise us, yn the wronge place, such as for ensaumple mass or hearinges concerninge hereditarie armorial bearinges, thenne we sholde ben lit uppe lyke Lollardes. If thou canst not hele yt, thou muste stande it."

"I WOLDE I KNEWE HOW OF THEE I MIGHT BE QUITTEN!"

Whanne Ich did retourne, Katharine said vnto me, "Thou didst not buye salt herringe!" Ich hadde to proffren her al of my yearly tun of wyn just to get her to keepe it mum.

Ich nevere saw the young man againe. The fayre reeve sans doute stil dwelleth somewhere in Kente, and Ich have herde fame of hym that he dide make a rime of Gawaine where Gawaine resisteth the ladye. And he dide make a rime of a Perle that was loste. And manye otheres. And Ich dide marrye myne darlinge Philippa, and dide sette up shop at the customes hous.

So yes, Ich knewe this makere of which thou spekest. Ich knewe hym wel. And for some resoun, whenevere myn thoghtes turne vnto hym Ich here some maner of softe chords playede on a giterne, and Ich se a smal, goldene statue recedyng awaye from me, which Ich take to be myn loste vertu. Love kan be a righte Lombarde, sometimes.

May love not be a Lombarde unto thee.

-LeVostreGC

March 26, 2006

Rider of Esement

Beinge a royale favourite ys not alle yt is crackede up to be, for My Lord Kynge Richarde redieth to goon aboute the countrye and visite wyth the locales, and he hath not a scrivener he trusteth for to maken his rydere, so Ich have been encoumbred by the taske. Ich thoghte of askynge myne owen scriven, Maister Adam Linkferste, but he ys oute of toune.

What beth a ryder, ye maye aske? Bifor for a kynge cometh to a manor or monasterie, he sendeth a purveyour who carieth the ryder, the which ys a document that listeth what maner of thinges the kyng shal need. Ywis, forto maken vertu of necesitee, peradventure yt shal plese yow gentils alle to reden of Kynge Richardes rydere which Ich have now made (whil myn owen propre custoume worke pileth up lyk undersized denim jacketes yn a hipsteres closet).

Incipit:

Lordlie And Royale Downtime Requirementz For Oure Trespuissant Sovereyne Richard Secound Of That Name By The Grace Of God Kynge Of Engelonde And Fraunce And Lorde Of Irelaunde

I. APPOYNTEMENTZ OF THE KINGES CHAMBRE:

ITEM. The Kynges chambre shal be adorned wyth tapestries depictinge the supremacye of a monarch over his subjectes by meanes of subtyl and lernede allegorie.

ITEM. The Kynges chambre shal be warmede wyth fire-herthes vntil a mannes brethe turne not into myste.

ITEM. Ther shal be a garden nigh to the chambre in which the Kyng maye walk, and yt shall be:
-Large
-Rayled all th'aleyes
-Shadewed wel with blosmy bowes grene
-Benched newe

Nota bene: Do nat forget to bench the garden a-newe, seriously. The kyng kan knowe a newe bench from an oold bench, and he wil nat hesitate to mencioun if a bench semeth a bit oold.

ITEM. The Kinges chambre shal be nigh ynogh to the chambre of Lorde Robert de Vere the Marquis of Dublin so that a dronken manne myght fynden hys waye along such a distaunce in the derke of night.

ITEM. the followinge victuals and beverages shal be available at alle houres of the day and night:
-Oystres yn gravy
-Henne yn broth
-Canterbury-fryede-Capones, XIV pieces
-Sardenez
-Strawberyes yn goode red wyn
-Wyn of whit and of red
-Sweete wyn
-II botels of brandye of the kynde VS, VSOP and AESOP.
-Champaigne sufficient for to fille a jacuzzie.
-Watir fayre and clene (MUST BE FAYRE AND CLENE)
-Blank chartirs

II. APPOYNTEMENTZ OF THE HALLE FOR FEESTES, LARGER GATHERINGES, BROWBEATINGE OF LOCAL NOTABLES, GIVING OF LAWE, AND LIGHT BEHEADINGS

ITEM. Yn the hall shall be sette the biggeste dangue throne that ye kan fynde. In no wys shal eny chayre yn the halle even compare to how bigge the throne ys. None shal sitte upon or touche the throne except oure lorde the Kynge.

ITEM. Halle feestes shal feature one (I) byrde course and two (II) fisshe courses and one (I) blancmange course and eek fowre (IV) courses involvinge pecockes and sixe (VI) maners of roosted flesh and also brede and spyces wyth ale and wyn enough to gladden the hertes of men.

ITEM. Aftir mete ther shal be AT LEESTE TWO OF THE FOLLOWINGE:

-II to IV wise clerkes that kan speken of cronycles of kyngez and other polycyez

-X pyperes, harperes, singeres, or sum combinacioun thereof

-I to III dancing bear(es)

-A childe uppon a chair who can jangle als a jaye and japes telle

Nota Bene: Yn no wys shal ther be nuts nigh any of Kynge Richardes foode. He hath a powerfulle aversione to the evil nut and doth turne red and kan scarce brethe. Any subjecte who so much as thinketh of nuts in the kinges presence shal be considred to have compassed the deth of the kynge and shal be hung and quartered as a traytor.

March 28, 2006

Flayme Werre

BSL! Mayster Johann Gowere ys all up in my bisynesse lyk galauntyne on a pyk. Nowe by alle the sayntz he stoopeth so lowe as to wryte nastie litel commentes on my blog.

Videlicet:

Myn Gentil Gefroi:

Ich am muchel wrothe at thy japes and hostyl wordes. Ye seem overe eager to maken me seem a smale and pityeful man.
Whatte have Ich wroght to maken my self so displeysing to yow?
Johannes Gowere
ps. my liverie is bettere and Ich do nat share it so freelye to harvest the gold of compleat strangeres.

O, pleyestow the martyr, Mayster Gower? Thou knowst wel my pleynte ayeinst thee, but so that Ich maye maken the roote and engendrure of myn anger cleere to all, Ich have writen a formal appeal ayeinst thee.

Videlicet:

SCIANT PRESENTES ET FUTURI and alle those who maye linke to thys page, Ich Geoffrey Chaucer in the presence of the Internette knowlechede thes wordes and typede them wyth myn owene fingres and thus Ich hereof appeale myn erstwhile freende and companioun Johannes Gowere that he ys a wanker.

ITEM. Thou hast removede mencioun of me from the secounde drafte of thy *Confessio Amantis*. WTS!?! & hereof Ich appeale thee John Gowere that thou art a wanker.

ITEM. Thou nedest getten a lyfe of thyne owene. Whenevir Ich wisshe to hange out with Tommye Uske or Ralph Strode or Sir "T-bone" Clanvowe and juste have some heade-to-heade tyme, thou art alwayes on aboute comynge alonge and then thou makest vs lystene vnto thy talke of moralitees and monkes and yt is ful borynge and maketh myn eyes to droope yn slepe. & hereof Ich appeale thee John Gowere that thou art a wanker.

ITEM. The tale of the Miller of Hendy Nicholas dide plese thee nat, the whiche is strongere affirmacioun that thou art a humorless wrecche than evene thyne intolerable *Miroir de l'homme*. & hereof Ich appeale thee John Gower that thou art a wanker.

ITEM. For lyke VI monthes thow hadst me callen thou backe immediatlie aftir thou called me because thou hadst nat the minutes. Thou shouldst have gotten a goode celle phone planne lyk everybodi els in the worlde.

ITEM. Thou nedst to getten thyn owene topics. Lucretia? Custaunce? Stop messynge up myn game.

ITEM. Ich do suspecte that thou beginnest to harbour unplesaunte thoghtes towards myn deere Kynge Richarde. & hereof Ich appeale thee John Gower that thou kanst not be verye enamourede of that heade on thyne shouldres.

ITEM. Thou art able to be boring in three languages.

ITEM. Althogh thou be rich yn landes and thus nede nat worke, thou japest at me for myn necessarie and profitable labour at the custoume hous and also thou disrespectest myn liverie the whiche ys not a coole thynge to do at alle. & hereof Ich appeale thee John Gower that thou art a wanker.

And of al thes matirs Ich stande redye to preven them yn whatevir maner be judged resonable. And Godde and trewthe shal deciden whethir thou beest a wanker or nat (but thou totallye art and thou knowst yt).

April 1, 2006

Mattirs of Bisynesse, Organisacioun, & Swoteness

Mes cheres lecteurez,

Ich do hope that thys newe syte for the blog plese yow as muche as yt pleseth me, for Ich do muchel relisshe myn litel florale bordere and smal illustraciouns. Ywis, Ich waxe fondre and fondre of my goode scriven and webmayster, hende Adam Lynkferste (confuse hym nat with Adam Pinkhurste, who ys a scabbye manne who did stele two large and creamye wheeles of chese from myn hous and shal nevere worke for me ayeyn!).

Litel Lowys my sone continueth to depely troublen myn herte. For he spendeth alle of hys tyme in hys chaumbre wyth his Exeboxe CCCLX playnge games of muchel violence. And whenne he ys nat killynge thynges on a screne, he listeneth to thys maner of musique called rap or sometymes hip & hoppe. And he careth nat for Boethius nor for the melodies of Machaut and Deschampes, nor euene for myn moste liveli tales of Alisoun and Nicholas. Lette alone the astrolabe. Ich haue decided that Ich shal wryte some verses of thys rap musique forto gladen myn litel sone and eek to maken othir yonge peple lerne of my tales.

That ys al for nowe.

LeVostreGC

April 1, 2006

Make Melodye Today

Ich praye that yow permitten me oon smal moment of sentimente.

Todaye ys the firste daye of Aprille. Bifor it was the cruellest moneth (whatever that meneth!), it was a moneth of coloures and cries, and pilgrymages. Yt was, Ich sholde saye, my favourite moneth.

Ich am nat oon to tooten myne owen horne, but todaye Ich wolde asken yow to declaymen my tales. To yowerselves, to yower frendes, or simplye in the marketplace or churchyarde. For charitees sake, ye coulde declaymen them to beggares, leperes, or humorlesse rogues who studien engineerynge. Wherever yow proclaymen them thogh, do yt so in loude voyse and cleere, for they are fooles who think that a poeme lith on the page aloone.

Yf thou knowst nat this maner of Englyssh, be nat ashamed. Yf thou kanst reden thys blogge, thou kanst reden yt. Talke to yt slowlie, as if it were an olde relative whom thou lovest verie muche, and yt shal talke back to thee.

"Whan that Aprill…"

April 6, 2006

Idea for a Poem

BXB&B! Ich haue devised an excellente plan for a worke of grete literarye merit, chock-fulle of sentence and solaas: the *Tales of Canterbury*. Peraventure, oon day school-childer alle across this great Erth shal reden of thes tales and thanke me for the delite they haue, much more delite than the distichs of Catoun shal euere brynge, or even the *Uve-passes of Wroth*.

Ich shal make a collecioun of tales with a central frame narratif, much lyk the *Tenne Dayes* of Giovan Boccacce, the whiche Ich loue so much that myn copye of yt ys fallynge into litel bits. But my tales shalle be tolde nat only by aristocratik sottes but by men and womyn of alle estaats. More jokes that waye! What ys funnyer than an argument bitwene a summonour and a friar? Thei shal be gadred in a compaigyne for to go to on pilgrimage, for trewely that ys when the weirdoes out of the woodwerke come.

Honestli, yt ys in sum parte sloth that thus driveth me, for Ich haue manye litel wrytynges heere and ther, svch as the tale of the two yonge knightes of Greece with funnye names, and the legende of Seynte Cecile, that wolde nat selle as independente volumes. But package them wyth severale tales of aventure and slapsticke? Bad-a-bynge, bad-a-boume. A devyce of marketynge moore cunnynge than a foxe that has jvst been made doctour of cunnyng at the universitee of Paris! A devyce of marketynge so clever that yt maketh Bill Ghates look lyk an apprentyce fishmonger! Ich am sorrye to be so prideful yn myn herte, but Ich am really psychede.

Thogh Ich am a man of litel lernynge and thogh Ich wielde an humble pen that kan nat be compared to the noble style of Cithero or of grete Dant who did trauel from helle vp to paradise, nevirtheless Ich do beleve myn litel tales shal be a mater of sum discussion and intereste for men and women who shal come aftir me in states vnborne and accentes yet unkennede. Keepyng this in my consideracioun, Ich do thus presente here to yow, gentil rederes, the notes concernynge thes tales that Ich made yes-termorn at the custoume hous. Myn clerkli mayster in freshman comp did alwey telle me that a wrytyng planne ys always a goode idea, and Ich tende to beleve hym since he ys now Archbishop, so he must have doon somethynge ryght.

Ywis, then, heere below followeth myn storme of braynes on this subject. May it plese yow to pardon me the seuerale unrelated nootes Ich haue made oute of ire or confusione, or concernynge litel dittees and balades the whiche Ich do penne almost constantly. Ich include al of the mattir, both kernele and chaffe, heere for the sake of Ladye Clio the warde of historyes and bookes, and hopefulli to answere future scholarlyle ques-tiones abovte the ordere and nature of my tales:

LIBER RATIONUM CUSTUMARUM REGIS RICARDI II—PAGINA XX

BSL! As yf strucke by lightynge—finalli a waye to get ouer myn writeres blok...
"Heere biginneth the Book of the Tales of Canterburye"
Howe coole doth that sounde? Organise ynto fragmentz, for Ich trowe that a worke in "fragmentz" shall appeale to Postmodernistes.

FRAGMENT I

-Intro/setup of frame: Something about Aprille—meetynge with the pilgrimes—pilgrimes in hir order and degre—the hoostes proposal.

-*The Knightes Tale*: A trewe tale that captureth the reale and authentic historicale feele of the culture and societee of Ancient Greece wythout eny imposicioun of ower current cultural standards. The tale shal include ancient Greek courtlie love, ancient Greek tournamentz, and ancient Greek Boethian meditaciouns on the universe. And eek the Knightes shal have avvesome names, swich as "Palindrome" and "Graphite."

-*The Milleres prologue and Tale*: The carpenter, hys wyf, the clerk, and the oothir clerk—absolvtely fabliaux!

-*The Reves prologue and Tale*: Not svre yet, but definitlie haue an ironike aubade and vse the word "fnorten", for "fnortynge" ys aboute the fun-nyeste worde of which Ich kan thynke.

-*The Cookes prologe and Tale*: heroik prentys named Perkyn Revelour sur-vyveth al thinges that wolde kepe a playere doun, meeteth Gros-Blanche, an famovs rapper, and hymself getteth ovte of the workshop and the street to bicom a star, all thurgh his hustle & flowe. Inclvde myn newe ballade "'Tis Difficult Out Heere to Been a Prentys."

XXX lastes of lether at iii pennyes subdsidie per laste is what? Goddes nvts, wher ys myn abacus? Yf Nichol Brembre hath taken yt ayein Ich am goynge to screame.

FRAGMENT II

-The Manne of Lawes Tale: Knighte of King Arthurez court goeth on queste to discouere what women want. Possibly the vote?

-The Dog-Maysteres Tale: The dog-mayster (talle, curtel of greene), his dogge, and his companiounes do fynde an olde wool-quaye that semeth to be havnted by a foule spectre. One of them has those fancie new eye-lenses, the which she doth frequently misplace. Eventuallie they fynde that yt is John Gowere who maketh the appearaunce and similitude of a hauntynge in ordre to kepe the quaye closid, for he disliketh the noyse of woole shipmentes when he writeth hys lame poemes. The dogge may-ster and hys meynee do counfounde Goweres plannes and at laste the vilaynous Gower sayth *"Cest conseil avreit eu success, si non pur l'interference de voz jeuenez meddleurs!"*

FRAGMENT III

-The Shipmannes Tale: Notorious and slightly crazed piraat John Robin helpeth a yonge smithe to wynne his noble ladye, and the yonge smithe helpeth John Robin to scapen from ghost pyrates. Howe avvesome ys that? Ghostes + Pyrates!

-The Prioresses Tale: Ich shal fynde sum edifynge storie of frendship and cooperacioun bitwene Jewes and Christian folk. Must make svre that Gower doth nat maken goode on hys threate to ascrybe to me through forgerie hys owene tale of Hugh of Lincoln fan-ficcioun, the whiche ys about as tolerante and charmynge as a badger on methamphetamynes.

-Sir Thopas: Worke ovte contracte with Thopas to tellen the story of his lyf? Tayle rhyme pleseth me and Ich kan nat lye.

-Tale of Melibee: Make vseful political allegorye wyth basic message: YE WHO RULE NACIONS, CALME THE HELLE DOUNE! Try nat to be excessifly borynge.

ther sholde be a daunce callede 'the bradshawe shifte'

-The Monkes Tale: Telle a series of amusynge anecdotes, all involvyng cheese?

-The Nonnes Prestes Tale of the Cok and Hen, Chauntecleer and Pertelote: A tale collecioun wythoute a beaste-fable ys lyk a fayre ladye withoute a goode foreheade.

Around the watir-cooler, Ich heare of more disputez concernyng herringe at Grete Yarmouthe. Ich do beleve God created Grete Yarmouth specificallye to bore parliamente to dethe—ick—back to my poeme notes . . .

FRAGMENT IV

-Sum wordes of the hoost to the companye: The hoost proclaimeth that tellynge two storyes ther and two storyes back ys right stupid and ympossible—everyone shal stikke to oon tale.

-The Phisiciens Tale: heere inclvde the storie of Appius and Virginia that Gower did stele from me to putte yn his stupide *Confessio.* Possibly add an extraneous bit about educatynge yonge ladyes at the bigynnyng? Now ther is oon thyng Gower ne knoweth no thing about: yonge ladyes!

XXXIV + C = CXXXIV

-The wordes of the Hooste to the Pardoner, and the Pardoneres Tale: Herein Ich shal expose the hypocrisie of the institutionale chvrch! Oones Ich do that, certes the dominacioun of simple folk by the greedie and violent thurgh the strangelholde of religious ideologie shal cease outrighte and the worlde shal moue ynto a more enlightenede age wher civic virtue and the lore of knowledge reign, and no monyes go to dishonest religious impostors. Or peraventure it shal be otherwise . . .

FRAGMENT V

-The Prologe of the Wyves Tale of Bath: Aske for a copye of thys from the Wyf whan she ys finished weavynge the t-shirtes for my blogge.

-The Wyves Tale of Bath: Stele sumthynge litel from Boccaccio? None of the chambre knightz and merchauntz do reden of Italien ficcion, so Ich am soooo yn the clere.

idea for a roundelay: ther mvste be some maner of departure from thys place / sayde the makere of jestes to the laroun / ther beth muchel confusioun heere, and Ich am troublede by barouns . . .

-The Freres Prologue and Tale: Recycle sermon exemplum heere?

-The Sumonours Prologe and Tale: Throwe yn euerythynge Ich kan thynke uppe about fartynge, arses, arses and fartynge, the arse of Sathanas, *et cetera.*

...God wille thes merchauntz euere calm downe abovte their nut-swyvyng woole? Ther ys a place in helle for misers, and Ich hope Ich shal be appoynted ther to prikke ther feete with my quill pen...focus, Geoffrey, focus, thou hast a poem to plan!

FRAGMENT B-12

-The Clerkes Prologe and Tale of Oxenford: That awfulle litel crypto-fasciste fable from Petrak, but make it a commentarye on how Phillipa doth abvsen me.

-The Marchantes Tale: Invente and popularise the terme "May-Januarie Marriage."

blogge t-shirtes sellynge welle! peraventure Ich shal buye Litel Lowys my sonne that turntable setup he wolde fayne possess...

FRAG VII

madam, ye been of al beaute shryne / as far as cercled is the mappamounde, / for as the cristal glorious ye—preene? ete a beene? acte obsceene? are peachye-keene? Thattes yt: shyne. Nowe, whatte doth ryme with mappamounde?

-The Squieres Tale: Jvst go bukke wyld wyth legendes and levitatinge horses and svche. They wil haue to invente speciale effectes ere they kan make a movie of this oon! Bifor wrytyng, possiblie get a hold of that straunge and addlynge weede that Tommy Vsk doth smoke, or peraventure sum intoxicatinge Balm of the Eest?

o seynt hyppolytuses turdes! simon burleye juste totalli caughte me checkynge myn freendstere accounte.

-The Frankeleyns Tale: Use advyce column for inspiracioun?

-The Haberdassheres Tale: Heroik Haberdasshere saues the globe of the erthe from a comete by making an protectif hatte for the worlde.

-The Carpenteres Tale: Heroik Carpentere saues the globe of the erthe from comete by making an protectif cupboard for the worlde.

-The Webbes Tale: Heroik Weaver saues the globe of the erthe from a comete by making an protectif mitten for the worlde.

-The Dyeres Tale: Heroik Dyere saues the globe of the erthe from a comete by making an protectif dye of indigo for the worlde.

-The Tapyceres Tale: heroik Tapycer saues the globe of the erthe from a comete by—BSL! in what maner shal a makere of rugges and tapestries saue the worlde from a fierye comete?

FRAG VIII.5

–*The Seconde Nonnes Tale*: Slip in myn litel lyf of Saynte Cecile heere.

o Sweete Euer-virgin Mothir Marye, kan Ich juste make yt thurgh oon mornynge without dippyng my quill in myn ale-cuppe insted of myn inkepotte?
–*The Chanouns Yemannes Tale*: Finallye an enemye everyone kan realli hate: alchemists.

FRAG IX

–*The Maunciples Tale of the Crowe*: Wille peple beleve that Crowes were oones whit as snowe? Peraventure nat, but yt shal be a storie of good relevaunce to an importaunt part of my biographie that Ich shal make cleare at sum later poynt.

–*The Knightes Yemanes Tale of the Englysshe Blancmange*: III freendes wishe to performe the acte of Venus, the whiche ys stille a mysterie to them, bifor they leave the householde of their mayster. To fulfill thys counsel, they do seeke advyce yn unusual places yn a series of misadventures. Oon of them doth fynde a straunge but appealynge yonge mayde who doth preface alle hir tales wyth "this oon tyme, at the convent wher Ich was raysed." Evventuallie, the freendes realise that the acte of Venus ys but oon of the manye gret offices of Love. Also putte yn sum amusynge sequence with a blancmange that is swyved.

CLV + CCIX + XLVI = ??????

FRAG 2,253

–*The Persouns Tale*: Vernacular pentientiale manuales sounde a lot more appealynge when they are ycleped "tales."

–*The Ploughmannes Tale*: Vernacular manuales on agriculture sounde a lot more appealynge when they are ycleped "tales."

–*The Hoostes Tale of the Mixinge of Drinkes*: vernacular recipees for grehoundes and grasshoppiers sounde a lot more appealynge when they are ycleped "tales."

–*The Ende*: the Millere doth winne the prise of a supper at hir aller coste. Peraventure include sum bit aboute how the redere ys the reale wynnere of the contest? No, that wolde be cheesiere than Gloucestershire.

Fynde a publisshere? Ich sholde telle Adam Lynkferste to starte buying the parchemin nowe…

April 19, 2006

Straight Out of London
(posted by Litel Lowys Chaucer)

Forsoothe the winterye windes do falle adown into the softe springe or some shizzle like that. HAHAHAHA GOT U—this iznt Geoff this is Lowys his son. I cant write all weird like Dad duz. I just write normal like everybod-E else.

I dunno why Dad calls me "Litel Lowys." Im like five inches taller than him. And what is up with his lame hat? Dude looks like a q-tip that got fat.

N E Way—Dad told me to put this entry up with my html skillz because Adam Linkfirst is away and Dad is out in Kent doing some stuff for our lord da King (trespuissant Richard Second Since da Conkwest Roy Dengleterre et Dirlande et Par Grace de Dieu Roy de Fraunce; Im getting an A in my heraldrie classe). So here I am to save teh day yo.

Big ups to all U gentils and churlz who read his blog like every day. You must not have N E thing else to do. PSYCHE! LOLZ I kinda want 2 put up some dirrty pictures or sometin' or copy that centerfold of Katie Swin outta my Valet magazine but then Dad would like sell me to Flemings or something he would be so mad. He loves this blog almost as much as he loves that wack poem he keeps working on at night about pilgrims and all that.

SHOUTOUTZ TO ALL MY FRIENDS YO—Humphrey I hope their not making you work too hard at tha ox2theford. Remember allz you gotta know for a benefice is "laudate" and somebody at court. And Jennet, aint no reason you gotta stay a recluse just because they walled you into that chirch. I got a chizel on its way to you LOLZ. Guy and Hugh I will C U tomorrow. You still owe me IIId. for the barge the other day.

So Dad is all like worried that I dont like all his weird ballad stuff and so he made this rap song for me. It was lying on my pillow when I woke up, all fresh ink drying on some nice parchmen. Which is kinda cool I guess except he like totally stole it from a classic rap track and that shizznit is so old you can look it up in the Domesday book. LOL! Im more into M et M and Fiddy Shilling and I have been gettin into some Reggaeton LOLZ.

Okay I dont wanna bore yall scholars and stuff, so I'm gonna post Dadz rap song. He tried his best even if it does kinda all sound like one of those commercials where some old guy is trying to rap and he soundz about as legit as a pope trying to be humble: "My name is Urban and I'm here to say / I don't like the schism in a major way" (adde in Cardinalz all beatboxinge). But go easy on him. Hez my Dad. It cant be easy walking around with that stupid hat on LOLZ.

Okay, peace out yall

-Louis Chaucer

p.s. anybody wanna buy an astrilable (sp.?)? I'll give it to you for one pound. Tell me soon OK before I put it on Craegslist

p.p.s OMG Crecy: Knight Commander is the best video game evir. All your Aquitaine are belong to us!

STRAIGHT OVTTA LONDOUN

a balade of hippe-hoppe par Geoffroi Chaucer

Straight out of London: lunatike freke namede Geoff C,
From the covin callede "Kynges Affinitee."
Men who confronte me beware my prowesse
Ich fight lyk Alexandre and talk lyk Boece.
Thou too shal see thys, if thou swyve with me!
The marshalsea shal nede to detainen me
Off of youre culorum, thatte ys how Ich am goinge outte:
For the drastye lollarde traytors, that ys showinge outte.
Gentils start to mumblen, they wolden rumblen,
Mix them and cooke them in a brothe lyk oystren.
This beth a plesaunt roundelay forto synge at morris
Wyth a romaunce like the rose so beloued of Guillaume Lorris.
Stressed-syllable poetiks ys my craft
Whanne Ich haue the custoume house ylaft.
Thow and Ich koulde goon pied-a-pied, yonge maye:
Ich breke statutz and hertes ech daye.
Nay ech weeke, ech monthe, ech yere
Vntil th'exchequer shal put me yn the cleere.
Whan thei audit myn accountes Ich seeke the vino,
For the labour doth chewe my brayne lyk Ugolino.
Yf my verse deliteth yow that ys my sole rewardoun;
Ich kan nat rum, ram, ruf: Ich am straight oute of Londoun!

May 2, 2006

To Kalamazoo wyth Love

O, swete ys the lusti moneth of May, swete aren yts floures and yts gentil zephyrs eke. Euen sweetre ys the facte that Ich am aboute to gette a really goode deale on some lande in Kente. Peraventure, eftsoon Ich and myn householde shal be far from stinkye olde Londoun wyth yts large advertisementz and yts almost constante factionale violence. Ich *so* do nat care whethir aldermannic elecioun goth by craftes or wardes; the whole mattir ys euen more borynge than the disputez in parliament concerynge the Grete Yarmouth herrynge monopolye. Haue not thes politicians eny lyves of ther owen?

Ther is oon othir enchesoun for the swoteness of Maye: yn this moneth ther ys the gatherynge of Kalamazoo. From alle laundes and regiones of the globe of the erthe, folke do come to talke of tymes of yore, to share academik werke, and to get rioutouslye dronke on free wine. Yt is, ywis, a jolie paradise ful of pleasaunte and lernede peple and muchel joye. Ther is also a daunce at the ende. Ich wolde haue visited thys yeere, but they rejectede my papere proposal. The lerned scolers did nat agree wyth myn interpretacioun of mynself.

Enyway, as Ich walkede yn a modest but fayre Kentish gardene, the whiche shall soon be myne owen, and thynkede on May, the loueres moneth, and on the feeste of Kalamazoo, Ich happed vpon the counsel of endityng wordes of loue for the vistores to Kalamazoo. Ich shall yive vnto them sum lynes of pick-vppe, with which thei kan earne the affecioun of that especialle homme or femme stayinge at Valley II.

Peraventure ye gentils do wondre at my givynge of aduice in loue, for Ich am a rolli-polli manne and haue nat yflirted wyth eny soule for mony longe yeeres. Philippa myn wyf wolde kille me with a blunt spoon yf Ich but thoghte amorouslye of eny man or woman bisides her fayre self. But thinke on thys, ye doubteres: that a whetstone is no kervyng instrument, yet it maketh sherpe kervynge toolis. Al thogh Ich knowe nat Love in dede thes dayes, Ich knowe muche of bookes and muche of myn owen past yeeres and amours.

And thus, lyk vnto a pale shadwe of Ovid, that grete writere of loue, lyk a verye *magisterulus amoris*, Ich gyve unto yow fayre folke thes lynes of picke vppe: sum shorte, sum longe, sum of noble caste and otheres churlishe, sum onlye vseful at Kalamazoo and otheres of applicacioun more general-ale. May the archere Cupide hitte the merke for yow!

GALFRIDUS CHAUCERES LYNES OF PICKE-VPPE:

–Do sheriffs administere thee to those who breke the kinges peace? Bycause thou lookst "fyne."
–Yf thou were a Latyn tretise Ich wolde putte thee in the vernacular.

-Ich do deuote myn diligence to studye of the anatomie of engendrure. Ich haue happed vpon an abstruse passage in the werke of Constantyne the Affrikan *De Coitu*, the which Ich kan nat construe. For lernynges sake and the benefit of wisdom, woldstow performe the acte of Venus withe me so that Ich may interpret thys clause in propre wise?

-Ich loued thy paper, but yt wolde looke much better yscattred across the floore of my rentede dorme roome at dawne.

-Art thou a disastrous poll tax? Bycause Ich feele a great risynge comynge on.

-Nyce bootes. Woldstow swyve?

-Thou lookst so mvch lyk an aungel that the friares haue lefte the roome yn terror!

-Shulle we maken the cindreblokke to synge?

-Woldstow haue me shyfte thyne voweles?

-Were thou yn my seisin, Ich wolde nevir escheat on thee.

-Thy beautee ys more intoxicatyng than the OVP open bar.

-Yf thy beautee were a poeme, yt wolde make Dante looke lyk Gower.

-The preeste telleth me that we aren more than VII degrees of consan-guinitee. Game on!

-Ich notyce that my demense and thyn do abutte. Wolde yt plese thee to consolidate ovre powere-base in the midlands?

-Makstow a pilgrymage heere often?

-Let vs breake oure mornyng faste togedir tomorrowe. Shal Ich sende a page wyth a message for thee, or shal Ich wake thee wyth an aubade composid *ex tempore*?

-Ich koud drynke a yearlye tun of thee.

-Ys thy father a makere of walles? For how else dide he gyve thee svch a tall and fayre forheed?

-Ich haue the tale of Lancelot yn myn roome. Woldstow rede of yt wyth me?

-By my soule, thou art a verye mappe of helle. For thy face lyk the rivere Styx wil make me swere oothes neuer to be fforsworn, and thy embrace lyk the Lethe shal make me foryet al else, and lyk vnto the Flegeton thyn arse ys ON FYRE!

-Woldstow be myn Gaveston?

-Howe abovte a blancmange and the acte of Venus? Whatte, blancmange pleseth thee nat?

-If Ich sayde that thou hadde a bele chose, woldstow holde it ayeinst me?

AN ADDICIOUN

Yet yeeres latir, whan Ich did travel with my Lord the Trespuissant Kyng Richard to Kalamazoo, my Lord the Kyng did trye sum of my lynes of picke-up. And yet my Lord had gret ire in his herte ayeinst me, for noon of my lynes did work for hym. So he founde hys owene, the which he seyd worked "lyk a charm." Ich haue recorded them heere appendid to this entrie, so ye kan see how differently a kyng and a middle stratum civil servaunt do maken sweete talke at the same conference.

THE ROIAL LYNES OF PICKE-UPE OF RICHARD II AT KALAMAZOO

–My Frensshe child bryde is at home. Shal we get it on?

–Yf thou yive me a buss on the cheek, Ich shal nat glare at thee from my throne.

–Woldstow lyk to see how much watir it taketh to wasshe the balm from an anonyted kyng?

–The lawes of Engelond are in my mouth, or sum tyme in my brest. Woldstow lyk to see what ys in my pants?

–Art thou a traytourous noble distrustful of my advauncement of inexperienced counselors and redy to use novel legal practices in parliament to violate my rule? Bycause Ich see thou art appealing.

–Woldstow lyk to make love? No? Well, hastow seen the 500 Cheshire Archers standinge over ther? How liketh thee thos apples?

May 11, 2006
Ask Chaucer Again

Mes cherez lecteurz,

Yt hath been many a moneth syn Ich haue thogte of the questiones and inquries that ye have sente vnto me for myn column of advyce. Yet Ich haue had sum smal tyme to looke ayein at them, and haue founde sum messages for which Ich kan yeven counsel.

BSL! Movynge hous ys a thynge of muche woe. Ich am boxynge vppe moste of my possessiouns so that churlez mayen brynge them to Kente to the newe house of the famille Chaucer. Lowys doth louren yn sadnesse of his departure from his freendes, and swete Philippa my wyf ys runnynge the whole showe wyth an accounte-boke yn oon hand and a large panne yn the othir. Ye may esily guesse wyth which oon she hitteth me vpon the hede whanne Ich trye to haue a sytte-doun. But by Seynte Ysidore, yesternighte the sterres al oon shone doun on my composicoun of responses, and my penne dide quicklie flye. So on to yower loial lettres!

Dear Geoff:

I'm changing the taps on a plastic bathtub. I've got a cranked spanner to loosen off the tail nuts, but I'm worried that the corrosion on the threads is so bad they're not going to come off, or that I might damage the fabric of the tub trying. Because I'm working in a restricted space (the cavity between the tub and the wall—about four inches) sawing would take ages, and the fact that the tub is plastic would make trying to burn the corrosion off pretty risky, too. I've tried loosening off with a synthetic penetrating oil, but all it seems to be doing is making the tails greasy.

What do you recommend?

Yours,

Frustrated DIYer

My deere Mayster Frustratede Dyere,

Ich do much wondre that a welthy mayster of the Dyeinge crafte swich as yowerself sholde haue a fyne and riche bathynge tvbbe with runnyge watir and yet haue nat the moneye for to payen men wyse yn tvbbe-crafte whane ye nede repairynge of the aforeseyde tvbbe.

For no man in hymself ys sufficiente for al nedes, and therewith as Aristotelis saith in his booke of Politique, diverse men aren ygrouped togedir yn citees and reaumes for to svpplie eche othir wyth their diverse skilles. Oon man cardeth the woole, oon man spinneth the woole, and an oothir dyeth the woole a fayre colour. Oon man ys skillede yn the husbandrie of beestes, an othir yn the preparacioun of java-basid onlyne gamblynge interfaces, and yet an othir in the produccioun of artificiale guacamole flavour for potato crispes.

Thus, Mayster Dyere, kepe ye to yower owen crafe of dyemakynge and dyeinge of textiles, and employe sum maysters of tvbberye to fixe yower bathtube. Also ye maye wisshe to haue installyd sum of those jacuzzi air-jettes; they are helle of swete aftir a longe daye of travel.

LeVostreGC

Dear Mr. Chaucer,

Okay, so there's, like, this guy at school and he is TOTALLY *hot and I think he likes me—like, he hasn't* SAID *anything? But Jamie heard from Marissa that Brooke had overhead him saying that he was completely into me!! And I like totally trust them? Except that this guy used to date M'lyssa and exes are like SO out of bounds, it's so not cool! But then she was all "oh, we're thinking about getting back together too" and the rest of us were just like, "umm, get over yourself?" and she was like "no", and we were like "yeah" and now she's not talking to any of us which is SOOO unreasonable, she is such a drama queen oh my god and she has the fugliest hair, she had it like slicked back yesterday and I was just like "what the hell?"*

So anyways, do you think I should go for him???

Love,

Hopeless Romantic

Ma chere Romantique sans Espoir,

Thou knowst wel the fayre couplete of Boethius his Consolation of Philosophie that saith "quis legem det amantibus, maior enim lex est amor sibi," the whiche in the Englysshe tonge doth signifie "love ys all kyndes of crazye."

Thus, thyn affecioun for thys manne of hotnesse doth surpasse eny bonde or promise thou hast ymade with Marisse. But onlye, Ich counsel thee, yf yower love doth drawe yts source from Cupides owen trewe arrowe, and yf yt ys sovereine and powirful love (and nat simplye a passynge fancie). So yf yt be trewe and honest love, proceede, wyth litle thoghte for the smal boondes yn fikel frendshep yforged. And yet, be nat cruelle aboute Marisses hairestyle, for as Cicero saith: "odium ludo non ludatori," the whiche meneth "thou shalt nat hate nat the playere but rathir the game."

LeVostreGC

Ma Cher Geoffery,

> *Myn clas was asked to post in yower blog. Perchance yow can shaer yower opynun of alle malle scoles and bathe owr clas in swich licour of which discussion is the flour. Euryone hath sumthing to saye on thys topic and we alwas wish to here them.*
>
> *-In Aprill Shoures*

Makstow a jape, yonge Aprille Shoures?

For both the litel scoles of grammar that aren connectede to chirches and houses of religion, and the grete scoles (by whiche Ich do mene thilke groves of lernynge at Oxenford, Paris, and Boloigne), are, alle and some, deuotede to the educacioun of men and boyes. Ywis, "all male" and "scole" are sikerly the same thyng. Spekestow of mervailles and fancies of straunge londes? For nevir have Ich herde of a woman at the scole of Oxenforde. Nevir have Ich herde of a woman who ys a doctour of theologie, or a mayster of artes or lernede yn physik.

Ywis, it ys a matir of sum consternacioun for me. Thogh mony gentil and noble wommen can lerne lettres at home for to reden scripture and othir werkes, in no wyse can they goon to studye the artes liberales or theologie. And thys vnjustice persisteth, thogh ther haue been and aren and shal be women nexte to which Thomas Aquinas shal seeme merely a coleric fat man wyth a good memorye, and Williame Ockham a faste-talkynge drunke wyth the occasionale interestynge insighte. For certes, Heloyse was a gode woman, and a lernede, as was Hildegarde the visionaire of Bingen. Hrotswit did wryte many a screenplaye and shewe many a film at Sonne-daunce. Marie de France did totallye popularyse the Breton Lai, and she wroot moore of helle than did Dant. And eek yn my tyme there ys Christine of Pise, who maketh moore money from her pen than Ich do. Alle of thes wommen are glories nat merely to their sexe but to al mortal soules heere on this erthe, and alle of them yshutte from prechynge and scolershipe merely by cause a couple men in the erly Chirche had verye difficult relaciounshippes with their motheres.

Nowe, as to whedir men and women sholde be yscoled togedir, that ys anothir matir and oon that Ich shal answeren oones women can actuallie goon to scoles. Ich do ymagine, thogh, that yt mighte be verye distractynge in the fayre moneth of Maye.

LeVostreGC

Gentil rederes, ye sholde knowe that several dayes aftir this poost Ich received a message from Christine de Pise.

TO: GEOFFROI CHAUCER (daliaunce@hottemail.com)
FROM: CHRISTINE (christine.de.pizan@walsinghampost.com)

Geoffroi,

BSL (By Seynt Louis)? Seriouslie. Knowstow nothing of historical women? For doctours of physic, why not Trotula? And knowstow nat of Novella, the legal scholaire and daughter of Giovanni Andrea? I'm a single mother in war-torn Fraunce and *I* can do better research than you. Step it up, big felawe.

What must I do to convince you and othere men that women have don and shal do gret thynges? Do I have to make a freaking allegorical treatys in which women build their own citee out of the gret achievements of their sistren? *Mon Dieu!* That gives me an idea...

La vostre

Chr.

p.s. You still have the third dvd of *The Visconti* season II that I loaned to you—please send post-haste. I want to watch the episode where Bernabo tells his therapist about his last duchess.

May 17, 2006

The Cipher of Leonardo

My gentil rederes alle, Ich dide thynke to teste out sum newe materiale on yow bifor Ich do trye to fynde an agent. Ich haue layde plannes for to enditen what Ich do calle a "cryptographic romance": all of the actioune and courtyle talk of a romaunce, but wyth sum puzzle solvynge and mysteriousness and sum thynge of an exposee of current eventes, corrupcioun, and the lore of heresie. Ich shal calle thys werke the *Cipher of Leonardo*, and Ich thynke yt "hath legges," as they saye in the Holy-Wood. Peraventure Ich shal put it in the tales of Caunterburye, to be toold by the Clerk of Oxenford. Here Ich shal pooste a "tesere" for thee; namely, the firste fitt of the poeme:

Heere Begynneth the Moost Thrillinge Romaunce of the Cipher of Leonardo

Oon night ther forwarde dide stagger, fayntynge,
A man hight Sawnieyre who knewe of payntynges.
Thurgh archwaye vaulted of the Louvre he passid
And grippede the nerest canvass as yf gassid;
A Carravage yt was, wyth gilded frame.
Ovt from the walle thys man dide teare the same.
In hepe beneth the canvas doun yfallen
From far aweye he herde th'alarme to callen,
And thoght hym "stille Ich lyve," and caste his eyen
Arounde the roome a refuge for to spyen.
As crawlede he forth a voys dide crye "Halt, stop!"
So close yt was! Wyth feare hys jawe did drop.

And ther thurgh irene barres he sawe a man
-for, Ich sholde saye, accordynge to the plan
Of Palais-Louvres securitee ful grete
By cause of the alarum above in lyne VIII
Ther hadde ydropped a gate of muchel strengthe
That trappid Sawnieyre yn that roomes lengthe.
The man on thothir syde (art thou stille wyth me?)
Was an albino, ful pale and straunge to se,
For nothynge striketh feere yn mortal soules
Lyk to the pale! A boate ful of hooles
Ich rather wolde thurgh sharke-rich watirs stere
Than oones come to an albino neere!
A longe-bowe from his coat the pale man drewe
And aymed yt at Sauwnieyre the trewe.
In accent odd, "Was litel vse to flee,"
He sayde, "Now wher ys yt? Thou must answere me."
"Tolde thee I haue," the gode man dide proteste,
"Of what thou spekst Ich haue nat the fainteste."
"Thou liest," th'albino sayde, "Thou and thy brotheres
Kepen sum thynge that by ryght longeth to otheres."
Adrenalin in Sawnieyres veynes dide synge,
"How might he," thoght hym then, "knowe of thys thynge?"
"Tonighte," pale weirdo seyde, "the rightful men
Thys thynge in seisin holden shal ayein.
Telle forth and lyfsblud for thynselfe reserve,
But telle me nat and by myn arwes thou sterve."
So Sawnieyre lyk Sinon storye tolde
False as the devil, and seyde yt forth ful bolde,
For he hadde yt rehersed many a yeer.
(Ye notice, O my gentil rederes deere,
Ich telle yow nat of what thys "thyng" might be-
Thys ys a tricke poetic vsed by me
To kepe yow yn confusioun most plesynge
Thurgh alle thys vague and nonspecific tesynge).
So, wyth the tale of thys McGuffin tolde
Sire Lilye-White did logh, "Ich knowe of oold
Thys storye false, for oothirs haue yt seyde."
Sawnieyre dide gaspe and blaunchen lyk a mayde:
Yf pale-face spoke the treuthe, than al the thre
Of senechaux (aske nat yet what they be)
Had dyede the deeth and tolde the selfsame tale.
Was no man evir yn gretere nede of ale
Than thys Sawnieyre, he was so reuthe.
"Whan thou art dede, no man shal knowe the treuthe
But me," th'albino seyde, and shot Sawnieyre.

Hys arwe sange yts hotte waye thurgh the aire
And lodged withyn the breste, o payne so soore!
Th'albino raysed the bowe for yet oon moore.
And yet within his quiver no arwes remayne
For whiche to dryve a passage thurgh the brayne.
"Suffir thy payne," the pale man toold Sawnieyre
And disappearede. By cause he knewe of werre
And eek of woundes he long agoon had seene,
Sauwnieyre did rekne he hadde minutes XV
Bifor the arwe keen wolde bryng his deeth,
And so he cast aboute wyth hys last breeth
To fynde whiche payntynge nereby he mighte see
Well suited to sum steganographiee
With which to leave a message or a clewe.
To knowe the rest: buy my book, redere trewe.

May 24, 2006

Wondrous Messages from the Internet

My gentil rederes alle, what merveilous werkes we see yn thys tyme. BSL!
Several tymes within one dayes space Ich am astonyed with the wonderful werkynges of the Internette. Trewely, yt beth a thyng of grete wisdam
and power.

Syn Ich have had thys blog for nigh an yeere, Ich do receive manye messages of emaile, of gret varietee in maner of speche and in importaunce.
Ywis, yt semeth me that Ich stonde within the dwellinge of the Goddesse
of Renoun or Fame, the ladye who knoweth all tales and tellynges yn
this world ymaad, and to her hous all rumoures and stories do come yn
the maner of pigeones flockynge to a man throwinge crumbes of breede.
Benedictee! so manye litel tales do flit toward myn inbox ech daye, nay
ech houre: sum of high sentence and muche lernynge, otheres of churlishe nature, sum tidynges of myn home of Londoun and sum of londes
ferne and straunge. Ther beth thynges of loue, and joye, and eek thynges
of muchel wo and lamentacioun. Ich speke nat of the emailes from my
freendes, such as Sir Simon Burley, Sir John Clanvowe, Ralph Strode,
Tommy Vsk et alii, Ich speke of thes messages from othirs of whom Ich
haue no acqueintaunce. Ich wene thei do sende them me by cause of myn
posicioun at the custoum house? Surely it must be so, for my fame as a
poete ys but litel, and thes messages come from alle ovir the globe of the
erthe.

Forto shewen yow the wondirs that awaiten me ech daye, Ich haue vsid the tooles of "cutte" and "paste" to presente yow the wondirs of myn inboxe. Heere are a fewe ensaumples:

I. *A fayre ladye of a far londe offreth me hir loue!*

TO: GEOFFREY CHAUCER (daliaunce@hottemail.com)
FROM: ABALIA OF SUSA (abalia@susa.co.pj)

RE: MAIL ORDER BRIDE FROM THE REAUME OF PRESTER JOHN

Good daye! Ich am ycleped Abalia. XXVII yeeres haue Ich dwelt yn thys worlde, far awey yn the lande of Prester John, yn Inde, wher the riveres of paradise do flowe ynto a see of gravel. Althogh thys be a fayre contree ful of precious stones and tables ymade of solid emeralde, wher even the tini-est tchotchke ys ycrafted of diamonde (seriouslie, Ich haue an adamantine shoe-horne), yet ther are fewe worthy men that dwelle herein. In deed, a lord hight Gatholonabes doth convince alle the yonge men for to joyne his cult of Assasines and they spende their tyme lernynge to kille silentlye and hide in shadowes. And thus no gentil man ys lefte for a yonge damo-sel swich as myn selfe, save for the wilde menne of the deserte who haue hornes of beastes and speke no human tongue, and thatte ys juste totally gross. Perhaps yt semeth foolish to yow, but Ich devoutely wisshe to fynde the blessinges of love matrimoniale! Ich do looke for a man riche nat wyth worldlie goodes, but riche yn corage and vertu, and thus Ich haue emailed yow. If liketh yow my message, and ye haue nat hornes and be nat an assa-sin, may it plese yow to sende an replye to me at abalia@susa.co.pj.

II. *An churlish proposicioun of anatomical alchemie! (Mayster Gower, peraventure thys shal be of aide to thee?)*

TO: GEOFFREY CHAUCER (daliaunce@hottemail.com)
FROM: AUGMENTULA SALES (492499@chanounsalchemie.com)

RE: BE SURE SHE CRIE NOT "TEE HEE" AT THEE

A man werkynge wyth an mighty plowe can just playne plowe a bettir furrough than a man with a tinye plowe! Woldstow haue a mighti plowe or a tinye oon?

Order AUGMENTULA todaye, and thou shalt experience the lyf-chaunginge benefittes thousandes of goode men haue whyle on the AUGMENTULA programme! Manye do witnesse grete increses yn the girth, lengthe, and potencie of the *membrum virile*, and do paye the debte of mariage yn gretere amountes than evir bifor. Finallie thou kanst marrye AND burne at the same tyme!

III. *A mightie prince of power asketh myn succour yn matirs financiale!*

TO: GEOFFREY CHAUCER (daliaunce@hottemail.com)
FROM: LEO OF ARMENIA (leoinexilevi@hottemail.com)

RE: THYN SUCCOUR YS NEEDED

Deere Sir,

Followynge the siege of the castel of Gaban and Oure subsequent capture at the hands of the Emir of Aleppo, we haue ben ythrowne into a state of complete confusioun, frustracioun, and hopelessnesse by Oure poore estaat. Oure royale person hath been subjectede to physicale and psychologicale torture by hethene captors in the toune of Cairo wher We nowe are helde prisonere. We do beleve that no Cristen soule hath the vertu or charitee to aide Vs, for yt semeth all the knightes and monarches of Europe are deef to Oure petiticiouns and bisy in their owene werres ayeinst ech othir.

Thou must haue herde, good sir, yn the newspaperes and the internette, of the perilouse state of Oure formere kingdom of Armenie, the whiche hath been ytaken from Oure rightful soverentee by the handes of the Mameluk Turkes.

And yet ther is oon othir matir. Ther are manye huge sums of coine and silver plate that We hadde ystored abroade at the tyme of Oure capture. Yn facte, the totale sum of riches still stored yn Oure name doth exceed MMMMMMMMM poundes.

We haue founde thy contacte informacioun thurgh Oure owen personale research, and, as a drowninge man doth reche for ony branche, We haue sette vpon the counsel of rechynge thee thurgh email. We place grete confidence in thee.

Due to the cruel shackles in which We are ybounde, lik to an newe Prometheus wyth the vulture of despayre gnawinge Oure liver ech daye whanne We thynke of Oure formere glorie and Oure fallen reaume, we kan nat go owerselves to an ATM. We wolde be verye grateful if thou wolde receyve the various summes of moneye due to Oure royal persone and take them into thy safe keepynge. Ower agentes abroade will be in contacte with thee as soon as securitee ys set uppe.

Oones We do manage to escape, We hope to settle somewhere plesaunte, perhaps Dorset for a while, and We shal receyve ayein the moneye whiche thou hast deposited, whilst yivinge unto thee a sum of thirty out of everie hundred poundes for thyn labour and thy loyaltee.

We will require thy telephone and fax numbres and thy banke accounte informacioun so that Oure chamberlain may transfer the moneyes unto thee. We wolde gretely appreciate yf thou wolde accepte Oure proposal yn goode faith. Plese expedite action by sendinge thyn replie to Oure chamberlaines email addresse *infra*.

chamberlaindeleo1133114@hottemail.com
En foi et espoyr
LEO VI D'ARMENIE

IV. *An appeale to the lustes of the bodi!*

TO: GEOFFREY CHAUCER (daliaunce@hottemail.com)
FROM: BROKERES OF ONLYNE EROTICA (spintrian1949@grapelane.co.uk)

RE: HOTTE HOTTE ACCIOUN

WITNESSE THE HOTTESTE ACCIOUN AVAILABLE ONLYNE!

MERELY I SHILLINGE PER DAYE

LADYES OF SPAYNE AND ITALYE, MADEMOYSELLES OF FRAUNCE, GIRLES OF WESTWALE AND ALEMAINE, DAMES OF ENGELOND

— ALLE WYTH FAYRE FOREHEEDS AND WELL-YWIMPLED! HOTTE COURTLIE ACCIOUN! GENTIL TALKE OF HAWKYNGE AND THE LORE OF CUPIDE, FAYRE SINGING OF THE DOUN-FALLE OF THEBES AND OTHIR MATIRS OF WISDAM! SOFTE AND CHASTE BUSSYNGE ON THE MOUTHE AFTIR LONGE TOURNEYS!

AND FOR BASER AND CHURLISHE FOLKE, LYVE WEBCAMES OF INNES OF THE STEWES, IN WHICH THE ACTE OF VENUS YS DOON PRIVILY FOR THYNE EYEN ALLONE. ALLE THE FRESHESTE STARRES, INCLUDYNGE ELEANOR RYKENER. TALES OF NERO AND CALIGULE AND OF THE MI NIGHTES OF ARABYE, AS WEL AS EXTRA-RANDYE FABLIAUX FROM FRAUNCE NEW IMPORTEDE. ALGATE IN IT GOOTH!

V. *And last but nat least, fortune doth smile vpon me!*

TO: GEOFFREY CHAUCER (daliaunce@hottemail.com)
FROM: FORTUNA MAIOR (audacesiuvat777@societastoletana.ed.sp)

RE: WORDES OF MUCHE POWERE

The anciente charme of the Romanes:

SATOR

AREPO

TENET

OPERA

ROTAS

Fortune shal rain doun favours upon thee withyn foure dayes of thy receyvynge thys charme of lucke in thy emaile, but onli yf thou passe thys message on to X othir peple.

Edward Kynge of Englande Thirde of That Name did recyve this charme yn emaile in 1346 and sente yt to ten of hys mooste noble barouns and WITHIN DAYES he dide haue a grete victorie at the battel of Cressy. Richard Lyons, merchante, did receyve thys charme yn emaile in 1376 and did nat sende yt to anyone and WITHIN DAYES he was accusid of foule corrupcioun in Parliament. Also thos who forward thys charme shal be immune to the Black Deathe and exchequer audit.

June 1, 2006

Deedes of Majestee

O the tene and vexacioun of beynge the humble servaunt of a grete Kyng. My Lord Kyng Richard hath caught me in the verray middle of moving my hous fro London to Kent. For todaye, as Ich dide looke ovir the laste of myn householdes posessiouns yn Aldgate of Londoun, bisi ynough with muche labour and thogte aboute wher to putte the lampe yn the rentede van and whethir Lowys sholde want the tee shirte he hath ylefte crumplide yn the cornere of hys roome, lo! an heraud dide appeare wyth a message for me from my lorde Kyng Richarde.

By Seinte Bartholemewes grille! Yt was no thyng othir than a royale writ *De flatteria scribenda*, the whiche doth demaunde that Ich wryte some small libell or brode-sheete yn prayse of Kyng Richarde contaynynge proofe of his vertu. Ich do translate the writ for yow heere:

> RICARDUS DEI GRATIA rex Angliae et Franciae et dominus Hiberniae ad suum carum servum Galfridum Chaucer salutem. Nunc est scribendum aliquid de flatteria pro nostra regali maiestate. Diu fructibus largitatis nostrae fructus es, et pauca pro nobis produxisti. Quaedam facta de quodam milite strenuo Carolo Norrys nomine in paginis internettae ad nostram notitiam advenerunt. Talia facta de potentia et sapientia nostra scribas.

"Richarde et cetera to hys deere servaunt Geoffreye Chaucere sendeth greetynges. Yt ys tyme to wryte sum thyng of flatterye for Oure Royale Majestee. Loonge tyme thou hast enjoyede the fruytes of oure largesse, and yiven litel to vs. Certayne deedes of a certayne bolde Knighte yclepede Karl de Norrys haue ycome to Oure Attencioun yn pages of the internette. Write swich deedes of ower power and wisdam."

Ywis, as thes thynges goon, Ich dide haue to stop my daye vntil Ich had composid and endited sum factes aboute my noble Lord Kyng Richard, the which Ich haue heere yncluded:

Toppe Factes And Deedes Concernyge The Mighti Kyng Richard

KYNG RICHARDE doth nat chase the deere. Chasynge doth implie the possibilitee that KYNG RICHARDE mighte nat catche the deere. KYNG RICHARD mounteth his horse and waiteth for the deere to die.

Whanne a dispute at Oxenforde did occur concerninge the trewe nature of the power of royale kyngeshipe, KYNG RICHARDE himself was acknowledged the wiseste doctour yn that lerned companie. Yet the kyng dide yive an answere of but two woordes onlie to the question "From whennes cometh power?" and hys answer was "KYNG RICHARDE."

The voweles of the Englysshe tonge weren supposed to shifte yn 1377, but KYNG RICHARDE tolde them to staye the helle where they were.

KYNG RICHARDE kan make Johannes Goweres poetrie interestinge.

KYNG RICHARDE doth nat consulte the bookes of lawes and statutez of the reaume. He kepeth the lawes yn his owene herte.

KYNG RICHARDE his touche kan cure scrofula. Yet he shal be soore hurt yf he catcheth scrofula, for nobodye kan touch hym.

The sonnes of the Great Khan do crye and waile with muchel a teere for thei knowe that nevir shal ther feestes be as royale and fayre as those of KYNGE RICHARDE.

KYNG RICHARDE was ful able to haue conquerede all of Fraunce longe agoon, but he thoghte that the "Thirtee Nyne Yeeres Warre" sounded bad.

Armor doth weare KYNG RICHARDE for proteccioun.

Oones, as the cronique doth reherce, ther liued a kynge hight Darius who dide gather hys thre counsellors and aske what was the strengest thynge: wyne, womman, or a kyng. And the firste wyse man dide saye that the kynge was the moost of strengthe, for he hadde powir over lyf and deeth. And the seconde dide clayme that wyne was the strengest, for yt doth bynde everi man far moore than ony kynge. And the thridde sage dide saye that wommen ben the myhtieste, for hir loue hath caused manye kingdomes to rise or to falle, and yet he dide adde that truthe was strenger than alle othir thynges, for in no wise may truthe be overcome. And then KYNG RICHARDE dide slaye alle of them.

KYNG RICHARDE doth nat sleepe; he exerteth his majestee while prone.

KYNG RICHARDE kan yive a summarie of Pieres Plowman yn undir a minute.

Whanne Parlemente dide aske for an accounte of the expenditure of KYNG RICHARDE his housholde, KYNG RICHARDE sente vnto them onlye a peynture of his visage ytwistede yn wrathe. Parlemente dissoluede ytselfe and the Knightes of the Shire dide flee to foreyn londes.

KYNG RICHARDE alreadye habet the corpus.

KYNG RICHARDE nedeth nat to buye riche furres of ermine for to make hys robes. The ermines themselves jumpe on to hys backe and do slee themselves for hym wyth grete blisse.

KYNG RICHARDE ys soore angerede at the clergie for infringement of copyrighte, for "The Peace of God" beth the name of hys right arme, and "The Truce of God" beth the name of his left arme.

At night KYNG RICHARDE hath brighte lanternes and torches al ybrennynge yn his chambre. Nat by cause KYNG RICHARDE doth feere the shadowede derkenesse, but by cause the derknesse ytself hath a grete feere of KYNG RICHARDE!

KYNG RICHARDE nedeth nat a hawke or faucon to catch a heron, for hys owne honde kan flye thurgh the air and kille any thynge.

Whenne God doth write lettres patente, he calleth hymself "Lord of the Universe by the Grace of KYNGE RICHARDE."

The Black Deeth had halfe of yts populacioun destroyede by KYNG RICHARDE.

Whanne he was borne, KYNG RICHARDE dide emerge from his motheres womb wyth sevene riche bishopes, a ful lernede confessour, severale dukes who aren hys freendes and counsellours, two yeomen bearynge banneres and ten menne of Gasconie ful redy to cooke a fyne feeste.

June 15, 2006

The Ocks Menne

Ah, the sweet dayes of somer are wel vpon us nowe, and longen folke to heare of superheroes, and storyes of aventure, of menne and womene wyth capes and funnye maskes who haue poweres. Ywis, Ich do awaite with grete anticipacioun the openynge daye of "The Man Who Kan Fly

Doth Retourne," and Ich was blowene awey to heare that ther shalle be IV (counte hem! IV!) villaines yn the newe filme of the Man of the Webbes.

And thus Ich haue sette aboute creatynge myn owene superheroes. Yt ys ful plesaunte to sitte and thynke of tales of marvelles al the while reclynynge in an adirondacke chayre yn myn Kentishe garden wyth the juyce of mojito. In but a fewe dayes Ich haue createde enogh storyes of superhero to fille manye a graphic nouele, feature filme or eek tie-in beat-em-up video game. Peraventure, oones Ich do complete the *Tales of Canterburye*, Ich shalle sette aboute enditynge the noble tale of... THE OCKS MENNE

Noble heroes from al estates of the kyngdom are broughte togedir by Professir William of Ockham, yclepede PROFESSIR OCKS, who ys confynede to a wheelchayre since that daye longe agoon when he dide soore wounde hym selfe wyth a deadlie razor of hys owene makynge. He doth seeke oute folke wyth speciale poweres of magicke, who shal kepe reson and justice in the reaume. Thei do fighte ayeinst the evil JOHANNES GOWERE (who hath no powere othere than to produce boredom, the whiche ys dedely enogh). The mooste famous and grete of the Ocks Menne do include:

THE PERLE MAYDEN: Thys ghoostlye spirite of a yonge girle weareth a comeleye garmente alle of perlez. She hath the powere to kepe eny manne engagede yn difficulte and intricatlie rhymynge spirituale discussion for seuerale dayes on ende.

THE COMMUNE VOYS: Thys right large manne hath an necke ymaad of iren and steele, the whiche kan be nat struck by no wepne. Beynge immune to beheadynge, he ys the onlie manne who hath no feare of speakynge the truthe yn parlement. Yn episode XII, Johannes Gowere doth trye to appropriate The Commune Voys but ys defeatede by his owene inherente elitisme.

PIERS THE PLOUGHMAN: Piers the Ploughman hath litel memorie of his birthe and rearynge, for he was the subjecte of a toppe-secret governmente experimente, the "PLOUGHMAN X" programme. Chancerye dide turne Pieres yn to the perfecte ploughman, to replace those who dide perisshe yn the grete pestilence. Thei dide putte plowes on Peres's handes, and dide yive hym the powir of regeneracioun yn caas he be ytrodden vpon by the oxene of the feeldes. Pieres made hys escape, and nowe doth labore on hys ploughe for us alle and showe us the waye of pilgrimage to truthe. Hys motto: "Ich am the beste ther ys at what Ich do, and what Ich do, Ich do for commun profit and the loue of Christ. Also Ich kicke arse."

BEVIS OF HAMTON: Bevis of Hamton ys a mighti knighte, thogh he speketh nat yn the maner of gentil folke, for oft he seyeth "hegh hegh hegh" and laugheth at the churlish japes of hys sworn brothir at armes, Childe Coule-Teste.

PICATRIX: Thys crafty Saracen magician doth come from Spayne. He ys mayster of magicke of the sterres. Wyth no thyng more than the kidneyes of a wolfe and a smalle figure of two toades jumpynge, he kan create enmitee bitwene thos who oones were freendes. He kan eek remoeve grisly rokkes blakke that hinder shippes from the see, and oft doth so to winne the loue of ladyes.

THE HUMAN ABACUS: Thys manne hath an abacus for an heede, and thus ys ful skillede at summes of nombres and calculaciouns. He knoweth the date of Easter for the nexte MMMM yeeres. He kan do the woole custoume accountes yn oon halfe of oon seconde, and thus his mariage ys ful blisful for he beth nat ycalled a "workaholic." The Human Abacus was an normal manne lyk thou or me, but then oon daye he was ybit by a radioactif abacus.

ANONYMOUS: Trewelye a thynge of fayerye, Anonymous ys sum tyme a manne, and sum tyme a woman, and eek sum tyme a large masse of peple. Yn the laste of those similitudes Anonymous doth brynge forthe large-scale sociale and politicale innovaciouns withoute leavynge eny trace. He hath a sister named LONGE DUREE. Whanne not fightynge euil, Anonymous writeth a grete dele of poetrie.

THE RECLUSE: Thys braue ladye kan nat be harmede for she ys wallede uppe yn a churche wyth no exit and onlie a smalle windowe out of whiche to looke and dispense spirituale counsel. She ys allowed to have one cat. Yn episode XLII, Gower shalle trye to deprive her of supplies of foode and watir for to slaye her, but the jape shal be on hym: she ys ful accousomede to fastynge for the grete sorwe and devocioun she hath to Oure Lorde.

THE YONGE MAGICALE BOWMEN FROGGES: Thes IV frogges dide swimme yn the streme nere an alchemistes hous and, thus touched by sorcerie, they did wexe large and stronge until they were as talle as men. Thei weren traynede by an hedgehog ycleped Shivere and haue lernede the artes of werre for to defende Engelonde. Augustinus doth fight with a longebowe, Ambrosius wyth a shorte bowe, Gregorius wyth two crossbowes, and Hieronymus doth kepe the arwes for the reste. Thei dwellen yn the seweres undir Londoun and eten blancmange wyth much relishe.

KALAMAZOO: Thys doughty knight kan gadir an hooste of werre of manye scolers, the whiche aren of litel use yn combat but might serue to distracte the enemye while the reste of the Ocks Menne do defuse a bombe or kille a large monstere. Kalamazoo hath the powere to intoxicate eny manne or woman at wille, wyth a depe and grete

intoxicacioun that doth laste for dayes. Hys secrete hideoute ys a
magicale place ycleped "Michigan."

June 23, 2006

She ys yong, sexie, and riche: Interview wyth Reims

Philippa hath pleadede for manye a daye that Ich fynde a waye to brynge
in more cash. The house in Kente ys trewelye a "fixere-uppere" and a
growthe spurte semeth to haue ycome to litel Lowys, for he devoureth
al the mete and drinke so that the reste of my meynee kan scarce fynde a
morsel or a droppe. The office of Justice of the Pees is right honourable,
but it bringeth in litel or no income to me.

Ich haue alwey thoghte myself to be a writer, so Ich shal attempte to take
on sum freelaunce worke. For that Ich do knowe manye a noble lord and
ladye, peraventure Ich sholde write articles for chronicles of societee and
fashioun. Here ys my firste attempte. A fayre ladye of courte dide jour-
neye to Kente with her retinue, and Philippa managid to score me sum
interviewe tyme. May it plese ye gentil folke to correcte eny mistakes
heere, and then Ich shalle sende it off to "Demoiselle" or "Vulgus" or
peraventure "Peple."

REIMS LAUNCECRONA nedeth nat an introduccioun to gentil folke; but ye
churles who lyve in smal holes and knowe nat of societee, knowe that
Reims beth the daughter of an riche stewarde and hosteler of Boheme,
who dide yplace her yn the courte of Anne of Bohemia. Aftir gode
Queene Anne did come to Englande to wedde Kyng Richarde, Reims
hath ben the talke of Londoun. The merchant Nichol Brembre hath seyde
that "a feeste withoute Reims ys lyk a Lombard wythout redy cash." And
the very paragon of fashion, Michael de la Pole, did recentlie remarke:
"Yt maketh litel difference if we winne Fraunce, for we have al redy ben
anonynted at Reims." The croniclez do reporte that she hath been sene
canoodlinge with no lessere a lemman than Robert de Vere, the hippe,
yonge favourite of Kyng Richarde and of late the Marquis of Ireland
(and eek, o scandale! a man yweddede to a grand-dogther of grete King
Edward).

> Galfridus Chaucer: Thou waitest upon—
>
> Reims Launcecrona: Ye —
>
> GC: Ich do beg yower pardon. Ye waite upon Goode Queene Anne, yet
> ye do manye othir projectes. How wolde ye descriven yower crafte
> and place in societee?

RL: 'Tis harde to saye. Lyk, I am a woman of businesse. I am an actresse. I do inspyre men of chivalrie to noble deedes. I do founde chantries ful of preestes who praye for the soule of my chihuahua, who of late did perisshe of the plague.

GC: Telle me aboute a daye yn the lyfe of Reims Launcecrona.

RL: Ywis, I do rise from my bowere and do washe myn selfe, and then, lyk, I throwe the watir doun to the strete for to coole the browes of poore men and labourers. For I am lyk alle aboute the charitee. Then I do haue meetynges. I do pose for peyntures for advertisementes or woodcuttes for croniclez, or I do planne the newe seson for my showe of televisioun.

GC: "The Lyf Symple?"

RL: The same. This seson we shalle go to a poore village the which hath had manye a yeere of dearth. And oure retinue shal lyk buye uppe al of ther beestes and corne that yet remayne, and we shal feaste vs fyne and passinge wel vpon those provisounes, and thenne we shalle mock the peasantz for their churlishe wayes as al the while hunger and nede do dryve them to desperacioun. We shal lyk make manye japes and jokes about the rough and foule visages of the peasantz, the whiche do shewe that thes churlez aren descendid from the lessir son of Noah and aren righftulli oure servaunts and we rightfulli the maysters. And yt shal be a rockinge good tyme wyth bikinis and sum hotte fashiones and mowre cleavage than thou kanst shoot a trebuchet at.

GC: And wher shal thys seson be yfilmed?

RL: The laste two seasonses we haue done yn Engelonde, but this oon shal be in Somerset.

GC: Do ye rede of the broadsheetes and the chroniclez to see what ys written of yow?

RL: Sum tyme if a chronicle hath an illuminacioun, I wil chekke it oute to see how cute I looke. But mooste of that writynge ys so smal and hard to rede. Thes clerkes and writeres and makeres of poesie aren such losers. I do haue much hatrede in my herte for thos folke who lyk sitte as stoones lyk al daye and al nighte for to write of riche and noble lyves that thei shal nevir haue. Thei aren alle probablie custoum house officiales or sum thynge!

GC: Do ye rede of blogges?

RL: Nay. I do nat wante to get too close or I mighte falle in.

GC: Whate saye ye? Ich undirstonde yow nat.

RL: I do not wante to falle in the blogge. Also, blogges are moost uncourtlie. And ful oft ther ys sum dead Pict at the bottom of the blogge.

GC: Of what occupacioun dide ye dreme whanne ye were a yonge girle?

RL: Saynte. Kanst thou beleve yt? I totallye wantede to be a saynte. But thenne I dide discouer that seyntez aren supposid to yive up the worlde and to spende their lives in werkes of devocioun and charitee. And so I thoghte, "that sucketh," and I decidede to be riche insteade. So nowe I haue bought manye a beggare, that I do feede at my cost, and oftimes I do commaunde them to thanke and prayse me so that I feele lyk a seynte, but I kan yet do the act of Venus and drynke depe of wyn and snorte the intoxicatinge balme of the East, the whiche no Seyntez do. For telle me, litel man, who beth the patron seynt of intoxicatinge balm?

GC: Ther beth none, my ladye.

RL: Exactamente, Jeffie. Thou shalt also fynde ther is no seynt of shopping.

GC: Nowe Ich am goynge to seye a fewe wordes, and yf it plese ye, ye maye responde wyth the firste thynge that cometh yn to yower hede whanne ye heare the worde that Ich saye. Peraventure thys shal bicom my schtikke.

RL: I dig schtikke. Go for yt.

GC: The Black Deeth?

RL: Bad skin.

GC: Chivalrie?

RL: Hotte dudes killinge.

GC: Kyng Richarde?

RL: Amazinge whyte foundation makeup.

GC: Professirs of literature?

RL: Vntil they owene up to havynge no ethical use, I shal nat respecte them.

GC: Confessioun?

RL: Hotness. My friare-confessour is sooo hotte. Lyk, he beth so hotte that thou nedest to put fowere of the letter t in "hotttte." Thank God spellinge is nat standardised yet, for we may neede moore than four of the letter t. Adam Pinkhurste kan nat make a fancie-enow lookynge "t" to convey the temperature of my confessour, Sir Penn Etrans-Domos. Caxton hath not "t" enow in hys cas of lettres to shewe how hot this friare ys. His *in principio* is insayne! O, pardon! I was so distractede. I lyk totallie lost myselfe. Hastow anothir worde for me, man?

GC: Nay, me thinketh that ys good enogh. Nevir in this interview haue ye been more wel spokene than yn this descrivynge of yower confessour. Now Ich wolde aske of yower grete fame. Manye a yonge ladye both noble born and lowe doth stryve to emulate yow in dresse and

manner, and manye a yonge manne of all estates doth wisshe fer-
ventlye that ye were hys paramour. Why are ye so popular? What do
ye thynke ys yower appeale?

RL: I am lyk a princesse.

GC: And yet with al respecte, thou –

RL: Ye.

GC: Ye come nat of blood royale...

RL: Silence, churl! Thinkstow that hath eny bearynge? Yt ys all aboute
      what peple weare and who they knowe. Ther aren no divisions eny
      more. Hastow nat rede that tradiciounal feudal bondes aren breakynge
      doun yn to a cashe economy? Be nat such a bastard about feudalism.
      It usid to be lyk "those who pray, those who fight, and those who
      werke"—but nowe yt ys moore lyk "thos who werke" and "me."

(at this tyme two large knightez of Reimses retinue dide haule me off by
my shouldres.)

June 30, 2006

Travel and Tales

Ich do humblie begge yower pardoun, gentil rederes. Bisynesse in Kente
hath been nippinge aboute myn heeles lyk vnto a wolfe or a beare, and
thus ther beth but litel tyme for my blogge. Beinge a justice of the pees
ys a real fulle-time deale, especiallye syn but fewe of the magnates on
the commissioun do evir bother to showe uppe. And Philippa ys on me
aboute payntynge the porche; yt is a contree hous, Ich telle her, nat the
Seynte Chapelle! But she recketh naught of my opinioun. And nowe,
by Seynte Elmo, Ich haue lernede that Ich muste travel to Italye on
bisynesse for King Richarde, so Ich shalle be far from my blogge and
my emayle.

Al the mene while, Ich continue to write of the *Tales of Canterburye*,
which drafte doth come alonge verye slowlie. To sette up the stories, Ich
am writinge a "General Prologue" in which Ich do telle of alle of the
pilgrimes and ther lyves, and Ich do liste al of the grete estates of societee. Alas, thogh, for toile and labour! For Ich did nat devise how manye
pilgrimes or of what maner, and now sum do nat fitte in wyth the reste,
so Ich muste cut them out of the final versioun. Ich shal liste a fewe of
hem for yow, my gentil rederes. Peraventure thes kan be putte yn to the
"Sentence and Solaas Special Edition" of the tales when they aren publis-
shede on dvd.

PILGRIMES OUT-YCAST FROM THE GENERAL PROLOGUE:

A PROFESSIR was there, yn clothes of grey
The whiche she boughte laste yeere for MLA.
Ful seuene yeere at grad schoole had she laboured
And yet ful litel Fortune hadde hir favoured;
For everie tale of hires was "welawey,"
And "publishe soone Ich muste or elles deye."
The scole she taughte at was ferre down the roade
And eek she hadde, Ich trowe, a fyve fyve loade.

A CLOWN ther was, and he wore yellow hose.
Ful white weren his chekes and redde hys nose,
Lyk to an Irisshe man in elder yeeres.
A horn he honkede right loude for to heere
And rode vpon an vnicycle faste;
No man on horse haue Ich sene make such haste
As thys performere dide vpon oon whele.
And yet, me wondrid at the childrene fele
That dide cry "no" and "harrow! help!" at hym.
For whanne he wolde a tricke or jape begin
No childe wolde staye to spyen out yts ende.
Trewelye, no gentil was this Clownes frende:

An INDIAN CHIEF, a COWBOYE and a COPPE
A WERKERE and a LEATHER MANNE (a toppe)
Did marche togedir in fraternitee
Al thogh thei were of varyinge lyveree.
Thei knewe sum auncient magicke remedye
For "Y M C A" dide they ful loude crye,
And lifte ther armes lyk vnto menne gone woode.
And eek yt semede their directions nere nat goode:
Thogh Canterburye-warde we headede Est
In unison thei seyde to us "Go Weste."

July 15, 2006

A Pyrates Lyf for Chaucer

Arrrrrgh, ye scurvie swabbes. Yt ys Ich, Geoffrey Chaucer, Drede Pyrate and Scourge of the Ocean See. Or at leest so Ich was 'til yestermorne, whanne Ich did at laste returne to my litel hous in Kente aftir a manye a daye. Ich hadde but scarcelie openede the door, yet right anon Philippa did seise me and remoue my ear-ringes and dide commaunde me to sitte yn the tubbe until the smelle of the salt-see and rum had departed fro me. She hath taken my parrot and putte it in a cage, the which newe settlement pleseth the birde right nat. She did telle me that Ich maye nevir ayein weare myn eye-patch if evir Ich wisshe to lay by her.

How did this hap? Ich shal tell yow. My journeyinge dide commence yn the accustomed maner, wyth muche planninge and manye lettres of passage from My Lorde Kyng Richarde. Ich was sente wyth my Lord Sir Edward de Berkeley to Lumbardye, ther to make negociacioun wyth Lord Bernabo about aide for Engelond in the grete werres with Fraunce. Our companie dide trauel by shippe along the costes, and dide reche fayre Milan. Al thogh trauelinge ys a payne in my butte, and my luggage was y-lost IV tymes along the weye, yt was all prettie okaye. By Seynt Isidore, ther ys a grand librarie and a fayre at Milan. Thos tyrantz do loue their bookes. Sey what ye want about their tackye horse statuez, but thos absolutist rulers gave Petrak grants lyk thei were candy, while Ich labor on my poemes on my owene tyme. O, the humanitees!

But by my feith, fundinge sholde haue ben the leeste of my worries. On the waye home, yn the greye morwenynge, the shipman espyede two blakke sayles at the horizon. "Alak!" quod he "We al shal be yslawe! For Ich do see the blakke sayles of the DREDE PYRATE ROBERTSON his two shippes, the *Caritas* and the *Cupiditas*. And the Drede Pyrate Robertson never leveth captives!"

Up wente the trompe, and wyth grysely soun out wente the grete gonnes, and heterly ower shippes dide hurtelene al togedir at oones. In goth the grapplinge-hooke, and the pyrates dide crye "arrrgh!" and shake their pegge-legges at us, and dide swash ther buckles ovir and cutte our rigginge. And Ich was dazed and fel doun.

Whanne Ich woke, Ich sawe IV faces peeringe a-doun at me, and yet they hadde but IV eyen betwene hem, for thei were pyrates alle. In sum way, my companiouns and my Lord Sir Berkeley had scapede, and yet Ich hadde ben ytaken by the pyratez for ransoum and putte on to ther shippe.

"Arrrgh," seyde a pyrate, "Wel mayst thou feere for thy lyf, for the Drede Pyrate Robertson cometh to thee, and he shal take thy kernele from thy huske."

"Aye matey," seyde an othir pyrate, "Thou spekest troth. Robertsones exegesis shal leve thee yn pieces!"

And ther he came, terrible for to looke vpon, wyth a parrot on his shouldre and a wide hatte wyth a skulle and bones y-crossede and a pegge leg and a copye of the *De Doctrina Christiana* by Seynt Augustine.

"Plese sire, plese spare my lyf!" Ich dide crye.

"Yt beth nat yn my power to maken excepciouns," the Drede Pyrate dide shrugge hys brode sholdres and the parrot dide moue accordinglie, "Oones worde doth leke out that a pyrate hath goon softe, peple beginne to disobeye. And then it beth no thinge but werke, werke, werke, al the tyme."

"Plese sir, plese, Ich nede to lyve!"

"For what reson?"

"For Ich haue begun to wryte sum *Tales of Canterburye*, and thei are but barelye bigonne. My name ys Chaucer, Geoffrey Chaucer, and Kyng Richard shal paye a pretti bountee for my hede, for whanne Ich was yonge Ich was y-ransoumed for XVI pounde, and now Ich am at leeste thries as hevy a manne as Ich was in thos dayes, when Ich served as a valet!"

He dide pause yn thoghte, and also dide consulte hys boke of Christian Allegorie, "Al righte, Geoffreye. Ich haue neuer hadde a valet. Thou kanst trye yt for tonighte. Yt most likely shal happe that yn the morninge Ich shal slaye thee."

For manye dayes he dide saye the same each night, "Good nighte, Geoffrey. Thou hast done wel. Maye slepe be swete to thee. Yt most likely shal happe that yn the morninge Ich shal slaye thee."

The pyrates dide take me as oon of ther companie, and dide yive me earringes (ouche!) and a parrot the whiche was a hand-me-downe from an oothir pyrate who hadde acquirede a moore colourful and impressive birde.

Ich dide lerne of the arte of spekynge lyk a pyrate, and dide swabbe the deckes wyth grete relishe. For Ich was so gladde of my lyf and my breeth that Ich wolde probablie haue enjoyede watchinge *Ishtar* yf thei hadde made me do so.

And thus al was wel, until we did redie to ouertake a Frensshe vessel. Thanne my legges dide aquaken and shiveren lyk two trees yn a storme. Ich felle adoun and blakeness coverede myn eyen. And aftir, the pyrates hadde muche disdayne and scorne of me, and the Drede Pyrate Robertson dide threten that he wolde make me walke the planke if Ich dide nat pulle my weighte.

But what coud Ich do?

"Ich kan nat fighte, nor take plunder and bootie," Ich lamentid, "for Ich nam nat a man of werre and of deedes of armes. Ich am a manne of ale and poetrie."

"Ywis, Mayster Chaucer, why shaltow nat then walke of the planke? Shaltow ete of ower foode and drinke of ower rum and do nat a thynge for vs? Yf thou kanst nat fighte, what kanst thou do?" And the pyrates all rounde me rattlede ther saberes.

"Ich kan..." and thanne my minde did seise vpon it, "Ich kan kepe accountez, and enrolle custoumes."

Yt took a litel convincinge, but Ich dide do muche for the crewe of the Drede Pyrate Robertson. Bifor my cominge, thei hadde knowne no thynge of kepinge of recordes and accounting, and thus muche had been poorlye spente and ther was muche waste and corrupcioun. But with my litel quille and my accounte boke (and my litel woolen hatte, the whiche doth helpe me to thinke), Ich did sette the shippes straighte.

Ich dide divide accountez in to plunder (commoditees ytaken from holdes of shippes, *viz.* wyn or wexe), bootie (goodes ytaken from passengers, *viz.* jewelerie, bokes, and incidentale items) and ransoum (selfexplanatorie) and Ich kepte thre columnes. Each takere of income wolde bringe me a slippe detailynge yt, and Ich wolde yive a recepite and kepe the accountes. Ich dide employe II clerkes, Barnacle Bille and Edward the Blakke-Sworde, who dide produce recordes and sende memoranda to Captayne Robertson. We dide balaunce the in-take of bootie/plundere/ransoum wyth the outlaye of wenchinge, parrote-keepinge, and replacemente of bodye partes.

Ich was full proude of my systeme! In no tyme, Ich was doynge complicated pyratical calculaciouns:

Exempli gratia:

II de Juillet—ytaken, the Frennshe shipe Sidan, XX lbs golde (plunder) + II locketes wyth jeweles (bootie) = spent on L eye patches + VII cutlasses + III hookes for handes.

IV de Juillet—ytaken, the Flandrishe shipe Hennepin, XVI lbs woole (plundere) + xx lbs emeraldes (bootie) + IV yonge fleminges (ransoum) = spent on iv parrotes + iii legges of woode + xii nights of ale and fayre wenches. I fleming remayned as a pyrate and now doth calle hymself by the pyrate name Hieronymus Bash.

And thus the dayes were fulle of accountes and the nightes were fulle of songe and rum, and Ich was, in my weye, verye happye. Yt was, Ich trowe, the beste vacacioun Ich haue ever taken.

And yet as Boethius doth knowe, all goode thinges must come to an ende. Oon foule daye, we sawe the shippes of the FEEREDE BUCCANEER DONALDSON, who dide seise ower shippes and capture the Drede Pyrate

Robertson and dide putte me ashore som where near Dover. And thus, wyth my parrot and my eye patch and my ear-ringes, stinkinge of rum and of see watir, Ich did come home. And thogh in sum regard Ich wolde fayne be on the fayre shippe *Cupiditas* on the rollinge see, yt ys still a thinge of muche sweteness to haue children to talke to, and a wyf to painfullye remoue ear-ringes from my ears, and a blogge to write vpon. So welcome me home, ye land lubberz. And thre cheeres for Philippa, who did kepe al in control the while Ich was offe havynge aventurez. And nowe, to bedde and to dreme of the see.

August 5, 2006

Ich Pwne Noobs.

O my gentil rederes, it hath been a thinge of muchel difficultee and laboure for to type euen the smallest entrie in myn blogge. For somer, lyk vnto a songe of Barri Manileau, hath ydrawn alle the spirit and vigor from my limbes and hert. For the gretre part of the hot moneth of July Ich satte in my garden on my comfortable lawn-chaire and langwisshed lyk vnto sum yonge lover who hath ydumpede been. Ich daubede myn foreheed wyth a moyste towel and did drinke mvch of somer drinkes swich as margaritae and daquiri.

By night, Ich busyede myself with wrytynge of my *Tales of Canterburye*. And yet methinketh that the somer hete did even then overwhelme my fantasie, for alle of the tales Ich enditede dide involve snowe and watir and plesaunte coolinge pass-tymes. In the Knightes tale, Ich wrote that Theseus did constructe a grete swiminge poole in which Arcite and Palamon wolde pleye of Marco Polo for the winninge of Emilye. The Nonnes Preestes tale was of a penguin ycleped Chanticleer. The Monkes tale was a liste of thos who stood in heigh degree and from yt felle and aftir wente on vacacioun in plesaunte tropicale isles. Alas! Yt semeth that Ich muste crosse ovt much of this werke and starte ayein from the beginninge. Yet peraventure Ich shal lete stande the Squires tale of Frostie the Snowman and how he was drawen limbe from limbe by Cambyuskan the grete kinge of Tartarye for to be putte in coolinge drinkes, and how aftir, Cambyuskan's doghter Canacee did fynde the corne-cobbe pipe and button nose and knewe of hir fadires crueltee.

And yet the thinge moost detrimentale to my werke did come nat from the hete, but from my son. Oon night, whanne Ich coud write no more, Ich herde from litel Lowyses room terrible soundes and grete crashinges and betinges of taboures. Quakynge wyth drede, Ich openede hys doore, and founde hym whole and sounde. "What maner of grete din ys that?" quod Ich. "Unwack yowerself a litel, Dizzad." Ich am playinge *Auriole,*" Lowys replyede, and did poynte towardes hys Exboxe CCCLX.

By Seynt Ninntendus, Ich thoghte to myself, thes aren thos "video games" the which Lowys ys alwey pleyinge. A grete curiousitee dide posess me, and so Ich askede Lowys to shewe me of the propertees of the games. He taughte me the lore of these merveilous stories, the which aren peyntures that moue and haue sounde and often are made yn Cipangu, and aren controllid by a small devyce or engine ycovered wyth buttones that ys helde yn the hand.

Heu michi quod sterilem uitam duxi iuvenilem! Ther were no swich games of video whanne Ich was a yonge man, and thus Ich knewe litel of the sport and mirthe that ys in hem. For soothly, thei aren quite clever and also do improue the coordinacioun of the hande and the eye. Lowys and Ich dide sette at pleyinge of the games and we stoppid nat vntil the cokke of morwenyge dide crowe. It rockede, and from thenne on Ich was caught in the trappe. Thus my *Tales of Canterburye* were on the back-burner yputte. Nowe the somer dayes aren fulle of reste, and the nightes fulle of games of video. Whanne Philippe chid me yestirmorn for pleyinge of youthful sporte, Ich tolde hir that thys was a grete waye to bonde wyth Lowys; she seyde in replye, "Whatevir happenede to helpinge hym wyth his grammer homewerke?" (for she ys a woman who loveth the laste worde moore than Anglo-Saxons love repeatid consonants).

Here beginneth the Descripcioun of the Ludi de Visionibus:

Syn ye, my rederes, are folke lyk myself who kanne noght of games of video, Ich shal heere descriven the wondirs of these tales and eek present to yow the moore notable games.

DONKEYE-KYNGE: Yn thys game, ye playe a peasaunt who hath yn his care a smal donkeye. Ye use the gentil beeste to dryve yower carte and to transporte donge, for which ye are payde ful litel, and yet ye muste kepe obeisaunt and meke to wards the bettir and mower substantiale menne of yower village. At the ende of XX minutes, a purveyor of the kinge cometh and taketh aweye the donkey, and then ye, the pesaunte, are sesed wyth despayr and do falle deed. Then ye, the playere, are rankid by how manye piles of donge ye hauen transportid and wyth howe much meekeness.

CIVILISATIOUN: Yn this ful lernede game, ye playe the ful course of civilisacioun on the globe of the erthe. Erst, ye do governe the civilisacioun of the Golden Age, and gathir acornes and the croppes that the erthe ytself doth yive forth withouten labour. Lowys sayeth that this part of the game "sucketh" for ther ys no werre or fightinge. And then oon of yower folke fyndeth golde in the grounde, and an othir discovereth iren for to make wepnes of werre, and thus the golden age doth ende. In sequence, ye playe thurgh the grete tymes of the Babyloniens, the Persyenes, Greekes, and the Romayns, and then ye come to the age of Steel, the which ys oure tyme, of longe werres and terrible, and of the divisioun bitwene the popes of Rome and Avignon and the Grete Pestilence. At the ende of the game, ye do muche penaunce for the sinnes of the werlde and thanne ther ys sum musique.

TROJAN KOMBAT: Yn this game of video, ye playe oon of the renouned knightes of Troye or Grece, and do battel yn single combat by pressinge the buttons on yower controller. My fauorite character ys Troylus! Everich caracter hath the same "basic moves," but yf ye presse the buttones yn speciale combinaciouns, the characteres kan do "special moves." Ich haue heere ycopyed the special moues for Troylus, for my remembraunce:

A + A + UP + DOUNE: The "Canticus Troili": it bringeth yn Pandarus to fight alongside Troylus.

A + UP + LEFT + RIGHT + B: The "Litera Troili": it maketh Troylus to sitte adown and rolle hys herte to and fro to seke how he may best descryven his wo to hys ladye (-a bit of a weird move, synce it dooth no thyng to help whan Troilus is getting upon the heed ypounded by anothir character).

B + A +DOWN + DOWN + UP + UP + A + CROSS YOWERSELFE: Maketh Troylus to speke of divine purveyaunce, the whiche doth paralyse yower opponente wyth confusioun.

And yet, wyth alle thes speciale moues, everye tyme that Ich playe Troylus, Lowys doth playe Achille, and Ich am defeatede. Lowys telleth me nat to throw the controller doun yn myn ire, for swich is the accioun of a "lamer."

GASTON DE FOIXES HUNTINGE AND HAWKINGE: This game doth make simulacioun of noble sportes, so that thos who aren nat of rich estaat maye ride of fyne horses and chase the kinges deere and go hawkinge wyth gode briddes of preye. This game taketh the name of the grete hunter and falconer Gaston de Foix, who hath IV tymes taken the prize of the Maysteres Tournament of Falconry, and twies won the daye at the PBH Championshippe of Boare-Huntinge. Manye a time haue Ich seene nobles go to hawke and hunte, and Ich do promise yow that this game ys verye realistic. At the ende of the hunte, noble ladyes come to the partye of hunteres and ther ys gentil talke of loue (presse B as faste as ye kan and ye shalle sigh wyth grete loue and affecioun) and al the while the churles preparen the deere for roastinge. Ye kan choose to playe as seuerale noble hunteres, yncludynge my lord Johannes of Gaunte (BSL! He muste licensed hys image to get sum extra moneye for his werres in Spayne).

AURIOLE: This game ys of the kynde ycleped "FPS," or "firste-persone sermon," in whiche ye see as yf out of the eyes of a noble prechour named Magister Chaplain, and ye traverse the countree prechynge to manye folke. Ye fynde manye bookes of storyes of deedes of seyntes and manye bookes of lore with whiche ye maye equip yowerselfe. My fauorite ys John Bromyardes *Summa predicantium*; it hath the longest range and ys effective upon alle classes of societee. Sum tyme yn the game ye encounter heretickes, and ye maye kille hem wyth the aide of the seculer authoritees. Yf ye haue grete success, ye receyve an auriole that shineth arounde yower hede. Ye kan also playe this game in competicioun wyth otheres "on-line," in whatte ys callid a "dethe matche." Ther ys a maner of speche vsid by thos who playe Auriole in "deth matches," the whiche jargon is newfangel and straunge to heere. To winne a game ys to "pwne" the othir playeres; conversiones thurgh yower prechynge are called "fragges," and thos who are of litel experience (lyk myself) are yclepede "noobs," or novices.

GRANDE THEFTE, COLLUSIOUN, AND MAYNTENANCE: Ich had herde of this game bifor, for manye a petiticioun hath ben yiven to the kinge in parlemente concerynyge the threte that thys game wille transforme children ynto violent felouns. Ich was astonyed to heere that Lowys had boughte it hym self, by bribinge a clerk of the video games store. And yet, ther ys litel mattir for worrye, for the game itself ys a satire of the disordred state of lawe in this contree. Ye run arounde and commit various actes of trespass with force and armes, and then use yower patrones and affinitee groupes to get yow out of prisone. Ther ys even a "mini game" yn whiche a sheriff doth presente yow wyth a writ to appeare in courte and ye teare yt yn piece-meale by pressinge the A button very faste. Ye gayne riche landes by doynge yower neighbours wronges and oppressiouns. Ye kan evene take the liverie of various corrupt local lordes and putte the robes and hattes and pinnes on and looke at yowerself yn the mirour. Althogh Ich trye to be a man of moralitee, Ich muste admit that this game ys ful of solaas. Every tyme Ich do commit trailbaston and hitte a lawyer ovir the heede to take of hys moneye, Ich do pretende yt ys that wankere Johannes Gower! Ywis, Ich do thinke that this game pleseth nat the menne of parlement for yt striketh verye close to the merke.

And so, my noble rederes, vntil the hete of somer fullie abate, Ich shal be up wyth litel Lowys, in hys attic room, playinge of video games and drinkinge depe draughtes of dewe from the mountaynes. C U L8re, gentilz!

August 15, 2006

Wondirful newes!

By seynte Edward! Yt hath ben a ful stressfule weeke, ful of much hastie and sodein laboure, but al of my effortes haue produced fayre and honourable fruyt thurgh the assistance of my frende and my Kinge.

Wednesdaye laste, Ich was yn my lawn-chayre slepynge aftir a longe night of pwninge noobs, whanne Ich was awaked by Tommy Vske, who had travelid as fast as he coud from Londoun.

Litel Vsk ys nowe a serjeant-at-armes for my lord Kinge Richard. And he thus broghte tidynges to me in execucion of his office. Writtes had ben ysent to everye shire for the eleccioun of menne to speke for the communes in parlement, and the eleccioun was to be held that Sundaye in Canterburye. And therfor my lorde Kynge Richarde had sente Vsk to telle me to runnen for parlement, for the Kynge seyde that he wolde lyk sum goode men and trewe and loyale to his majestee to be ther attendaunt vpon the parlement.

"Thinkstow that folke wille voten for me?" quod Ich.

"Hekke yes. Ich wolde vote for thee," he spak.

"And yet, what skille haue Ich?" Ich askede.

"Thou hast a sweete litel woolen hatte. And thou art prettye good at enrollinge accountes, plus thou art lyk the onlie guye in the shire who ys enditinge a lengthie frame-tale collecioun in the Englysshe tonge."

With gretest haste, we travelid to Canterburye, and ther dide campaigne amonge the peple. Vsk did helpe me by vsinge his skilles of drawinge to make cunninge billes and posteres for me, the whiche we putte vpon the dores of chirches and of grete halles. We also hadde manye a litel signe of liveree on whiche was writ "VOTE FOR CHAUCER." By cause we hadde the aide of my lord the kinge, we were greetede wyth grete favour and supporte by the bettir men of the contree.

And thus thurgh the intervencioun of Vske at the beheste of my Kynge, Ich am nowe a KNYGHT OF THE SHIRE! A MEMBER OF PARLEMENT! Ye do heare me correctlie, good gentils: in but a fewe monthes Ich shal goon to parlement at Westminster to represente the shire of Kente, and be priuy to the grete speches and wise conseyles of grete lordes and lerne of grete affaires of the reaume, and eek Ich shal complayn aboute the smal detailes of lyf and the lak of stedfastnesse and of good dentale care for al of my constituencie. The parlement comenceth on the firste daye of October. Ich am so excitede. This parlement is goinge to be wondirful!

August 21, 2006

Serpentes on a Shippe

Al of Londoun ys aflame wyth newes of the grete entertaynment of *Serpentes on a Shippe*, the which ys perfourmed ech daye by the men of the gild of beekeeperes (and thus ys ycleped a "b-movie"). Ich haue just nowe retourned from a trippe to see yt wyth Litel Lowys and Tommy Vske. Whan Ich was ther, Tommy founde for me a copye of the romaunce in fyve chapteres on whiche the performaunce ys based, and Ich shal pooste yt heere for yower redynge.

SPOYLER ALERT: If ye haue nat yet seene the performaunce of *Serpentes on a Shippe*, rede nat of the following romaunce, for it doth telle of the manye suprises and straunge eventes that happen in the course of the storye, and thus it mayhap shall lessen yower enjoiement of the performaunce yt self.

The Noble Tale Of Sir Neville De Fraunce & The Serpentes On The Shippe

Maad ynto Englysshe from the Frensshe bokes by John Malory

To my son, Thomas, wyth fervent wisshes that ye caste off yower youthful wylfulnesse and growe to be a law-abidinge man of great worship

Chapter the Ist

Hit befelle uppon a day that SIR SEAN, who was a yonge knight and a gentil, dide wander as adventures wolde gyde hym nere to the fayre citee of Honolulle. He lepede on his hors from manye an heigh hille yn slowe mocioun yn the maner of a goode knighte and a valyaunte. And whan it was nyghe none, Sir Sean cam to a grete bridge that was made of oold by the Romayns, and from that bridge did hange doun-ward an eremyte whos visage was ful hewn and bledde and al his clothes and the place aboute weren bloode red. And Sir Sean askede hym what he did ther and wherfor he was hanged and who had so grievousli him woundede; "Fle from this place, Sir Knight," he seyde, "For the man cometh who did thes woundes to me and he is a grete kynge but a felon and a traytour and hys name is THE KYNGE MAUVAIS SANS MOTIVACIOUN and he hath doon this to me by cause I haue stood ayeinst hys grete outrages and felonies."

Then Sir Sean did see manye knightes comynge to that place and so he hid hymself among the bushes. And Kyng Mauvais came wyth his knightes and dide kille the eremyte. And Sir Sean made to fle but his bootes made a sounde and the knightes spyede hym and gave hym chase. And thogh he scapede from hem, thei sawe wher he rode and knew of his lodging. Therwithal Kyng Mauvais sente thre of his knightes to Sir Seanes lodging for to slayen hym for he had sene hys foule deede. And thus cam aftir vespers Sir Stuntman Number Oon and Sir Stuntman Number Two, son of Expendable Extra who had done manye deedes in the dayes of Uther Pendragon, and wyth hem Sir Stuntman Number Thre.

And so the miscreant knightes wolde break ope the doore of Sir Seanes room and slaye him foullie, but that SIR NEVILLE DE FRAUNCE cam and seyde to Sir Sean, "Sir Knight, if thou shalt do my biddynge than thou shalt scape wyth thy lyf," and he bad Sir Sean to hye hym from that place. And then Sir Neville made hym redy. Wyth one spere he smote hem downe al thre over ther horses croups. This kynde of thynge was ful yn his style, for hys verye wallet hath "bad motherswyvere" on it ywrit.

Chapter the IInde
Then Sir Neville told Sir Sean that they must cross the see to the court of the grete King Arthur, for Arthures puissance coud bringe Kyng Mauvais to justise. For Sir Neville was yn the Feudal Bureau of Investigacioun. And so the two knightes cam to the coost of the see and ther thei sawe a rich vessel hilled over with red silk and thei cam to yt.

"Master mariners," seyde Sir Neville, "We muste make passage yn yower firste-classe section, for I bringe a witnesse to the courte of Kynge Arthur." And the mariners and the maydes on the boate assentede, thogh manye a rich burgois dide grucchen much at levynge first classe for coache.

And thus the mariners made hem redye to sayle across the grete see. In first classe Sir Neville and Sir Sean talkede of matirs of prowesse and knighthode, and, doun in coache, manye a stereotype did sitte and make conversacioun. Ther was a PRIORESSE, who lovede hir smalle dog, and also a SQUIRE, who mad manye songes of rappe and had TWO FAT KNIGHTES wyth him, and also a WOMAN WYTH A BABYE AND AN ACCENTE, who coud muche of plesaunte folke remedyes and TWO FOUNDLINGES who travelid all al oon, and an ANTISOCIALE ENGLISHMAN and also a gret manye EXPENDABLES.

And Kyng Mauvais bethoghte hymself how Sir Neville was a man of muche power and coud nat be bestede by knightes; and so Mauvais turnede hym to trecherie and sorcerie. Withinne the hulle of the shipe he had privilye yputte manye a caske fulle of serpentes and wormes and foul addres, and therto he put aboute the boate a philtre ycleped Far-Amoun by the Arabes, the which maketh serpentes to freke the helle oute and starte juste bitinge eny oon thei see. And wyth alchemy Mauvais sette the lockes of the caskes for to bursten whan the boate was yn the middel of the see. And yn this wise nat oon of the securitee gardes did knowe of the ambusshe of the serpentes that was to be, even thogh thei did make al the passengers remove ther toothpickes and lettre-openeres and especiallye ther jarres of oyntmentz and sportes-drinkes. And thus the vessel departed wyth the serpentes hidden vpon it.

Chapter the IIIrde
So whan the ship had on the ocean saylede for two houres and was on the rollinge wawes of the see, anon the lockes of the caskes breste forth and the snakes weren loosed. Right so the hoolde of the shippe was fulle of al maner of serpentes that hisse and crawl vpon the erthe, such as amphisbanae and aspides, vipers the which aren sum tyme called berardes, and bosk-addres and cheldires whos bite causeth shakynge and sodein deeth, egges-wermes and water-naddres, slow-wormes and ophites and manye othir thinges that movede serpentli. And syn thei had brethede depe of the Far-Amoun, thei were wood as if thei weren on cracke.

Thus cam the snakes in the coache seccioun of the vessel, and ther was much noyse and screminge and manye EXPENDABLES weren eten and in the naughtye partes ybitten. The ANTISOCIALE ENGLISHMAN dide throwe the dogge of the PRIORESSE to the serpentes for to make them delaye, and yet he too was eten by a grete wyrm. And the SQUIRE did showe that for all of his bling he was but a cowarde. And the WOMAN WYTH A BABYE AND AN ACCENT dide scape wyth her babye and her accent.

Sir Sean herde the noyse and fayne wolde haue gon doun to the coache seccioun. For neyther he nor Sir Neville had seene the snakes, but herde onlie the cryes from below and knew nat what happede. And so Sir Sean got hym up to move but Sir Neville seyde, "Sir Knight, whan first we met I toolde thee that if thou sholdst do my biddynge, thou wolde lyue, and in ower aventurez it hath happede thus that thou hast no reson to distruste me. Thou must bringe thy witnesse to Kyng Arthurez court, and thus stay thee heere the while I figure out what the helle the noyse ys aboute. Mesemeth peraventure that the folk haue realised how litel legroom remaineth yn coache these dayes and do give riot and protest." And so Sir Sean stayede put while Sir Neville went doun to ward the noyse.

Chapter the IVthe

Sir Neville cam to wher the folke of the shippe wyth the snakes yfought, and he sawe the bodyes of the dede and the sight grieved hym sore, for the battel had waxed passinge hard and the folke had little wherewithal to defend hemselves. And Sir Neville then fared wood as a lion and with his swerd he cutte in twayne the snakes that at him lept.

"Builde a walle for to kepen out the serpentes," he seyde, and the folk obeyed hym and piled up ther luggage, the whiche did stop the onslaught of the serpentes as an othir walle had long agoon ystopped the onslaught of the Scottes. And the WOMAN WYTH A BABYE AND AN ACCENT coud sum thyng of leechcraft and so put salues and poulticez on thos who had been bitten and yet had nat perisshed. And oon of the FOUNDLINGES was bite and hys arm was sore sore.

And the SQUIRE was losinge yt and seyd "O Jesu, defend us from death and horrible maims! For I see well we be in grete peril of death, for ther aren snakes on ower shippe and thei are angrie at sum thyng."

And Sir Neville seyde to him, "Yes, I marvel how thei cam vnto this ship wythout wittynge of us alle. Yet nowe ther beth litel hope but to fighte hem."

And Sir Neville and the SQUIRE and al men on the shippe alive who coud beare armes dide marche ayeinst the serpentes and do grete bataille and long war. But the snakes were full of ire and of venym and were still passinge y-riled-uppe and thus gave grete assaut in returne. And thus the battel stood wyth manye dede on eyther syde.

Chapter the Vthe and Finale

Then Sir Neville and the men who with him fought did drawe togedir and Sir Neville seyde, "Litel it availeth us to fighte wyth thes snakes. By cause thei do not jouste as knightes do, nor do thei make fayre parlay whan thei aren captured, but rather in the nature of beestes thei bite the helle ovte of vs the whole tyme." And thus thei made retreat to behinde the walle.

Then ther was a crashinge grete and terribil, and the sound of the sayles droppinge on to the decke. In the winde the ship did founder. Vp staires, Sir Sean did checke wyth the mariners and finde hem all y-slawe by the snakes, and the snakes had occupyed the wheel of the shippe and the mappe of navigacioun. And Sir Sean cam doun and toold Sir Neville and Sir Neville was passinge wroth and seyde, "That ys ynogh. I haue hadde it wyth thes cursed by Seynt George snakes on this cursed by Seynt George shippe!"

"What haue ye seyde?" askede the PRIORESSE then.

"I did curse the snakes," seyde Sir Neville, "and therwith the shippe, in the name of Seynt George who ys a patron of valour and chivalrie."

"Ywis," seyde the PRIORESSE, "yower cursinge hath borne good fruyt, for methinkede whan I herde ye speke thus that the arme of man, eek even of a mighti man swich as yowerself, is but a litel thinge compared to the grete power of God the which is dispensed thorow the mediacioun of the seyntez. And thes serpentes the which do make werre ayeinst us aren figuraceouns of the sinne of ower firste parentes who weren by a serpent deceyved, and thus thei signifien that we sholde seeke nat strengthe in knighthede but in prayere and devocioun. For syn we face thes foule serpentes, mesemeth we must seeke succour and aide from the gret seynt who is the enemy ysworn of al maner of serpentes."

"Dang, babye," seyde Sir Neville, "ye speke gret wisdam."

And alle the crewe prayed to Seynt Patrick and thorow hys mercy the serpentes were slayne every oon of hem and the shippe came safelye to shore.

Good Lord saue us alle yn swich a maner as thou hast saved Danyhel in the liones den and Jonah in the wales bellye and saue us especiallye from Snakes on the See, in the name of Jesu ower Lord and Seynte Patrick.

HEERE ENDETH THE BOKE OF SIR NEVILLE DE FRAUNCE AND THE SERPENTES ON THE SHIPPE BY JOHN MALORY AND MAY ALL GENTLEMEN OR GENTEL-WOMEN THAT REDE OF THIS BOOK PRAY FOR ME WHILE I AM ON LYVE AND ALSO GO SEE THE MOVIE ADAPTACIOUN AND BUY THE MERCHANDYSE THE WHICH INCLUDETH TEE SHIRTES AND ALSO SMAL MODELS OF SNAKES

CHAUCERES PARLIAMENT JOURNALS

September 16, 2006

Parliament Journal: Unpleasant September

It hath been longe syn Ich haue writen eny thing for my blog. *Pour voir dire*—oops, rathir: For to speken trewely, ther beth but litel mirthe and solaas yn myn hous, and lik-wise in al the houses of Engelonde. Al the moneth of August and nowe yn to the temperat moneth of September, mony tidynges haue yronne thurgh the reaume of a great fleet of shippes that the Frensshe haue gadrid at Sluys. Every shire feareth an invasioun!

And thus Philippa is al vp on me about goinge to Londoun for Parlement. Ich am yerne to goon to speke of the gret matirs of the reaume wyth ful loial corage, and to peraventure do sum "networkinge" that may winne me a bettir job. And yet Philippa wisheth me to stayen at hoom.

Alwey she saith thus: "Forwhy dide Godde yive thee eares, Geoffrey, whan thou opst hem nat to eny sense? Thou art ever froward, that dare I swear. Al the folke of London murmren as bees doth in an hyve that the Frensshe shal eftsoon come to Londoun-toun and maken siege and assaut vpon it. Kanst thou, Geoffrey, holde off the knightes of Fraunce wyth yower games of video, or wyth yower litel woolen hatte?"

And she hath a poynt, for Tommy Vske hath written me of the hullabaloo that taketh place in Londoun thes dayes. Al who kepen menage –oops, rathir: kepen hous—in Londoun haue been commandid to laye doun store of provisions ynogh for III monethis if the Frensshe should make siege. And sum men of Londoun, Ich trowe, haue torne doun the houses that stood neigh to the walles, to make hem moore redy for defens. And the fishmongeres have preparid greet trebuchets—oops: machines of werre— with whiche they shal hurle salt-herringe at the foe-men whanne they come up the Thamis. The poulterers haue trained XL cokkes to fly wyth bombes of fyre and poudre yfastned to ther talons, and droppe doun vpon the shippes of the Frensshe. Ther haue eek ben sum suggestions involving serpentes. And sum men flee the citee, or dispend al ther worldlie goodes for thei thinke they shal haue but litel tyme left to lyve as fre men.

And eek no soul speketh wel of the Frensshe in al of Engelonde. Ywis, in eny phrase or name which bifor had the wordes "Frensshe" or "Fraunce," nowe for loue of Engelonde and Seynt George and good Kyng Richard al men say in sted "Magna Carta." And thus we eten of "Magna Carta fries" and "Magna Carta breed" and do ower legal pledinge in "Law Magna Carta." Ich chide litel Lowys for "Magna Carta kissinge" on dates and the whil Ich wayte up for hym to return Ich do rede wyth muchel delit the *Lais* of "Marie de Magna Carta." Syn everychoon pretty much still useth the Magna Carta language for commerce, and chevisaunce, and lawe, thinges are a bit of a mess, consideringe Magna Cartish phrases keep up-y-cropping.

And thus al is nat wel chez moi—at myn hous. Parlement—oops, a big meetinge? A big talking? Ywis, let us leave that oon in the original Magna Cartish. Parlement shal be a tyme to speken of gret matirs, for the kinge nedeth moneye for defens. No matir what Philippa saith, Ich feere no Magna Cartish invasion of Londoun, and Ich shal go and speke for my shire. Eke, Ich shal pick up sum of my annuittees and also Ich am supposid to testify for my lord and buddy Sir Richard Scrope yn a conflict about his coat of armes. And it shal be good to see Tommy Vske ayein. Also, it wolde much plese me to see thos trayned attak chickens.

Ich shall writ ayein whanne Ich come to Londoun! The Parlement openeth on October Ist. Ich haue ben toold that ther shal be a recepcioun wyth shrimpe cocktailes on the first daye. Also, my lord the kinge hath sente me a liste of "talking poyntez."

Le Vostre—oops, Yoweres Trewely,

GC

September 30, 2006

Quick Chekke-in

This is juste a smal missive to saye that Ich am heere in Londoun and redy for Parlement in Westminstyre on the morwe. Tommy Vske was nat able to offer me hospitalitee for—By Seynt Valentine!—he hath sum ladye stayinge over. Ich know litel of her saue that she beth ycleped "Margaret." He promiseth me that we shall brunchen togedir sum tyme this week. He beginneth to throwen hym self aboute as if he were all that and a bagge of oat-cakes. *Nichil asperius paupero cum surget in altum.*

So, beinge thus sexiled, Ich haue taken the hospitalitee of my verye talle frende Guillelmus Langlande. Livinge in a cotte in Cornhulle wyth a lanky angrie poet, hys wyf Kytte, and hys doghter Calotte ys nat exactlie myn idee of a holidaye, but Ich wisshe to kepe my parliamentarye fee for to purchasen sum bookes, so no fancie hostelrye for me.

Eny way, Ich am vsing the wireless at Paternoster rowe, and a scrivener is yivinge me dirty lookes. Moore to come whan Parliament beginneth.

October 5, 2006

The Opening of Parlement, and Ich am Traytorously Deceivid

O straunge worlde, for the dayes are fulle of selcouthes and no thyng is as it semeth. Alwey in my fantasie syn Ich was a yonge man, Ich thoghte Parlement to be a grete and noble assemblee, wher the wisdam of the reaume was spoken in the presence of oure sovereyn kynge for the sake of the commune good. But al thing in this worlde adoun is lyk vnto a cake fulle of beares: on the outsyde, it appeareth delicious and plesaunte, but inside yt is crawlinge wyth beestes that wisshe to clawe thee to deeth. For nowe Ich see that Parlement is fulle of thretes and secretes, and matirs derke.

On Sundaye night, the daye bifor the grete openinge of parlement, ther was a speciale recepcioun for folk lyk myself who had come to Parlement to speke for the shires. This feeste was held in the halle of the Exchequer, wyth the tables of rekynynges laden wyth metes and drinke. Michel de la Pole, the Earl of Suffolk and Chancellor of the reaume, frende of Kyng Richard, was ther, and he did shake the handes of al who were presente, and callid vs by oure names and bad vs drinken depe of the ale and maken murye. He yaf vs alle small billes, the whiche contayned the poyntez which we were to speken of for the good of the reaume, and he avised vs to keep the smalle billes secure.

The small billes were covered wyth thys text:

TALKYNGE POYNTEZ FOR PARLEMENT FOR THE LOIAL SUBJECTES OF KYNG RICHARD AND HYS CHANCELLOR MICHEL DE LA POLE

Whanne a felawe member of Parlement or a cronicler or othir member of the media doth aske yow of the business of Parlement, ye shal saye the following:

I—THE REAUME IS IN GRETE PERIL FROM OURE GRETE ENEMYE FRAUNCE, IN GRETER PERIL THAN EVIR BIFOR:

A. A Frensshe flete has gadrid for to make invasion in ower lande.

B. The Frensshe shal turne alle of our filmes in to non-linear meditaciouns on lyf and deeth both insouciant and weightie.

C. The Frensshe shal destroyen the Englisshe language and create a world maad only of voweles.

D. The Frensshe shal covir Engelonde wyth cafees wher yt costeth more to drinke coffee sittinge doun than standing up.

E. If alle else faileth, repete "grete peril, grete peril" lyk vnto a psalme.

II- OURE KYNG RICHARD TO PROVE HYS WORTH SHAL MAKE A GRETE EXPEDICIOUN OF ARMES OVIR THE SEE AYEINST THE FRENSSHE FOR THE FOLOWYNGE RIGHTFUL CAUSES:

A. We fare bettir to fighten the enemye acrosse the see than heere in owere owene lande.

B. The Kyng is mighti and fullye committede to the governement of his reaume and ys not a "wussy" as sum sclanderers haue seyde. Nat to name eny names, but Henry Bolingbroke hath been pretty critical of the Kyng.

C. Yt is right and proper to pursue the Kynges clayme to the crowne of Fraunce.

D. We muste winne honour.

E. The werre has nat even lastede C yeres yet. Yt is too soon to throwe in the towele.

F. If alle else faileth, repete "winne honour, winne honor" lyk vnto a psalme.

III- AND THUS WE NEDE AIDE SUFFICIENT TO PROTECT THE REAUME AND MAKE PURVEYANCE FOR THE KINGES EXPEDICIOUN:

A. That is, alle the cash we kan get from the contree.

These thinges mesemed good and ful of wisdam, and fayre to speken for the safetee of the reaume. And yet, Ich sawe but fewe men of Parlement ther in that halle. Ich trowe, ther mvste haue ben gadrid on that night but halfe the men that cam to Westminstre for parlement. For the communes aren manye, and this felaweshippe was smal. And manye of hem who stod ther wyth the Chancellor were knowen to me as frendes of the kinge and loyal servauntz to hys majestee.

And yet litel me thought of thes thinges, for the ale was good and moyst and fre of charge. Ich dranke depe and talkede wyth manye men, and we swalwed gret draughtes for the Kynges helth. Tommy Vsk did come and we did talke of this and that. Ich askid Vsk whedir all the men of parlement had been called to this meetinge, and he seyde, "Every liege at parlement loial to the Kyng hath ben callid heere tonight, but nat the foule churles who wolde arguen ayeinst the wyse counsels of the Kyng and the Chancellor."

The moon brightli shone, and Ich was alle fordronken so that Ich coud scarce feel my owen legges vndir me. Drink had me daswed. Ich knewe Ich coud nat retourne to Langelondes hous. It was too far, and eek the alliteratif tonge-lashinge Ich wolde receyve from William about the gluttony of my drinkinge ("ye ram rum too rough") wolde be moost peyneful. Thus Ich took my reste at an inn that stood nigh to the palais of Westminstre. Ich payde the keeper for a room and did climb the stayres to go to slepe. On the stayres, a fayre wenche cam me-towardes. She must haue ben but of XVIII yere of age, wyth heere as yelwe as flaxe ysponne. She was ful moore blisful on to see than is the newe pere-jonette tree.

"Hi, uh, were you at the meeting?" quod she.

"Fayre mayde, mene ye the meetinge at the Exchequer wher the talkinge poyntez weren yiven vnto vs?"

"The, uh, talking points. Yeah, exactly. Good. I'm the handmaid for Sir…Roland…de Quelquechose. He was at the meeting and he, uh, well, he got a little drunk."

"Goddes curse on men who are dronkelewe and guzzleres of ale," Ich sayde, and then burpid in a maner uncouth and my face wexed reede wyth shame. And yet the fayre wenche spoke further.

"Well, so Sir Roland made like Lot with the beer and all, and he kind of lost his talking points. He's got me running around trying to find other men, uh, loyal to the king who might have them. Could I just borrow your talking points? I'll make a fair copy for Sir Roland and you'll have them back before you know it. I'll just put them under your door in the morning. Pretty please?"

"No thyng wolde greter plese me than to do courtesie to yow and to yower mayster the goode sire Quelquechose, O mayden swete and fayre," quod Ich, and bente me lowe to honour her and yaf hir the talkinge poyntez. And than Ich stumbled to my slepe.

And yet when Ich woke, no oon had putte the bille of talkinge poyntez backe vndir my door. Ich askede the inn keeper if a braue knight ycleped Quelquechose had taken his reste ther, and the inn keeper seyde he knewe no swich name, but it semed to hym that it mente somethinge. And thanne Ich asked of the fayre wenche, who she was and whider she had com, and the inn keeper tolde me that he knewe her nat but that she had come ther yesternight at the tyme of vespers and she had hunge around talkinge on a verye expensive celle phone and makinge snarky remarkes.

And as Ich stod adased and wondired on what thes thinges coud mene, it cam to my memorie that it was Mondaye morne, and the daye of Parlement! Ich hoofed it to the halle of Westminstre, and entered it in last nightes clothes, stinkinge lyk vnto a table of beer pong.

O the pompe and majestee! Ther was a grete thronge of peple, gentils and men of richesse fro the shyres, and grete lordes wyth their retinuez, alle assemblid in the Paynted Chamber of Westminstre. Ther were merchantz in liveree of manye coloures, knightez sadde who had served in werres, and professional politicians who shifty semed. Bifor hem alle sat Kyng Richard in hys splendor, and bifor hym was Michel de la Pole the Chancellor.

The Chancellor bigan to speke, and he toold of the resons for the callinge of parlement, and he did in grete voys and loude, and wyth fayre speche. And yet noon of yt was newe to me, for it was alle the poyntez of talkinge that Ich had rede of at the recepcioun yesternight: that the kinge was to make werre vpon the Frensshe, and that the communes should commit ther shires to yive moneye for the werre, and eek he gave the resons forwhy, *et cetera et cete-*

Ich sterted, for som oon clasped me by the shouldre. It was Tommy Vsk, and his eyen were fulle of ire.

"Hastow sene this?" he askede me, and he yave me a hand-bille, whos title was, THE PRIVEE TALKINGE POYNTEZ YIVEN BY THE KYNGE VNTO THE CONSPIRACIE OF KEPTE HOUNDES AND SERVAUNTZ HE HATH CALLID TO PARLEMENT TO SPEKE OF HYS OWN SPEDE AND NAT OF THE GOOD OF THE REAUME BUT ONLY FOR THE AVARICE OF HIS COUNSELLORS, NOWE PUBLIS-SHED AND EXPOSID TO ALLE TREWE COMMUNES OF ENGELONDE AND WYTH REFUTACIOUNS.

"That looketh bad," Ich seyde.

"Bad in deed," he sayde, "Sikerly, ther hath ben a leak."

"That smelle ys juste my clothes from last nighte," Ich seyde.

"Nay," quod he, "Ich mene ther hath been a leak in ower securitee. Alle folke of Londoun haue thes billes, and thei aren posted on everye chirche-dore. How has this come to pass? Hastow yiven thy liste of talking poyntes to any oon?"

"Nay, to noon but the loial mayde of Sir Quelquechose."

"Ther beth no knight of that name in the Kinges faction," seyde Vsk, "What maner of mayde was she?"

"Gent. Smal. Ye knowe the type."

"With yelwe hair?"

"Yis, sikerly."

"Geoffrey Chaucer, thou sely foole, thou hast discovered the kinges secretes to Griselda Mars, Girl Detectif in the servyce of Henry Bolingbroke!"

But we coud talke na moore, for the speche of de la Pole was finisshed, and alle the communes wente awey to the Chapter Hous of the abbey for to speke of the respons thei sholde make to the demaundes for moneye, and Ich wente with hem in my capacitee as elected representative of Kent, and Vsk ranne off on busyness of his owene.

O, my rederes, ther ys much moore to telle of, but my handes are sore and myn eyen are blered and myn herte filled wyth doute. Soon Ich shalle telle yow of what bifel in the Chapter Hous, and eek what Ich lerned of the plottes and plannes of the factions. And yet Ich tremble as Ich type, for Ich scarce knowe wher my loyaltee stondeth.

October 31, 2006

Parlement Continueth, and Ich See a Visioun

God shilde us fro meschaunce! Whanne Ich last had tyme and space to enditen of my aventures at parliament, Ich hadde ben tricked by Griselda Mars yn to handynge ovir the talkinge poyntes of the kinges loyal men. Ich lerned this just as Ich had to goon wyth the othir communes to the chaptir hous in the Abbeye of Wesminstre, the which ys the place allotted for the communes for ower smell pleseth nat the lordes in the Palais.

Whanne Ich entred the chaptir hous, Ich sawe al the communes: the goode knightes and burgeses and men of wit and lerninge who had com to speke for their shires and citeez. And sum Ich sawe ther were Kynge Richardes men, who had ben at the recepcioun the night bifor. Mesemede these men suffred thilke same gret unese that bugged me, for all ower talkinge poyntez had ben disclosid.

Vp roos thanne a knight that was helde wys, by leve and by conseil of othir that were ther, and seide: "May the Lord blesse vs all! Gentils, ye all haue heard how Chancellor de la Pole hath tolde vs a tale of the causes of this parliament, how he hath seyde that ower lord the King nedeth gret amountes of cash and taxacioun for his werres."

"Yay!" Ich roos vp thanne and spoke with noble steven, "For the Reaume mesemeth is in gret peril from the malicious Frensshe, in greter peril than evir bifor. For a Frensshe flete hath ygadrid to make invasioun vpon ower lande. Gret peril! We must all drede the peril! For the Frensshe shal turn al of our filmes in to non-linear meditaciouns vpon lyf and deeth both insouciant and weightie. And eek thei shal destroyen…"

"Namoore of this, for Goddes dignitee," quod the knight, "What maner doofus artow, that thou rehersest the talkinge poyntez of the kinge? For thei haue all been addressid and defeatid. Ay, the Frensshe do seeke to make werre vpon vs, but the moost freshe newes saith that their fleet is all kindes of disorganized and bad wedir hath y-messed-vp ther shippes. No attack loometh as yet. As for the threte thei pose to ower cinema, Ich wolde thinke that *Love, Actuallye* doth prove that ower cinema is a threte vnto itself."

And ther was muchel laughter. And the men of Kyng Richardes faction did glare me-vpon as if to seye "do nat make thinges werse."

And the knightes speche continued: "And thogh the threte from the Frensshe yet remaine, even thogh ther flete cometh nat soon, yet ther is a greter threte: for we knowe that the houshold of the Kynge is full of fooles and liares who take the money of taxacioun and spende it to ther owen avantage. Nat oon grot that is y-gadrid gooth to the defens the reaume, only to the vainglorie of the kinges false freendes. Michel de la Pole buyeth much land wyth money he hath from the king y-stole. And what man kan speke fully of the surquiderie and ill conduct of Robert de Vere, whom the king hath—in blindnesse of this mannes baseness—raysed to the ranke of Duk of Ireland? Ay, verilye this fals de Vere who hath yiven up hys lawful wyf to gallivant about wyth Reims Launcecrona. And thuswise the hard-erned goodes of ower constituents go to buye mower bottles of balm-infused vodka for Launcerona and de Vere's table. Certes, good sires, in no maner shal the Frensshe werre be broghte to good conclusion vntil the Kyng assent to the advyce of his noble uncles and of his cousin, Henry Bolingbroke. What say ye?"

And al assentid wyth oon voys.

Wel, almost al. The Kinges faction did slip out stelthily lyk vnto the audience of a conference panel whan the wyne hour hath alreadye started. And yet Ich moved nat to go wyth hem, for it semed that the knight spak trewthe, thogh it semed lyk tresoun.

And at that verye moment, Ich felle doun in a swoon. (Ich haue been fall-
ing y-doun into swoones pretty much on a dailye basis evir syn Ich haue
been slepinge in William Langelandes gest-room and etinge hys food.
Methinketh the meales in his hous are full of pejote and valium. The man
hymself ys basicallye a narcoleptique).

In my swoone thus, Ich dremte that Ich was yn a feelde wyth singinge
briddes in the trees and a river cler as crystal. And nigh my feete were V
smal figures. Thei were made in the forme of liouns. And oon was azur,
and an othir was as grene as the feelde. The thridde was as red as blod,
and the ferthe was yelwe lyk the blosmes of the dandelion. The Vthe smal
figur of a lion was blakke as the night. And Ich picked up the liouns, and
niste what thei ment or who had made them, or why thei were in the
grasse in my allegorical landscape. Ther was also a smal perle next to the
liouns, but Ich ignored it by cause Ich figured som oon els was lookinge
for it.

And thus Ich wandrid holding the smal figures of the liouns, vntil Ich
cam to a man who was clothed al in blak.

And he seyde to me, "Gode sone, what cariestow in thy hondes?"

And Ich seyde, "Smal figures of liounes."

And he seyde, "How many?"

And Ich seyde, "Fyve."

And he seyde, "Trewelye, my son, thes fyve liounes signifien thy fyve
senses, which sholde telle thee wher thy trewe path lieth in this matir of
Parlement. For by sight thou knowst sum thing of the matir at hand, and
eek by thy hearinge, and folowingly thurgh touch, smel, and tastinge.
But thou hast nat putte hem al togedir."

And thanne Ich knewe, for Ich put the liounes togedir and thei formed
the figure of a mighti knight and a wise, lyk vnto the knight who spak.

"Behold! Put al thy senses togedir and thou getest the figure of Voult-
Roune, which bitokeneth 'turne in secret.' For my sone, thou must joyne
wyth thes folke as thy fyve senses say. For thou seest wyth thyn eyen the
sory state of the reaume, and thou herest wyth thyn heringe the wordes of
this knight, and thou touchest the matir wyth thy minde. And thus…"

"What about smel and tastinge?"

"Sum tymes the allegory worketh nat out completely. And thus, Geoffrey
Chaucier, thou must go wyth thy felinge. Dostow trust this knight and
wisshe to helpe the communes ayeinst de la Pole?"

"Ich do!"

"Thou must speke wyth greter felinge, for I heere thee nat."

"Ich do!"

"What?"

"Ich DO!"

At which Ich wook, and sawe the communes weren deep in debaat. And sum oon had at that moment asked the question, "Who wisheth to go wyth me to get the secret evidence ayeinst de la Pole?" And by cause Ich had screamid "Ich do," Ich was chosen for the job.

And thus Ich was no lenger a trewe aye-man of the kinges faction, but a man who wolde folwe thes communes to remove de la Pole from offyce. And Ich was scared that Tommy Vsk would at me be soore y-pissed.

Of what then happed, vpon the journey to fynde the evidence, Ich shalle write soon.

And who was the man in blak, ye maye ask? Ich knowe nat, but it semed he stood within a burninge ringe of fyre.

Syn Parlement was so wonderfully ful of aventures that yeer, Ich koud nat commit much of yt to the blog, forwhy Ich was in gret feere that my dealinges and doinges should be knowen by myn enemees. Trewely, yt was a tyme of cloak and dagger, involving sneaking yn to houses and wiretapping hotel roomes. Ich got a bit on the bad syde of my Lord Kyng Richard, and he did nat talk to me for a while after that.

By cause Ich koud nat write on my blogg, Ich kept a seryes of notebooks. In them, Ich recorded al of my doings and eek the secret talk of the communes, and also the matir of ower meetinges wyth gret nobles and eek Kyng Richard hymself. Ich kept the notebookes yn a suitcase and broght them back hoom.

The funnyest thing happened, thogh. On my way back from Londoun, the suitcase disappeared. So no lyvyng soul shal knowe the exact role that Ich, Geoffrey Chaucer, did pleye in the Wondirful Parlement. O meschaunce! O coincidence foule!

[*Editor's Note:* The "Parliament Journal" posts relied on consultation of published historical accounts, including the *Riverside Chaucer*'s introduction, Pearsall's biography, and C. Given-Wilson's *Parliament Rolls of Medieval England*, as well as Ronald Butt, *A History of Parliament: The Middle Ages* (London: Constable, 1989), and Nigel Saul, *Richard II* (New Haven, CT: Yale University Press, 1997), especially pp. 148–204.

In addition, Chaucer's vision above is inspired by Matthew Giancarlo, "*Piers Plowman*, Parliament, and the Public Voice," *Yearbook of Langland Studies* 17 (2003): 135–174.]

November 23, 2006

Bibliomania

Geoffrey heere. Many aventures haue me befallen sithen Ich haue elected ben to speken at Parlement for the sake of the realm, and eek ther ys much for me to tellen yow of, my goode rederes, but for nowe Ich wolde speke of sum thyng yet more paisable and swete: buyinge hell of newe readyng material.

By seynt Jerome, gentil folk, Ich nede no *Philobiblon* of Richard de Bury to instructe me of the grete power and vertu and joie that is to be found in bokes. As messire John of Gaunt loueth women, so Ich loue bokes: without limit or discriminacioun, Ich loue them oolde and newe, short and longe, Frensshe or Latin or on Englysshe tonge, of heigh sentence or of lowe japerye, from the smalest leef of parchemin to the gretest volume clad in blak or reed wyth commentarye and big honkinge metal claspes for fasteninge it shut.

Thogh the quiet lyfstyle of Kent pleseth me much, yt is right hard to fynde goode bokes ther, so as Ich make my stay in Londoun for Parlement, Ich haue been going crazy about the purchasyng of bokes. Euery daye Ich visit the scriveneres for to see the newe bokes and maken requestes for copyes. My shire doth paye me IV shillinges for ech daye Ich am in parlement, and by cause of al the monkey business of this straunge parlement yt is lastinge longer than a voyage to Spayne. By cause Ich lodge myself with my frende Langeland, Ich spende but iii pens for a capon ech daye (and a somedeel greter amount for ale, wyn, and batidas), and thus a gret surplusage of cash moneye remaineth for the acquiringe of newe bokes.

Sikerly it taketh nat a wise philosopher to reken that the rederes of my blog peraventure wolde wisshe to knowe of the bokes Ich haue picked up or planne to buye, so heere Ich shal liste sum notable ensaumples of my haul of ink and wordes:

Battelstar Ecclesiastica

by Johannes Wycliffe

> In this boke of science ficcion, a man ycleped Wycliffe is the bishop of the gret chirche of Seynt Paules, the which is lyk vnto a mighty shippe and kan moue thurgh the voyde of the planetes. Al othir chirches on the

earth haue ben destroyed by the deuil and his feendes, who haue taken on the visages of men and look exactlie lyk friares. Ther is a mighti ladye of feyth called Margery Starbaxter, who ys a loyal warryour for the chirche and sleyeth the friares. And eek ther ys a traytour named Belshazzar who doth see visions of a sexie friar yn his heed, the which friar telleth hym to betraye the goode folke of Seynt Paules. Sum oon nedeth to jump on this sucker and turne hit in to a series of television.

The Harley Lyrics

by Anonymous

Oon of anonymouses bettir workes, thes poemes are ycopyed fresshe from a manuscript contaynyge many othir thinges. Thei are songes of loue both goostly and bodili, and oft speke of a knightes loue for his horse, the which he calleth hys "motourbyk," upon which he "liveth to riden, and rideth to liven." Othertimes these songes speke of a knightes affecioun for his "chopper" (his axe?) or his "hogge" (why raiseth a knight pigges?) or his "mama" (gentil remembraunce of oones mothir ys fayre and chivalrous). Heere ys oon ensaumple of this straunge but plesaunte verse:

> Maketh motor for to runne;
> Shoopen vs to to heigh-waye;
> No aventure shal we shunne
> In what-evir cometh ower waye.
>
> Yn the smok and lightening,
> Blastes of hevy metal.
> Wyth the wind goon racing-
> The felinge is so goode.
>
> An hendy happe ichabbe hent,
> From nature pure we aren sent
> Vndyinge we kan make ascent
> For borne we are to waxen woode.

The Doctours: The C and I Moost Dangerous Scholastic Thinkers in Europe

by Archbishop Thomas Arundel

This boke pointeth out the dangerous doctrine of many of the doctors of theologie and maysters of the artes who teche yn the universitees and scoles. For many of these folk, thys boke telleth me, teche nat simply the dogma of the chirche but also injecte heretical doctrine from auncient philosophres and thus pose a grete threte to ower future ecclesiastical administrators and preestes. The worste by far ys Thomas Aquinas, who hath argued, drawing from Aristoteles principle of the first entelechy, that the forme of the soule containeth the sensitif and vegitatif soules, in contradiccioun of the gret tradiciouns of the chirche. Ich drede what shall come to pass yf thes techinges are allowed to poyson the mindes of goode Cristen folke.

Piers Plowman: The I-Text

by William Langelande

This boke confuseth me, by Seynt Charles Borromeo, so Ich do copye the text from the back of the avertisement:

"Ye gentil folke haue rede the compact A-Text, haue thrillede to the cliff-hanger endinge of the B-Text, and haue enjoyed the occasional addiciouns and politicallie prudente modificaciouns of the C-Text. If ye haue got Piers-fevere lyk we do, ye haue probablie even hunted the bootleg market for the fabled Z-Text. NOW PREPARE YOWERSELVES TO EXPERIENCE THE EPIC TALE OF PIERS THE PLOWMAN YET AGAIN IN A RELATIVELY NEWE WAY. The I-Text of Piers Plowman ys available on the I-Bokes web-syte. Ye kan download a passus for a mere XCIX pens and carrye the boke around on yower I-Pamphlet for esy readynge whil in Parlement, while sayinge matins, or just when sloshinge around the feelde yn the bitre cold. Ech I-Text passus featureth even more intricate changes to the texte. Who will establish the power of the king in the prologue of this versioun? How will the elaborate grammatical metaphor get even more complicatede? Don't miss Passus V: the I-Text version includeth an expanded *apologia pro vita sua* the which narrateth Willes earlier experiences as a clerke in a department store and hys misshaps in the datinge world of 1360s Londoun. HOW CAN YOU RESIST THIS AMAZING AND CONVENIENT WAY OF SEEING THIS ACTION-PACKED CLASSIC IN YET ANOTHER SLIGHTLY DIFFERENT FORM? Go to the I-Bokes web syte and download the Piers Plowman I-Text today. *Legal information*: the ink vsid alloweth you to make but V copyes of the poeme in to yower owen household boke or pamphlet and doth nat permit excerpts or trademarked character names to be included in rebellious let-teres. Eny sign of tresoun shal be punisshed wyth death."

The VII Habits of Heighly Effectif Hangers-On

by Thomas Vsk, Serjeant-at-Armes for his Trespuissant Majestee Richard Kyng of Engelonde

Sithen Ich haue just spoken of oon of my frendes bokes, yt semeth proper to maken mencioun of the othir. This litel volume is in no wise semblable to Vskes earlier *Testament of Loue*, but rather yt is a pamphlet of "helpe-thi-self" that telleth how to survyve in Londoun factional politics. Vskes maner of late doth bringe me grete unease; mesemeth he hath grown too grete for hys britches. But yet to return to the matter of hys boke, he maketh seven poyntes of conseil, the which Ich shall liste for yow heere:

I. Be Proactif at Changing Alliaunces
II. Yet Begin Thy Werkes Wyth Thine Eternal Ende (RESPECT!) in Thy Minde
III. Paye Heed to First Thinges: Who Kan Yive Thee Bettir Livery?
IV. Think Winne/Winne: Thou Shalt Winne Honour, and Thy Former Allies Shal Winne Exile
V. Seek First to Vndirstond the Factional Situation, & Aftir Make Thy Loyaltee Undirstood to Thy Sovereign Lord Kyng Richard
VI. Synergize Boethius and Love Allegory and Sum Thyng About a Knot into a Literary Werke Proclaymynge Thy Trewe and Honorable Nature
VII. Drop Names of Famous Writers Whom Thou Knowst As Often As Possible (for as Geoffrey Chaucer the gret poete and my faste and loial freende hath seyde: "For may no man fordon the law of kynde")

The Stoner Letters

Compiled from the collecioun of the Stoner Family

Ich am crazie about readynge of the histories of families and specially in hire owen wordes. This boke doth collect the writinges of many generaciouns of good gentry folke in the shire of Oxford, their letters and their bokes of accountes and charteres. Oon the straungest thinges of families ys the similaritee shared by parents and childer. For the Stoner family semeth consistentli to seke certayn items from age to age. To wit:

1290 Accounte of Household Expenses of Richard de Stoner:

> *X poundes for potato crispes*
> *III poundes II shillinges for poster wyth a wizard and sum skeletons that sheweth well and fayre vndir black-light*
> *IV poundes X shillinges III pens for a balle for to pleyen hack-the-sack*
> *II shillinges paid to Harold Chillouttent esquire for restraininge of John Stoner who kynde of freaked out a litel*

1380 Edmund de Stoner to John Bounge, Grocer of Londoun:

> *Dude, please sende lyk a wagon full of potato crispes for the munchies soore possess me. And eek plese sende newe bulbes for the black light; Ich kan scarce see the orange dragon that decorateth the basement. Of gretest importaunce, telle my servaunt to return right quick, for Elisabeth hath gone oon toke ovir the lyne and hath just now lokked hirself in the tower for feare that all folk aren set ayeinst her. My servaunt*

kan fynde me outside of the tower. Probabli I wil be lyk playinge hack-the-sack or just chillaxinge.

Trewely, kinship runneth deepe and strong in the Stoner blood!

Thogh this be but a smal liste of bokes, peravanture yt yiveth yow a samplinge of the manye deliteful purchases Ich haue in Londoun y-maad. And now, Ich am off to grabbe yet oon more book bifor Ich muste cacche my coach back to Kent.

January 5, 2007

Margery Kempe at MLA

My gentil rederes, Ich haue a text of gret sentence to share, thogh nat by me ywritten. Ich haue many freendes across thys gret erthe and oftimes they sende me their werkes. Oon of hem ys a ladye of much spirituale knowledge who oft writeth of her aventures. She hath sent me thys her latest tretys, the which speketh of a straunge festival ycleped MLA. Be this MLA of fayerye or of devilrye Ich knowe nat. Ich nam nat no theologien, nor nam Ich a mystique lyk my freend Margery. Ich shal poost her boke heere and ye maye maken yower owen interpretaciouns.

Date: 3 Janvier
From: KEMPE, MARGERYE (desperaathouswyf@kempesoflynn.com)
To: GEOFFREY CHAUCER, M.P, J.P., D. D. S. (daliaunce@hottemail.com)

RE: MY MOOST FRESHE AND NEWE TRETYS ON MLA—FOR YOWER BLOGGE

Here begynnyth a schort narracioun for synful wrecches, of the gret merci that ower Lord Christ Jhesu did unto a synful caytyf at the rite of MLA amonges the paynims and the scolers of blakke magick. (Thys synful caytyf and creatur is callid Margerye Kempe and her bookes can be yfounde in many fyne scryvyneres shoppes).

I: In the seson of Cristemasse, thys pore creatur and caytyf did fynd herself in a straunge launde. For sche had maad passage to Ba'alt-Ymoor, the which citee she thoghte was yn the launde of the Sarazines ner the citee of Jerusalem. And she had gret compuncion and wepynge for the synfulness of her ignorance of geographie, for Ba'alt-Ymoor was in no wyse close to tho placez wher ower Lorde dyed on cross, but was in sted across a gret see and ytself was a place of passinge foulness wher ffolke did etyn only of the crabbes that walked on the floor of the bay Chesupyk and did watch the filmes of Johannes des Eaux. And thys creatur was sore afreyd of the synneres of that place and so sche went forth northewardes on the heigh-way XCV. Yet the way was long and her feet ached swich that she threw off her Manohlo Blahnikes and sat by the syde of the heigh way wepynge. And this was on the feest of Seynt John. As thys creatur lay in contempla-cyon, sor wepynge for the peyne of her feet sche prayid to ower lorde for deliverance from this launde. And ower lorde seyde to her, "A, dowter, why wepest thou for the peyne of thy feet for thou knowst how soore my owene feet were woundid on mount calvarie? And therfor to bringe the to spiritual helth and contemplacioun I shal sende thee on a desperaat tryal and a terribil oon amonges devils and their ministeres and necromanceres. For thou shalt fynde a tan stacioun wagon that schal be ful of clerkes and thes clerkes shall take thee to the moost terribil place on al the erthe." And the creatur seyde, "A, Lord, what ys this place that ys the moost terribil on erthe?" And the lord seyde to her, "It is callid MLA."

And right so it befel in dede that a stacioun wagon did pulle up and a voys from it seyd, "You going to Philadelphia?" And thys creatur seyd, "I go to MLA," and the voys seyde that MLA was part of Philadelphee and thus sche cam with hem. And in the vehicle was a cumpany of thre yonge scolers, to wit one woman and two men. And thys creatur spak to them and seyd, "Tell me what maner ffolk ye aren." And oon the men seyd, "My dissertation addresses the pressing question of the relation of *The Owl and the Nightingale* to the paradoxes of materiality and to changing ideas of spirituality at the same time that it questions what I would call outmoded models of allegoresis. Essentially, I propose that this heavily mediated text engages with debate poetry not as a generic exemplar but rather vis-a-vis an interstitial combination of truth claims and bestiary passages about cephalopods." And thys creatur was soore confusid, and sche prayid to ower lord and wepid gret teares for the passioun of the child Jesu who had been born in a maunger to take awey the synnes of all ffolke and also to deliver her from MLA. And alle the cumpany did wepe with her vntil the ladye who drof the van schouted at the oothirs and seyd, "Could you please be quiet? I'm trying to listen to the sparque-notes for *Cursor Mundi*." And thys creatur knewe litel of thes wyse clerkes wyth whom sche travilid and she askid what maner ffolk thei weren. Oon the men was named Genderstudyes and the othir man was named Faulknerstudyes and the woman was named Medievaliste. And thei were from Bigresearchuniversitee.

II: Than thys creatur and her felawshep cam to Philadelphee wher thys MLA did stonde. And Sir Genderstudyes seyd that al the cumpany scholde be herberwyd in I room togedyr and this creatur assentid for sche had but litel goold. And thei took hostelrie at a gret paleys called the Merry Ott and thys creatur seyde, "Forsooth thys name ys contrarie to the wordes of ower lorde for we oughten nat be merrye but rather we oughten be sadde for ower synnes." And Dame Medievaliste seyde, "That's pretty Robertsonian of you." And thei cam to the room and sche had gret feere for her chastitee but eftsoon sche saw that the yonge clerkes cared oonlie for lamentaciouns and for gret studye of manye smal pieces of paper and the seyinge of preieres yn quiet voys and sumtyme gret wepynge. Thus sche feered no triall of hanquie-panquie from thes folk.

Thys caytyf had ben in many cumpanyes and in all of hem sche had ben the moost ful of wepynge and sorwe. But amonges the thre yonge clerkes, and amonges the othir yonge scolers in the Merry Ott, sche felt lyk the oonly Cristen soul whos puppy had not given up the goost the day bifor. Trewely, thes yonge folk wyth hir lamentaciouns and hir gret vigiles and fastinges did semyn to be trewely greved by the synnefulness of the world. And thys creatur tryed to cryen and wepen wyth sumwhat greter force and yet sche stil semed to be right joyeful in comparaisun to thes scolers.

And thys creatur had grete wondir at the holiness of thes yonge clerkes, for thei weren nat full of pryde and vanitee as were the friares and bishoppes yn Engelonde who lyved in ese and wyth pleasaunce. And sche wondrid that Ower Lord had in his revelacyons to her seyde that MLA was a desperaat and terribil tryal, for to her it semed the oonlie place on erthe sche felt sort of normal. And sche seyde to Ower Lord, "A, Lord, wherfor sholde I feere thes folke? For thei aren lyk the Harlem Globetrotteres of self-mortifica-cioun." And Ower Lord seyde, "A, dowter, ask thes folke to what seyntes thei prayen and thou shalt see wherefor thou sholde be greatly afrayd."

Than sche askid the clerkes to which seyntes thei prayid, and nat oon of hem did mencioun an holy cristen seynt. For sum clerkes seyd thei prayid to Seynt Budtler, and sum to Seynt Sedgewicke, sum to Seynt Foucauld, and sum to Seyntes Deleuse & Wauttaure, and sum to Seyntes Jamison and Egleton, and eek sum to Seynt Blume. And lo thys creatur had gret feere and terror for thes weren nat the names of holy Cristen seyntes. Thes names weren al straunge and were nat writ in ony legendes of seyntez and thus thei weren assuredly the names of devylles and feendes of helle. And thes clerkes seyd thes devils gave hem grete powers for to undirstonden textes and to gloss hem, and also gave hem poweres to deconstructen thinges and to unpacken thinges and to see the privee menynges of wordes.

Than the creatur knewe that al the semynge holiness of thes yonge clerkes was but devocioun to ower goostly enemy, and their gret piles of papir were but devylles writtes and their gret tomes weren but grimoyrez and bokes of necromancie. She tok hede to listen to the murmuringez of the clerkes, and thei al spak of "My dissertation addresses the pressing question of..." the which ys nat a prayer but an incantacioun. For sche did suspect that thes "dissertations" were gret actes of devocioun to the devils who had swich straunge names. And than sche fled doun-stayres to get a frappucino for sche was so soore adraad so sche cam to the elevatours.

III: And yit thys creatur got out at the wronge floore for sche had so much drede, and sche found herself in an halle. And ther thys creatur saw II men clad in clokes, and oon wyth a laurer wreath vpon his heed wyth a mighti grand nose. And the othir did shimmer lyk vnto the proiection of Princesse Leeah that out of RII-DII's holographick projector y-came—for it semed hys body was goostli. And thogh thes men spak nat on Englysche, Ower Lord gave her grace to undirstodyn hem. And yet thogh sche herd hir wordes, thei made but litel sense.

(he wyth the nose and laurer wreeth spak):

> "O great Mantuan, you who lead me through
> This hostelry of madness, at your will,
> Inform me what transgression caused these souls
>
> To be so foully ensepulchred here,
> Among such reams of paper and such cries.
> Do we draw near to hell's frost-covered core?"

(he who did flicker lyk a flourescent light yn the bathroom of a nightclubbe spak):

> "O Tuscan, at the gates of Albuquerque,
> We should have leftwards turned our path, for see:
> This is not that despairing pit we seek,
>
> Only its earthly image, where the faction
> Of those with suits and snappy colon titles
> Comes to seek reward at price. Let's go
>
> And feast upon some cheesesteak ere we leave,
> For in the miserable place we seek
> The only snack is Ruggieri's head,
>
> And I could use a nosh."

And as thys creatur stood in gret mervayle at thes men sche saw nat that a door had opened behind her. And a man yn a navy blue suit cam out of the door and addressid the creatur, saying, "Are you the twelve thirty?"

And the creatur seyd to hym, "Sir, I am afreyd of the folk heere and I prey yow nat be desplesyd yf I ask yow to take me into secrecee and safetee from the many cruel folke and necromanceres who are heere."

And he laughed, "That's one way of putting it. Please, come in."

Than in the room thys creatur saw the two felawes of that man, and the man bad her sit vpon a smal chayre while he and the oothirs sat vpon a bed. And sche bigan again to be soore adrad, for thei also had many paperes and portfolios and semed to be necromanceres and clerkes of derke knowlech. And it semed thei wolde interviewyn her, and sche was basicallye hyperventilatinge and about to freake the heck out. Owr mercyful Lord, spekyng in hir mind, blamyd hir of hyr fear, seying, "Why dredist the? Why art thou so aferd? I am as myghty here at MLA as in the paleys of a Bishoppe or in the land of Judee. Why wilt thou mistrustyn me? Suffyr paciently a while and have trost in my mercy. Wavyr nowt in thy feith and answir all questions quicklye and honestli and make sure to emphasyze thy research."

And the man in the suit put doun hys papirs and portfolios and seyd, "I'm very sorry, but we seem to have misplaced your cv. Could you please refresh us on your name?"

"I am a wrecchid synnere and a pore caytyf who seekes God. And for that sum call me a lollard and a heretik."

"Okay Ms. Andaheretic. We were all very interested in your work; really, it's very affecting. Could you tell us a little about your future plans?"

"I schal spekyn of God and chastise folk that sweryn gret oathes whersoevyr I go, unto the tyme that the pope and holy chirche hath ordeynde that no man schal be so hardy to spekyn of God."

And oon of the mannes felawes than seyd, "So you work on control of speech in religious discourse?"

"I praye that Ower Lord Jesu may grant me the grace of undirstondynge yower discourse, madam. And eek I wepe for synnes, rathir a lot of wepyng for ther are rathir a lot of synnes."

"Okay. Well, could you describe for us your teaching style? How would you, say, teach a lesson about this religious discourse your project deals with?"

"I preche not, ser, I come in no pulpytt. I use but communicacion and good wordes, and that wil I do while I live."

"That's great. It sounds very student-centered. Now, as you know, research is very important in this department. Do you have any plans for publication?"

"Sir, unworthy creatur thogh I am, I was oones charged that I schuld don wryten my felyngys and revelacyons, so that the goodnesse of Ower Lord might be knowyn to alle the world. And so I had it wryten doun by a man from Dewtchland and then a preest put it into Englysshe."

"A book, really? You've got a book already?"

"Two, in feyth, sir."

"Well, that's very impressive for a junior faculty appointment. Look, I know this isn't supposed to be done, but I think I speak for all of the committee when we say that we're very interested in your application. But we've had problems in the past when candidates couldn't—well, you know, they couldn't make their personal lives really fit with their plans. Now, you don't have to answer this, but—what is your family situation?"

"I have a good man, a burgeys of the town of Lynne, to myn husbond."

"Oh, overseas. That's—unfortunate. Do you think that will be a problem, you know, bringing him over?"

"I prey yow, ser, put me not among men, that I may kepyn my chastitee. Myn husbond gaf me leve wyth hys owyn mowthe that I schold goon on pilgrimage and livyn out of hys presence."

"Well, Ms. Andaheretic—may I call you Alollard? I know this is quick, but I'd like to extend the invitation of a campus visit. You sound exactly like the kind of candidate we could do with at our institution."

And thus thys creatur now dwelleth at a universitee in Amerique wher she giveth instruccion in the wayes of Ower Lord and sche ys called assistante professour. Her studentz drawen much edificacioun from her wepynge and her research scavenger hunt assignmentz. And sche praiseth Ower Lord everich daie for he did deliver her from the necromanceres and the sorwe at the hostelrye of the Merry Ott and the derke rite of MLA, in the maner that he deliverid Danihel from the Liones Den and Jonah from the Whale and Sir Neville de Fraunce from the Serpentes on a Shippe. And thos of the universitee scholde knowe that thys short tretys counteth as a publicacioun towardes tenure for it was blinde-peer-reviewede by II hooly eremites. Worschepyd be God. Amen.

[*Editor's note:* The above entry silently works in verbatim passages from the *Book of Margery Kempe*. The entry allows the *Book*'s text to answer questions in an MLA interview. During Margery's interview, the lines beginning "I am a wrecchid...," "I schal spekyn...," "I preche not...," "Sir, unworthy creatur...," "I have a good man...," "I prey yow, ser..." appear in the same form that they do in Margery's text. I have used the TEAMS edition of *The Book of Margery Kempe*, ed. Lynn Staley (Kalamazoo: Medieval Institute Publications, 1996).]

December 2006

Freestyle Joust and Oath of Brothirhede

The followinge eschaunge of wordes did develop on my blogg. Thogh Ich was sum thyng irous at first, yet Pees and Concord smyled doun upon both myself and Sir Baba de Brinkman, who maketh rymes of my rymes. (*www.babasword.com*)

A comment of myne:

> Ywis, long haue Ich loued the mad rhyming skillz of Baba Brinkman and had hym y-listed in myn sidebar. Nowe, wolde that he wolde make sum mencioun of myn blog! (And thogh it peyneth me to shewe myself as an proud herted man, by my soul Ich thynke that myn owen songes of rap are phattre than his). -LeVostreGC

A comment followed from Sir Baba de Brinkman hymself:

> Check it:
> Every man is proud hearted
> Until he gets outsmarted
> So when this battle is over
> Just remember how it started...
> Peep the dialogue, you've got two eyes blocked, one by a mote,
>   and the other by a log, as I weave my words around you like
>   a quiet fog, if you're lonely, buy a dog, but if you're bored and
>   misanthropic, try a blog.
> Apparently I'm a superior narrator, while you're an inferior parroter,
>   a mere imitator of a lyrical character, which means I'M the OG's
>   clear inheritor.
> I'm part of a mass movement, makin' rap music for the average
>   human. You're obviously a sad, clueless grad student, laughing at
>   the world 'cause you assume it's half-stupid.
> Now, faux-Geoffrey, you've been vivisected by the pen of a scribe
>   whose mind has never rested. I love getting tested by clever jesters,
>   but never question my dedication seeing Chaucer resurrected!

Respect for the blog, good sir,
Baba Brinkman

And thanne Ich joyned the battel wyth sum wordes of my owene:

Yower dedicacioun was nevir yet my *quaestio*,
So wherefore this assaut of wordes so wilful and so nasty, yo?
Ich made a pleiful japery invitinge games of rhyme
And nowe ye waxe wood on me lyk hyenas full of Zima?
Ye maye possess a funnye shirte in anachronistic style,
Ye maye also make mp3s yower cofferes for to fille,
Ye are in dede a man of wit for to speken veritee,
But sir, yt semeth ye haue not a drop of charitee.
Inheritaunce is partible and falleth vnto alle,
Ther beth many vacant chaires in poesies halle,
So wherfore claim ye sole seisin of my tradicioun:
Ich list yow in my sidebar—and ye come forth to piss me-on?
Nor overpasse moot Ich nowe yower vileynous *ad hominem*
Ayeinst thes poore grad studentz—for haue ye evir met with hem?
Ich see ye haue attayned degre of magister of arts,
So know ye nat that lerninge ys a wheel on wisdames cart?
Wherfore must scolers and studentz put up wyth so much crap
Whan it is thei who edit bokes of which ye make yower rap?
But all of that doth miss the poynt (thogh poynted be yower wordes);
Telle forth my name my gentil frendes, both feithful churles and
    lordes!
Ich am ycleped Chaucer, a pilgrim on the strete.
Ich seke to swinke for solaas of every soule Ich mete.
So wherfore faux ye me, my foe? Fo sho ich foe nat thee:
From litel woolen hat to shoes, Chaucer, Ich am he.
Yower movement may be mass
but by Seynt Loy it lakketh class.
Day to day half million websyte hits, Ich make the peple laugh.
Ich wryte for studentz in heigh scole, and thos of foreyn landes
Just as ye do, rude Baba (thogh no mic in my handes),
For researcheres who werke fulle harde, for professors who swinke,
For gentil folk who of my werkes haue nat yet rede a winke.
Thogh my blogge be nat composd wyth parfait ars grammatik
Ich yive a taste of England past, so stop wyth al yower static.
Blending truthe of historye wyth snark and gentil fun,
Ich mix the yore and now-a-dayes for the good of all and sum.
Philanthropee is what ye fynde yf ye peruse my syte:
Jolitee and swete joye in every kilobyte.
A misanthrope yet nevir Ich was, and if ye thinke me swich
Ich prove it in refraynynge from callinge yow a—name.
So look within yower herte, BaBard, or selle it for anothir
That will allow yow to rejoice in the werking of yower brothir.

And thanne, lyk a gentil knight Baba did propose a trews and ooath of brothirhede:

> Hats off to you, noble Geoffrey.
> I admit my words were a bit crueel, but keep in mind that you did call me out. I am well quyted, and I concede that our mission is the same (nor can I compete, it seems, with your army of fans).
> Let us be henceforth brothers in arms, spreading your fair Tales to the ends of the earth, you in cyberspace and me on the airwaves.
> Your i' faith,
> Baba

To which Ich respondid:

> Mon Cher Frere Baba,
>
> By Seynt George, that ys a fayre and gentil message, and Ich am right grateful for yower courteous wordes. Ich wyth al myn herte accept yower offer of brothirhede. If evir ther beth sum waye for me to assisten yow in yower projectes, thogh my skill be but smal and my blog but a litel thing of bits and bytes, ye maye simply informe me and Ich shal rallye to yower syde. Yower freendship pleseth me more than to haue al the wyn of burgundie and al the stout of dublin. To Canterbury!
>
> LeVostreGC

January 12, 2007

The V Thinges Meme

Ich haue now twies y-tagged ben for the "V thinges ye knowe nat concerning me" meme.

A meme, gentil rederes, is a smal taask the which oon writer of blogges performeth and then passeth on to othirs for to doon themselves. Mesemeth ther aren many memes yn the court of King Richard (at which Ich and my famille did spende the holidayes), swich as "King Richard now uses a smal scrap of cloth to clene his nose: YE MUST ALSO SO DOON OR YE SHALL HAUE YOWER LANDES FORFEIT AND YOWER HANDES CUT OFF" or "King Richard now uses a smal metal rod wyth a cup on its end for to drinken of his soupe: YE MUST ALSO SO DOON OR YE SHALL HAUE YOWER LANDES FORFEIT AND YOWER HANDES CUT OFF."

And yet for to speke of moralitee, a meme ys a thing that draweth attencion to the habits and natures of folk and tendeth toward pride and surquidrie, for the doing and making of memes prompteth folk to talk at gret length of their maners and opiniouns and historyes. And the word ytself containeth the truethe of this lesson in its verye spellinge, in the same maner as yn the langage of the Romayns the word signyfiynge frendship or love, *amicus*, cometh from the word for hook, *hamus*, for freendes and loveres hook yn to ech othirs soules lyk vhelcro. And thus considereth that the word meme ys writ "me me," and thus a meme is a reduplicacioun of a singuler self and a gloryinge in ego. Ich wolde that sum wyse folk sholde make "theethees," the which wolde be actes of charitee and goodnesse that yive vnto othirs. Ich haue a theethee for yow, my gentil rederes: yive a freende a copye of my poemes for the feest of Seynt Hilary.

But to retournen to my matir, Ich haue ben asked to participate yn a meme, the nature of which is to telle V thinges that fewe peple knowe concerning me. And thus Ich shalle do so, for to be gentil and curteis towardes thos othir bloggeres who haue me y-tagged.

V THINGES YE MAYE NAT KNOWE CONCERNING GALFRIDUS CHAUCER (YET EFTSOON YE SHALL KNOWE YF YE REDE BELOW)

Iste thinge: Whan Ich was yonge, oon yere for Christemasse my fadir announcid that he wolde buy me an Englisshe longebowe for my gifte, so that Ich mighte practice the art of archerie and lerne to defend the realm. Ich soore resisted, seyinge "Ich shal shoote oute myn eyen." Every daye of Advent he wolde speke to me sayinge, "Jeffie, ye shall haue a fyne longebowe for a gift at Christemasse." And Ich wolde saye "Nay, fadir, Ich shal shoote oute myn eyen! Yive me rathir a boke of Cicerones *Dreme of Scipioun* or peraventure a gothic belt." And whan Christemasse cam, the presente was in sted a gift certificate for pizza, for my fadir is a good man and a mery.

IInde thinge: Ich haue a cat named Christopher who loveth marshes and swampes. Ich haue composid a poem to hym entitled *Jubilate Stagno.*

IIIrde thinge: After a short misundirstondinge, Ich haue joyned in sworn brothirhede wyth Sir Baba de Brinkman, a good man that maketh dope rymez of my poemes for the delit and edificacioun of studentz. Knowe all ye haterz present and future that thos who wolde mess wyth Sir Brynkmann shal also get a tun-full of Geoffrey. Ich am soore annoyed to heare that sum folke see nat the worthe of hys makinges and musique, and that sum write him saying that Ich wolde nat be plesid to heare of his rappe. Litel knowe that many a song of rap doth pleye on the stereo in my car, and that Litel Lowys and Ich do bobbe oure heades up and doun to the musique wyth muchel relish. *Noli nothis permittere te terere*, Baba: Ich mynself haue receyved swich criticism. Ywis, whanne Ich gan writen myn poemes yn fyve-stress ryming englisshe coupletes, oftimes Ich got muchel grief from snooty nobles who seyd: "La poesie est proprement composee en langue Normande, gros vilein avec ton petit chapeu de laine! La langue Anglais est langue des pesauntez et labourerz & nest nemye belle! Par Seint Eloy, cest langue Anglais est seulement pur escrivre le doggerel alliteratif, come les poemes del horrible escripteur qui sappelle Anonymous." O, fooles all: for Englisshe has bicom the hot newe trend and Ich am on top of yt a-surfynyg! As Dant the Italyen seyd: "ther is oon thing worse than to have tales of yow y-told, and that is nat to have tales of yow y-told."

IVthe thinge: My biggest compleynt: Whan wil folk stop saying Ich nam nat real? Whan wil thei stop asking for my "real name"? What part of G-E-O-F-F-R-E-Y C-H-A-U-C-E-R do thei nat vndirstonden? An editor from a major magazine did contact me to aske if that fyne publicacioun mighte printe a part of my poost concerninge internette abbreviacions. Thys was gentil and did plese and honor me gretli, and Ich consentid. And yet thei wantid to yive credit to "Geoffrey Chaucer (aka your real name)" and thei wanted to knowe what Ich do in "in real lyf." Whan Ich toolde hem that my trewe Cristen name was Geoffrey Chaucer (Galfridus *in Latina*) and that Ich am a justice of the pees in Kente and a member of parliament, thei seyd thei coud nat print it. For thei seyde thei coud nat printe writinge "without attribution to a real person." What am Ich, liver y-chopped? Reality ys harder to com by than a duchy thes dayes, mesemeth.

Vthe thinge and final: Helas, in the custom of thes memes, much of the aboue ys complayning and whining. And yet peraventure that ys in my nature. For whan Ich was yong, Ich was sum thing of a goth (or gothic): the which ys a depressid yong person who wisheth to be part of an ancient culture. Ich wrote lettres to my gothic frendes yn Visigothic script, and studyed Jordanes boke ycleped *Getica*. At night, Ich went to goth clubbes—constructed wyth horshoe arches withouten key-stones—at which Ich was ycleped "Alaric" by my freendes. Ich dressid mynself yn rough robes wyth big ornate belt buckles, and oones Ich got in trouble wyth myn parisshe preest for pretendinge to be an Arian. Ther was many a feud bitwene the Visigoths who lovid the musique of soft ethereal synthesizers and the Ostrogoths who listned to the harshe musique of guitares and powernoyse. And everichon complained about the musique at the club the while smokinge clove cigarettez. Yt was pretty foolish, to think back upon it, and yet being a yonge goth was part of who Ich am. It dooth myn herte boote that I have in a club freakie y-got to The Systren of Grantmercy. Certes, being a goth led me to lerne of Boethius, who was by the goth Theoderic murdred. So a shout-oute to all yonge goths out ther: *sai atgaf izwis waldufni trudan ufaro waur me jah skaurpjono, jah ana al lai mahtai fijandis jah waihte ainohun izwis ni gaskathiith*, children of the night!

March 9, 2007

My New Anthologie

An idea for a project hath in myn herte taken root. Ywis, ye remembren that Ich bought many a book whan in Londoun. And yet, for ever-ich book that Ich did buye, yet myn desir for to rede did growe. Ich went from autobiographie, to self-helpe, to westernes, to poetrye—and rederes, whan Ich to poetrie came, Ich found that ther was no collecioun of poetrye the which had all the beste poemes yn it. For trewely, al the colleciouns of contemporarye poetrye are but poore thin thinges. And thus, at the prompting of Philippa, who seeth shillinges undir every mannes foot, Ich haue taken up the businesse of sellinge myn owene anthologie of poetry:

Galfridus Chauceres Anthologie of Poetrie in Proper (Middle) English

Ich am in negociaciouns wyth several scrybes and scryveneres to produce thys fyne book. Ye maye look for it at booke-stores neare yow, or contact Hippolyta on-lyne and haue it delivered to yow by warrior-women of the Land of Femenye.

Heere ys what thei call a smal "pre-viewe" of the gret poemes ye shal fynde in myn anthologie. Ye shal see that thys gret book containeth poemes by cherles and kynges, the wel-knowen and the anonymous; poemes of hard livinge and beere and poemes of gret beautee.

The Fortnights Run Away Lyk Draught-Oxen Behinde the Barn
by Carolus de Bois-Quasqué

> I was goinge somewhere
> like chirche

but Ich got round to Betties
and she had sum ale going
and spices and al that maner merde
and Ich seyde to myself
"Swyve this"
Good beere, and sat ther
Cess and Watt, elde buggere Tim Tinkere,
Clarice Cokkeslane—helle, Ich hadde a thinge
a couple yeeres ago wyth her
back whan Ich was deep yn to the horses.
Had a beere.
Clement and Hikke had sum bull-merde thing up
wyth a cloke and hood, sum exchaunge;
sum men aren alweys thinkinge money
but for me yt ys eyther beere or Mahler or swyving.
Moore beere from Bettye, alewyfe divyne,
Beere lyk continuous blood-
And the sonne-set red lyk an appel.
Belly rumblinge lyk a swyving bulle
Up to goon
Pissid on the bar-walle, long ynogh to singe a snatch of opera-
Fell around swyve-all y-blente.
Sum oon carryed me hom-ward
Sleped for dayes yt semed, al blak;
Ich heare myn wyfes voys
"Hank, 'tis Sonday"
and Ich seye
"Where is the bolle?
Ich want a drynke."

Thys Is Just to Saye
by Nostre Trespuissant Kynge Richard II

We haue had y-slayn
the knightes
that were in
Newgate

And which
ye were probablie
wisshyng
vs to pardoun

Forgyveness
nevir!
The lawe of Engelonde is ower will and lieth in ower breest, knave.

Kublai Kahn (Or, Marco Polo Lieth Thurgh Hys Teeth)
by Sir John Mandeville

In Xanade a mighti soudan yclept Kublai Khan has ther ymaad a place
of leysure neer the watir ycleped Alph the which is heeld hooly by the
saracens and is neer to greet cavernes. The walles and toures of that place
do mesure an greet span, that is to say x myles, and ther are also many
fayre gardyns right plenteous of fruyt. And ther was als wel a crevyce the
which ran doun the hill toward trees of cedar, at whos bottom was a well,
noble and faire, and at several houres of the daye it wolde yive spoute and
russhe with watir. I, Iohn Mandeville, saw this, al thogh I had nat bathed
for mony dayes and thus myn hair did float in a maner straunge and myn
eyen did flash for I had no thyng to eten of ther but honeydew melons and
sum horses milk. And al folk did daunce thryce around me in their pagan
maner. Weirdoes.

Whan Adam Dalf
by Anonymous

Whan Adam dalf, and Eve span,
Who had to write two bookes to get tenure?

The Daye Ladye Blaunche Perisshyed
by Sir John Clanvowe

Yt is terce in Londoun, a Tuesday (or peraventure a Wednesday)
Two dayes bifor the Feest of the Exaltacioun of the Holy Crosse, aye,
Yt is MCCCLXVIII or peraventure MCCCLXIX and Ich go to get
    my bootes shyned
for Ich will ryde my palfrey toward Northampton
by vespers and then go right to sup
and Ich knowe nat thos folke who shal me feede
Ich walke up the strete, thikke of air, the sunne gynneth shynen
and Ich ete of a blancmanger and sum corny ale and buye
an ill-fauored pamflet of NEW BOHEMIAN WRITINGE for to see what
    the poetes
in Bohemia aren doynge thes dayes
Ich go on to the exchequer
and Mayster Stondecart (firste name Laurence oones Ich herde)
looketh nat at the posicioun of myn accounte stones on the felt for
    oones in hys lyf
and yn MAYSTER PYNKHURSTES shoppe Ich get a litel Machaut
for Geoffrey wyth illuminaciouns by sum Parisian, yet Ich do
thynk of Boece *de Consolatione*, translatid Jean de Meun or
Langlandes newe A-Text *Piers* or *Yvain* or *Lancelot*

of Chrestien, but Ich do nat, Ich am stedfast to Machaut
aftir well nigh fallynge a-swoun wyth quandarynesse
and for Gower Ich just repaire to the CHEPESIDE
taverner and ask for a botel of god Rhenishe wyn, and
than Ich go back whence Ich cam to Soperes Lane
and the grocer nigh the Pageant Wagon and
lightli demaunde a carton of spyces of pepir and oon
of galyngale, and a PROCLAMACIOUN wyth her visage upon it
and Ich sweat muchel nowe and Ich thynke upon
leaning on the chambre door at the Abbeye of Reading
whil she did daunce so comlily, carole and synge so swetely
that my lord Duk John and al and mynself brethed nat

Jesu Me
by Dame Julian of Norwich

Hethen slaye yow;
Ovens are hotte;
Inquisitores flaye yow;
And plague-sik haue snotte.
Abbesses growe fatter;
Prechours moote wirche,
Pilgrims oft chatter:
Wall me in a chirche!

May 25, 2007

An Appoyntment

Myn gentil rederes, the joly tyme of Averille and May hath not been of
much jolitee to me. In feyth, Ich haue had but litel tyme to look upon
the newe floures and heere the smale foules doyng their thinge, for cursid busynesse hath fallen a-newe vpon me. Ich was prikked to take thys
biswinkful newe labor by grete nede, for whan Ich maade myn accountes
Ich discovred gret dettes and but litel revenue. Thomas, who ys wyth my
Lord John of Gaunt in Spayne, had gret need for moneyes to buye a newe
Blakkeberrye (for his hath been y-swiped by the Frensshe), and Lowys
hath taken up an internship for the somer wyth a Man of Law and thus did
need many a fyne robe and tie. Ywis, Lowyses raiment on moost dayes ys
but a tee shirte and jeans that falle nigh hys ankles for thei aren so loose.
Performing the dutees of a Justice of the Pees ys helle of interestinge (chee-
fly whan we usen blacklites at a crime scene) but it payeth slightli less than
nothinge. Ech daye, the many notyces did arryve from the Master of the

Carde and from thos whom Ich owed dettes, and at long laste Philippa did take the mattir into her owen strong, usually shakinge with anger, handes. In myn owen name and in myn owen script she wrote to my Lord Kynge Richard and asked if ther was sum posicioun available.

And so, my freendes, Ich haue bicom the Clerk of Kinges Workes. Myn abacus, the which was in the store-room yput wyth Lowyses astrolabe, now gooth with me wheresoever Ich go lyk vnto a new, wooden, boringe Ruth. Everich weekend, meseemeth, Ich must go to Westminstre, or to the roail palais at Sheene, or to sum smal manor at which several important but unwiedli obiectes are kept that must, withouten delaye, be brought to sum oothir smal manor. And the clerk bifore me did leeve thinges in a soory state. Ich do beleeve that myn predecessour was yiven his knowledge of letteres by chikkens, for hys writinges and accountes aren moore lyk the walking up and doun of several hennes than any maner of human script. Peraventure he was bisy eetinge seed and clucking, for he did but litel of hys job: many an angrie gardiner or ice sculpture maker hath contacted me and yiven me muchel guff for not havynge been y-payed for labor in the kinges servyce. And get me not started concerninge the stonemasones union. But the cash beginneth to flowe. And thus myn owen accountes shal be made wel by my labour on the accountes of the propertees of my Lord the Kyng.

November 12, 2007

Chaucer the Hooly-Woode Scabbe

Yf ye wonder, lordinges and ladyes, wher Galfridus Chaucer hath been, the answer is: in a verray purgatorie of busynesse. It pleseth me litel to labour as Clerk of the Kinges Werkes, and yet labor Ich muste, for Philippa forever addeth to our hous yn Kent and litel Lowys is beginning to speke of applyinge to Universitee next yeere, the whiche surpriseth me gretely: paraventure it is the ale of Oxford that lureth hym, not the bookes.

My lord Kyng Richard is a man of muchel ymaginacioun and many needes. Ich had thoghte that beinge Clerk of the Kinges Werkes wolde involve sum smal calculaciouns of repaires to palaces and castles, or perchaunce sum litel arrangement of walls to be buylt and an odd tournament heere and there. By Seynt Barbara, not in eny way!

Kyng Richard and hys fauorites Robert de Vere, Justice Tresilian, Bishop Neville, Nicholas Brembre and Michael de la Pole (the which clepen themselves the "Brat Packe") alwey asken me to arrange sum project of construccion that semeth a thing of fayerye. Fountayns of red and whit wyn in Hull? Chekke. A reenactement of the battel of Hastinges wyth dogges and cattes in armour? Chekke. A monster trukke rallye the which involveth a trukke that transformeth yn to a dinosaur? Chekke. Makinge a giant elephaunt walk the stretes of Londoun? Chekke. A Carolingian Renaissance fayre? Chekke (thogh that was prety esy, for it was minuscule). Mesemeth yf thes counsellors to the kyng do not get their spendinge and extravagaunce under control, sum thyng bad myght happen.

But thys weekend my lord the Kyng and the Brat Packe haue gone to the Malvern hilles for sum maner of mystique ritual in which thei shal "fynde themselves." And so wyth a litel fre tyme, Ich haue returnid hoom to relax and watch sum television. No thyng wolde plese me moore than to sit yn myn slothful-knave chayre wyth a caipirinha and catch up on sum muste-see tv. Or so thoghte Ich.

Yet allas, allas, the *Lex Murphiae* holdeth alwey trewe. In that gret and magique land ycleped Holy-Wood, from which cometh many a joieful showe of televisioun, the poetes and scrybes haue putte down their pennes in protest of the avarice of large corporaciouns. Al the gret tales and comedyes and shewes of talk haue y-ground to an halt and are no thyng but reruns.

Ich do thynk that the writers of Holy-Wood are goode folk and trewe and sholde continue their protest, but Philippa hath toold me that thys coud be an greet opportunitee for myn owene writinge (for alwey Ich am scribling sum poem or anothir or having some idea). So Ich am going ayeinst myn owene conscience to propose sum shewes of televisioun. Peraventure the mightie corporaciouns and compaignynes of produccion wil choose me to be an writere of televisioun ones thei see my wondirful conceptes heere on thys poost of blog. It peyneth me soore to be an scabbe and an protest-lyne crosser, but my sonne wisheth to goon to Oxford and my wyf desireth a patio. Forgive me, o ye merveillous writers of Holy-Wood: Chaucer nedeth a newe payre of shoes!

Ich haue purchasid sun-glasses for my meetinges and Ich haue practiced swich importante phrases as "Wayt for yt—wayt for yt" and eek "This will blowen yower mind" and eek "Ich wolde absolutely love to heare what revisions the sponsor hath suggestid for my script." Myn experience at court shal serve me wel.

Heere, withouten further delaye, O Executives of Entertaynment, are my proposales for shewes.

The Televisioun Lyne Up of Galfridus Chaucer, Clerke of the Kinges Werkes:

Sectes in the Borough: This hot and explicit showe wil handle religious dissent yn a more free and open way than evere bifor. Carrie Baxter is an underground writer of Lollard tractes in Norwich and the oonly thynge she loveth moore than questioning the validitie of the institucional church is her III best freendes: sexie Samantha, who seduceth many a preeste; intellectuale Charlotte, who speketh out ayeinst women being unable to preche; and Miranda Kempe, who receiveth visiouns from God. Thei meet every week to rede of the Bible in Ynglisshe and talke smacke about pilgrymage sites. Carrie is alwey resistinge the temptaciouns to submit to the orthodoxie of the Church, personifyed by Archbishop Thomas Arundel, whom she clepeth "Monsieur Grand." (Paraventure for a cabel network, by cause main-streme audiences aren not redi for frank depicciouns of heretical practice?)

The Gower Report: Thogh Johannes Gower ys an horrible wankere, yet hys churlish maners and hys gret pryde and surquidrie aren ful amusinge to watch. Yn this showe, Johannes Gower wolde speke to the audience of hys writinges and hys gret feare of beares. He may weare hys robe of a man of lawe wyth its striped sleeves and shal stand in front of peyntures of hymself. That ys so Gower.

Flight of the Lombardes: In this syde-splittinge comedic satyre, two yonge Lombard marchauntz, named Brentano and Germano, comen to Londoun to make their fortune wyth trading and finaunce. Thei aren also makeres of songes, ditees, roundels, and ballades, the which thei singe as commentarie to their aventures in love and businesse in a mildly self-deprecatinge maner. Their gretest ballade ys cleped "Tyme of Busynesse," and gooth sum thing like this:

Ywis, it is tyme of Busynesse. Aw yeah.
How knowe I this, askest thou?
For yt ys Wednesday,
a day not forbidden for tradinge and bargaininge by the lawe of Holy
     Churche.

Yea, for al is right, condicciouns are perfect
for Busynesse,
for thou hast sheeldes thou wishest to selle in exchaunge
for merchaundise thou hast bought in Flaundres.
And Ich haue soore nede of thy merchaundise.
Aw yea. And Ich am yn my red hose, the which aren cleped
Busynesse hose.
Doinge exchaunge and bargainynge.
Doinge exchaunge and bargainynge for two.
Doinge exchaunge and bargainynge for two

Florins profit. For two florins profit is better
than the profit of one shilling.
I schal put it on thy taille.

Hawk the Bountie Hunter: Thys showe shal deele yn the materes of kinges
and gret affayres of state, and thus shal be ycleped a roialtee showe. Ich
shal arrange for many cameras of televisioun to followe the gret merce-
narie Johannes Hawkwood, who hath risen from lowe birthe to serve as
a puissant man at armes in Italye and hath y-weddid the fayre dogther of
Bernabo Visconti.

The Privy Seel Offyce: Thys offyce of clerkes and scrybes produceth manye
documentz and eek muchel laughter. An hilarious ensemble cast of quirkie
folk shewe the dailye japeries and jolitee of roial bureaucracie. The privy
seel offyce is run by Michael Scot, who doth gret deedes of magique
and yet kan nat conjure good fortune for hymself. Yonge clerk Tristram
Canterbury soore loveth the receptioniste Ysolde Beesley, but sche ys to be
married to an oothir man. Yet Tristrames loue sickenesse preventeth hym
nat from makinge an ape of the haughtie clerke Gareth de Schrewe, who
oftymes findeth hys quill and ink put ynto a jello mold. Both Tristram
and Ysolde mocke Gareth, callinge hym "Beaumains." (Ywrit in collabo-
racioun wyth Mayster Thomas Occleve).

Doctor Hwaet: Thys showe doth chronicle the aventures of a solitarye one who
must wander the wayes of water on the rime-cold waves, mindful of miser-
ies, yn a large device ycleped the TOWAERDES (the which ys a grete magique
ship disguised as a burial mound) that alloweth hym to travel in tymes to
come and also yn the places that ben past and the far landes of fantaysye.
Alwey he sercheth out and protecteth a poem ycleped *Beowulf* the whiche
he saveth from a fyre and also turneth yn to several filmes in order that the
beautee of Grendeles motheres heigh heeled feet may drawe newe rederes to
thys tale. "That ys fanTASTick," he saith yn the rare tymes whan he ys of
good chiere. He fighteth many enemyes, includinge the Cybermonks, the
Daneleks, and folk who thinke that "Geats" is pronouncid "geetz."

February 22, 2008

Lament for Sir William

My gentil rederes, yif it be nat oon thynge, it is an oothir. For a while,
Ich was bisy with werke building a "fortified compound" for Kynge
Richard. It semeth parliament was merciles this yeere. That did ete up
much of my tyme ovir the seson of Yule.

And now of late, Ich haue been soore depressid to heare of the deeth of
my freend Sir William, yclept Ulrich of Liechtenstein for a certayn tyme,
with whom Ich did travel in Fraunce about XXXX poundes and a half

head of hayre ago. Ich haue sat in my room going thurgh oold joustinge programes and thinkinge of thos jours d'alcyone.

Thogh my pen is but a sely thing, moost fit for ditees and smal jokes and puns, yet Ich koud nat but trye to write sum few lynes of rym for the memorie of my good freend, the which Ich share heere. Ich knowe that newes of his deeth hath long ben publisshed, and many wyse folk have seyd thinges of hym, yet tak this rym-doggerel for my part, a poore candel for a goolden shryne.

A Compleynte on the Deth of Sir William Thatcher, Sumtyme Ycleped Ulrich Von Liechtenstein

Yif al the woe and teeres and hevinesse
And eek the sorwe, compleynte and wamentynge
That man hath heard in thes yeeres of distresse
Togedir were y-put, too light a thynge
It sholde be for this yonge knightes mournynge.
Withouten hym this world can no wey plese,
Fulfild it is of shadwe and disese.

In sorwe and teeres and eek in hevinesse
Stand Roland, Wat, and Kate, his compaigyne
(And eek myself, the forger of noblesse):
Sir Deeth wyth falshede and wyth sorcerye
Hath slayn thys knight who never feered to dye,
Of honor nat of lyf took Ulrich kepe.
A see of teeres nys nat ynogh to wepe.

Proud Deth, yower trophie is our hevinesse,
Your heraud may ful loude yel and crie,
For thou hast slayn the flour of hardinesse:
Sir Ulrich knewe the herte of chivalrie,
And evir daunce he coud to melodye;
A silent yere he spent oones in a toun
In Itaylye to understonde a roun.

This feble world fulfild of hevinesse
Offreth us nat but wo, O welaway!
No thyng it hath may us give restfulnesse,
For yisterday was noblere and moore gay
Than thys clipt peni that we hold today.
On Ulrich spende yower XII last silver teeres
Syn now departid aren hys golden yeeres.

He chaungid hys sterres, ros out of lowlinesse,
Bicam the man that fyrst did make me thinke
Our dedes nat our birth bring gentilesse,
And when Ich was depe in the dice and drinke

He bought my pants ayein, it is no nay.
May hevenes blisse repay that charité!
For blessed on erthe are al who had the chaunce
To walk the gardyn of his turbulaunce.

★ ★ ★

A NEW ORDER—GEOFFREY CHAUCER HATH AN EXTREME BLOG: GO ENGLAND! YT IS RAD!

Thomas Favent, and the Lords Appellant

Bitwene the monethes of July of 2008 and Maye of 2009, the Lords Appellant did seize the control of my blogg as part of their campaign of publicitee. Thei renamed the blog, clepyng yt by the foul and overlie trendie designacioun: "GEOFFREY CHAUCER HATH AN EXTREME BLOG: GO ENGLAND! YT YS RAD!"

Thogh thys appropriacion did payne me soore, peraventure sum of yow may wisshe to knowe of what was poosted by thes folk and their hired flunkie, Thomas Favent.

July 24, 2008

A New Order

WELCOME TO THE INNOVATYF RE-BRANDINGE OF

GEOFFREY CHAUCER HATH AN EXTREME BLOG: GO ENGLAND! IT YS RAD!

PRESENTID BY THE LORDS APPELLANT:

Thomas "The Swan" of Woodstock, Earl of Buckingham and Duk of Gloucester
Richard "Horsie" FitzAlan, Earl of Arundel
Thomas "Yogi" Beauchamp, Earl of Warwick
Henry "S-Collar" Bolingbroke, Earl of Derby
Tommy "Featherweight" Mowbray, Earl of Nottingham

YWRITTEN BY A GLOBAL TEAME OF CREATIFS AND TRENDSETTIRS ASSEMBLID IN FELAWESHEP WYTH MUCH COFFEE, AND Y-EDITED BY:

Thomas "Favor Fave" Favent (formerlie director of chihuahua trakkinge and parliamentarie gossip for GAUCHER Media)

INTRODUCCION BY THE LORDS APPELLANT

Welcome, gentils and churles alike. We haue looked at youre emailes thurgh our constant and completelie legal secret monitoringe of communicaciouns, and we haue wisely and graciously seen that the whole globe of the Erthe doth lament the lakke of posting on the blogg of a certayn Galfridus Chaucer, formerlie of the customes hous and until recentlie clerke of the kinges workes, and synce June an absent fathir, distractid soule, companion to a wandering king, and balm-addled layabout. Well, the longe tyme of yower waiting is ovir, for heere ys the new GEOFFREY CHAUCER HATH AN EXTREME BLOG: GO ENGLAND! IT YS RAD!.

Ywis, we Lords Appellant haue re-branded and re-concepted thys blog. We haue replaced Chaucer wyth a top team of new media specialistes. This is nowe a blog that ys dedicated to bringing yow the hottest and moost up to date content about the worldes of entertaynment, political societee, hangings, filmes, culture, quarterings, and defense of the noble realme of Engelonde. Prepare to be virtuallye beaten ovir the head and neck by the sheere force of the hot and up to date content ye shall see on this blog. Ther shal be verye funnye thinges. The thinges ye shall see shal be so funnye they shall maken yow to "laughen out loude" (LOL). They may even maken yow to ROFLAYYHBB ("Rolle on the floor laughing as yf ye haue been beheaded"). Ther shal also be much newes of Engelonde and ower gret effortes to kepe yt safe from the foul Frensshe folk, who seeke even now to destroye ower language and ower large estates. Nevir bifor did loue of the realm of Engelonde and hot and up to date content come togedir in a productif and profitable webbe-twopoint-o fusion-synthesis as they do nowe in GEOFFREY CHAUCER HATH AN EXTREME BLOG: GO ENGLAND! IT YS RAD!.

We requeste that all ye folk who reden of this blogg do signe the loialtiee oath in the commentz to assuren us that ye aren nat Frensshe spyes or folk who wolde overturn the gret proceedings of the moost recent Parliament. Yf ye signe nat the loailte oath we shall come to yower hous wyth our retinues of armid men and we shal show yow the latest hot and up to date content in opinioun-chaunging. (see end of poost for oath)

Go England! Trust us!

—Tom, Dick, Tom, Harry, Tom

And nowe a woord from yower newe editor, Thomas Favent.

The Editor Answereth Yower Queries

How hangeth it, ladyes and lordes? This is nat Geoffrey Chaucer. Geoffrey Chaucer ys chubtastick and hath a smal woolen hat the which was cool back when round tables seemid lyk a fresshe idea. Chaucer, my darlinges, hath left the building. Ich am Thomas Favent and let me telle yow Ich am a lot thinner and a whole lot moore fun to make out wyth at large outdoor summer-tyme festivals. Ich am so totallie ypsyched to be runninge this syte and providinge yow wyth the hottest and moost up to date content concerninge the mattirs aforemencioned by the lords appellant in their grace and wisdam.

Nowe, Ich imagine ye are going "what the swyve?" (WTS?) right nowe, by cause that thinges aren a littel different around heere than what ye haue seen bifor. Wel, Ich am heere to telle yow that CHAUNGE IS A GOOD THYNG. Sum peple think of chaunge as the werkinge of a capricious fortune upon the blisful stabilitie of lyf, but Ich prefer to think of chaunge as the force that kicketh boring people off of the island. All webbes must be blown by the winde so that the spider maye re-cast them, and thus yt is wyth thys websyte, blown by the wind of clene and pure chaunge into the newe and awesome shape yt taketh bifor yower eyes.

So that Ich maye yive sum response to yower questions about the gret chaunges of this blog, Ich haue arrangid a liste of questions that haue come thurgh email, the which Ich shall answir in order. Suspend yower wondir, rederes, and all factes concerninge this blog and the recent lakke of postinges shal bicom clere thurgh my crystalline prose.

The Facoundely Answered Queries (FAQ) Concerninge Thys Blog

1. *Where the hell is Geoffrey Chaucer?*
Geoffrey Chaucer hath been verye busy ovir the past monethes assistinge King Richard wyth King Richard's rehabilitacioun. King Richard hath been in a bit of a funke (see belowe). Currentlie, Geoffrey Chaucer ys with King Richard in Las Vegas. The two of them left in June, after a period of gret distraccion. The paparazzi do saye that bifor he left, Kyng Richard waxid poetic about a maner of quest involving drivinge to Las Vegas and drinking much wyne and the inhaling of gret quantitees of aromatic balm. Chaucer semed uncomfortable.

2. *Why is almost everyone involved with this new blog named Thomas?*
Go to Canterburye, chekke the name on the shryne, and light yowerself a clue candle, doctor of theologie.

3. *What has been happening in the last couple months? It's something to do with parliament, right?*
Ye are correct. Yn Februarie, the Lords Appellant (listed above in their grace and wisdam) did bring the concernes of alle the peple of the realme to parliament. They did saye that the counsellors and men who surroundid

King Richard were corrupt and rotten and thes evil counsellors did hate the realme of Engelonde. Thes evil counsellors (the "Brat Packe") did kepe King Richard from thinkinge of the safetie of the realm, so much so that he thoughte to make peace wyth the foul Frenssh. He also spent a lot of moneye on thinges lyk giant water parkes wyth ancient mythologicale themes (q. v. "Styx Flags") and did depryve the gret nobles of the realme of their landes. But the realme neded nat to suffir until it dwindled and bicam prey to the foule Frensshe. Nay! Sum of the gretest nobles of the realme did heare the people complaining of the woes of the realme, and thei rose up to challenge the vicious scum who did surround our King Richard. Thes gret nobles and saviors of the polity do call themselves the Lords Appellant (because thei are so appeallinge). The Lords Appellant usid the rightful and proper force of parliament to put the fals counsellors of King Richard on tryall for tresoun and to bring gret peace and order to the realm by deelinge wyth them.

Best. Parliament. Evir!

Consideringe all the deelinge that had to be done, the parliament did laste for many monethes, and Geoffrey was kept bisy making thinges for the kinge (includinge a fortified bunker the which was nat fortified quite ynough). This parliament went off and on until June 3rd, upon which daye Geoffrey and Richard drove off and haue nat been yherd from since.

4. Who were these counsellors?

The foulest of the dangeres to the realm were Nicholas Brember Mayor of London, Alexander Neville fals Bisshop of York, Robert de Vere supposid Duk of Ireland (and kynd of too close wyth the kyng), Michael de la Pole supposid Earl of Suffolk, and Robert Tresilian once Chief Justice. Yet their were many othir folk, swich as the knights Berners, Burley, Salisbury and Beauchamp and also the small folk Thomas Usk and John Blake. The lords appellant in their grace and wisdam exiled or executid moost of them.

5. Executed?

Ye kan nat make an omelet wythout hanging and drawing and quartering a few egges.

But wait, I heard a rumor that Thomas Usk didn't actually die, but instead was saved at the last minute by Dr. Hwaet and his beloved companion Wat Tyler. They replaced Usk with a robot that looked like a person but could really only walk and recite basic liturgical formulae.

When the lordes appellant fynde the source of the crakke ye are smokinge, in their grace and wisdam thei shall destroye it to make safe the healthe of the nacioun and to quell swich fables and ficcions. Dr. Hwaet is a ficcion. Even yf he did exist, the idea of a totallye ancient alien with an accent from Norwich ys ridiculous.

6. *Lots of planets have a Norwich.*

BE SILENT or the lords appellant yn their grace and wisdam shall knokke yow the helle about the head. Next question, peple.

7. *Hey, also: Why was a blonde new wave woman singing in the palace when Richard said goodbye to De Vere?*

Ynogh of the rumores. Wheniver ther ys political activitee the chronicleres just start blabbing about eny thing. Wheels of fyre. Talkinge wax hedes. The Thames dryinge up. Alienes from Norwich wyth burial mounds bigger on the insyde than on the outsyde. Pop icons singinge "Everichtyme We Saye Farewell." Seriouslie people, hyre a serjeant at law and get yowerselves a clue in fee simple! Thes chronicleres are all basicallie writinge Gerald of Wales fan ficcion inspyred by badly-kept monastic cheese. No more queries about unusual events surroundinge the parliament.

8. *Okay, fine. So the parliament happened and Chaucer went away to Vegas after a hard time. Why are you running his blog?*

The lords appellant in their grace and wisdam are verye interested in media saturacioun. Thei aren aware that at oon tyme many folk did rede of this blog and fynde joye in it, so nowe thei seek to exployt that fact, fynde thos peple, and provyde them wyth hot and up to date content and also newes of the defense of the realme of Engelonde ayeinst the foule evil of the Frensshe.

9. *But it's not your/their blog?*

According to propertie lawes written in the tyme of the kinges great grandfather and far too complex for ye to undirstonden, the blog did revert to the kynge when Geoffrey Chaucer entered a gazebo in May wythout a hat, and then thurgh a certayne arrangement of inheritance decreed by an ad hoc committee of judges the rights *de escriture* for the blog did fall to the second cousin of the Duke of Gloucester, the which cousin upon halberd-poynte did gladlie relinquish hys ownership of the blog and thus the blog fell ynto the hands of the Lords Appellant, who haue arrangid it all nyce and hyred a teame of writeres and we haue a studio wyth bean bag chayres and chartes concerninge which animal image will make folk buye which Latin pop album. And so it is as clere as ys the sumer sun: the blog ys oures.

10. *How did you get his password?*

Yt was taped undir Geoffrey's desk.

11. *You searched his house? Wait. Did you people do anything to his family?*

Ther ys no need to worrye, thei are all fyne. Bifor Geoffrey and King Richard left for Las Vegas, King Richard did leave gret summes for to keep the meynee at Geoffreyes hous. Litel Lowys ys doing a summer internship and preparing for universitee in the fall. Philippa ys fixinge up the garden hous and doing pilates. And Thomas as always ys wyth John of Gaunt, Kinge of Spayne, handling thinges on the continent.

12. *What do you think about the fact that the first-ever international conference on John Gower just took place?*
We heere at GEOFFREY CHAUCER HATH AN EXTREME BLOG: GO ENGLAND! IT YS RAD! do support and love that Gower conference wyth all our hertes. John Gower hath alweys been a fervent supporter of whoevir is in power. We do nat undirstond why Chaucer hath swich a bugge yn his butte. Peraventure yf Geoffrey sholde evir come back from Las Vegas we maye let hym poost hys owene reacciouns to the conference. But that day may nevir come.

Okaye, that ys ynogh questions for todaye. Look forward to exciting newe pro-England content in the dayes to come on GEOFFREY CHAUCER HATH AN EXTREME BLOG: GO ENGLAND! IT YS RAD!

The Extremely Awesome Loialtee Oath

Please put yower name yn the followinge loyaltee oath and poost it as a comment or else we will disinherit yower male heirs in perpetuity. All commentes shal be screened to prevent treason and Frensshe spyes.

Ich____do affirm the actes and decrees of the parliament of this yeere and do agree that it was right to reform the ill governement of ower King Richard in order to bring peace and justise to the realm and nevir shall Ich speke against the Lords Appellant at eny tyme yn the future. Ich do abhor and reject the ridiculous rumor that Thomas Usk was saved by Dr. Hwaet bifor beinge executed. Ich do sweare to return to thys blog and enjoy its hot and up to date content. And Ich do sweare, no mattir what lord Ich folowe or in what lande Ich dwell, nevir to betray the realme of Engelonde to the foul Frensshe. Signed this____daye of ____; also, yt ys my trewe opinion that the hottest and moost up to date content these days includes the topics____,____,and____, all of the which Ich wolde rede wyth gret gladnesse and joye and loialtee to Engelonde.

August 5, 2008

Televisioun Wythout Mercy
by Thomas Favent

• *Spayre the hanginge, spoyle the incipient discourse of nationalisme*
What coud be hotter than televisioun? Market surveyes shewe that many folk watchen of yt. Thus, we must bend it to ower will or breke it all to pieces.

Last week the Lords Appellant in their grace and wisdam did taken control of the programminge of televisoun netwerkes in order to preserue the values of Engelonde. All of yower fauorite shewes got a make-ovir. Peraventure ye haue been over-bisy wyth toyle during the week (hanging flagges, translating Anglo-Norman romances into Englisshe, spitting south-wardes) and haue nat been able to catch up on developmentes on all yower fauoryte showes of televisioun. Worry nat! Television Without Mercy provideth thes wittie and concise recaps for yower informacioun. Go Engelonde! Here ys what ye maye haue missed:

GOSSIP GIRL: Spotted: at the Tower of London ys Gossip Girl herself, who hath been ycaught by the diligence of Henry Bolingbroke. She ys taken to Tyburn and hanged. Ye who heare the recap of thys episode, think on what a thyng it is to be a gossip and a teller of tales. Beholdeth the rewardes of telling the pryvytees of othirs upon a blogge! Be ware, lest in yower owene blogges ye bicom jangleres and telleres of tales! Thinketh on yt and in yower myndes rekeneth how deedes haue their endes. Thus endeth the episode.

FLIGHT OF THE LOMBARDS: Thys episode openeth with the Lombard traderes Brentano and Germano yn the stokkes, for Henry Bolingbroke hath discoverid their plan to import fals currencie ycleped lusshebournes ynto Engelonde and eek corner the market on silk and sweet wynes. Brentano and Germano suffer long yn the stokkes and beg for mercy yet thei receyve yt nat. Thei beginnen to singe a roundel but Bolingbrokes men stuff their mouthes wyth cloutes and ragges. Ye who heare the recap of thys epsiode, think on what a thing it is to be a fals marchant and a foule usurer and eek a writer of humorous folk tunes. Beholdeth the rewardes of destabilising Englandes currencie! Be ware, lest in yower owene dealinges ye bicom fals traderes and usurers! Thinketh on yt and in yower myndes rekeneth how deedes haue their endes. Thus endeth the episode.

DEVELOPEMENT ARRESTID: All the membirs of the de Blouth familie were yhangid for tresoun in the yeeres of Kyng Edward and thus ther beth no resoun to recap this shewe.

SCRYBES: In thys episode Adam Pinkhurste writeth every manuscript in Engelonde evir, just lyk in every othir episode.

WEEDES: Thys episode openeth wyth Nancie yn the court of Thomas Arundel, Archbishop of York, who sitteth in gret judgement along wyth Henry Bolingbroke, who hath captured Nancy. Thes two gret lordes, oon of the church and oon of the lande, ask Nancy why she doth spreade the heretical writinges of the lollardes and thus doth sowe weedes in our cleane corn. For the teachinges of heretics are lyk weedes, the which strangle the good croppes. Ye who heare the recap of thys episode, thynk of how gret a sin it ys to befoule the feeldes of feyth and loialtee wyth the weedes of heresie and conspiracie! Thynk howe thes weedes of sin do dull the mynde and ynspyre the eatinge of the fatteninge twinkies of rebellion and the fingre-stayninge cheetoes of misfortune! Thus endeth the episode.

SO YE THINKE YE KAN DAUNCEN?: Thys episode openeth wyth all of the contestants in front of special guest judge Henry Bolingbroke. Oon by oon, he asketh each if he or she kan daunce. Yf he or she kan nat, ther ys a hanging. Ye who heare the recap of thys epsiode, think on whether ye kan dauncen, and what ye wolde saye yn front of nat only an earthli judge, but eek the high Judge himself upon hys throne at the final daunce. KAN YE DAUNCE? KAN YE? ANSWIR WEL OR THOU SHALT DAUNCE IN FLAYMES. Thus endeth the episode.

Next week on televisoun: XXIV houres a daye of footage of the battel of Cressy. Go Engelonde!

August 26, 2008

Hot Newes on Blazing Fellow
by Thomas Favent

Watbethup, homeskilletes? Yt is I, Thomas Favent, the lovelokest bloke on the blokke, bringinge yow hot and up to date content that shal provyde extra value in yower fast-paced web II.0 lyves. I am certayn that many of the rederes of this hippe (and loial) blog are the kynde of folk who wolde come from every shires ende unto the festival of Blazinge Fellow. Talk about hot; this oon ys a scorcher.

Blazinge Fellowe doth take place in the moneth of August, begynning on the feest of the moost Blessid Bartholomewe the Apostel and rokking on for several dayes until its awesome and radical conclusion: the applicacioun of flaymes to the Fellow. At first celebrated by a gatheringe of hip and hard-lyne bishops led by Henri "Defensor" Despenser of Norwich, Blazinge Fellowe hath nowe grown into a gret gatheringe that attracteth Ms and Ms of participants. Heere ys a quick and dirtie faq (facoundeley answered queries) on Blazinge Fellowe.

• *What is Blazing Fellowe?*
In the dayes of the celebracioun of Blazinge Fellow, many peple come togedir to express their joye and devocioun to the institutional Church

and the law-makinge State in fantastic maner. Thei weare costumes from beyond yower imaginacioun. Forget friares in brown robes or blakke robes; haue ye gentils evir seen ORANGE ROBES? PAISLEYE? Yower mynde will be blown. And the throngs! Sondry folk, clerkes, bishopes, fanatic laypeple, summoners, deacons, cellarers, abbots, venture capitalists, and novyces all gather in a gret hoost to make art and to set fyre to the Fellow. Thes "Blazeres" consume gret quantitees of wyne both white and red and do sniff of balm and yet staye within the boundes of temperance, for it ys all done wyth the approval of the Archbishop.

• *Where is Blazinge Fellow held?*
Blazinge Fellow is held in Smithfield or, as yclept by Blazeres, "The Feeld." The wethir on The Feeld oft presenteth gret discomfort and inconvenience to Blazeres, as yt can be slightli humid and also rayne and eek hayle are nat unheard of. When stayinge in the feeld, yt is best to bring an umbrella and a smal tent, thogh many folke develop elaborate paviliouns the which do surpass the beautee of the pavilions of Sarrasens and even Fayerye ytself, and yet they staye within the boundes of humi-litee, for it ys all done wyth the approval of the Archbishop.

• *What kinds of Public Art are There?*
Draconian enforsment of orthodoxie is nothing without sum interestinge public art. Blazeres organise yeerly into "theme cloisters" to yive beautee unto The Feeld and to distribute beverages and balm. Each theme cloister is devoted to a different aspect of ower deep and orthodox devocioun to the Institutional Church. Sum theme cloisters celebrate the virtues: Chastitee Cloister yiveth awaye beltes and saltpetre, Prudence Cloister enacteth the tale of Melibee and hys neighbores ("hey kids, get off my lawn or Ich shall slaye yow"), *et cetera*. Othir cloisters are full of gret won-deres and mystiques. Ich once stayid in a stylite cloister. It was tops.

Ther ys also a cloister of miraculous women from Flanders who kan survyve in ovens. This yeer Ich heare thei shall be bringinge microwaues. Astonishing! And yet yif ye asken me, sum of the art ys a litel wack. Ther aren large sculptures the which look lyke giant hollow stone chicken men on legges made out of trumpetes and filled wyth smal birdes playing the harpe. What maner of bosh ys that?

• *Do people get naked?*
Ywis, sum tyme ther ys nakedness and bodye-payntynge, and yet it ledeth nat to the synne of lecherie for the bodye payntynge is moostly pictorial narratifs of the punishementes of purgatorie (and yit sum still falle into errour and sinnes of the flesshe, the which is lamentable but pardonable).

- *Where can I buy a Pardon?*

Pardones are soold at several posiciouns around the feeld. Yf ye aren anticipatinge a particularlie elaborate synne, ye must consult the central pardon offyce at the hospital of Rouncesvalles biforehand.

- *Where can I find a Physician?*

Synce all of the uryne of Blazeres ys a uniform color (cleere), physiciens may nat make diagnoses and thus often humoral imbalance gooth undetected at Blazinge Fellowe. Be sure to consult early on wyth yower owen physicien or at leest a learned local vicar yif ye haue a tendencie towardes humoral imbalance and are planninge to attende Blazinge Fellowe.

- *When is the Fellow Emblazed?*

The Fellow ys emblazed on the final night of the celebracioun, aftir a lengthi heresie trial. The stake ys set up in the middle of the feeld, neere the usual spot for execucions. Yf the Fellow recantes of hys heresie, sum tyme he ys yiven a repreve and ther is no emblazinge. Yet feere nat, for yf the Fellowe recantes, a prisoner from Newe-gate ys emblazed in his sted. And yet thei nevir blaze as brighli as do the heretickes, the which aren full of the sparkes of sin and rebellioun.

- *What is the meaning of the Fellow?*

The fellow to us doth represent on the allegorical level all of the dirt and faultes that we wolde wasshen from owerselves. The emblazinge of the fellowe ys a commitment to directinge owerselves wyth more passioun and more institutional support to being the best folk we can be. Yt is an act for stablisshinge pure feyth in good government, good religioun, and good use of ower leisure tyme.

On the literal level the fellow doth represent a man who hath been found a heretick and is being burned and shoutynge wyth a loud voys. Sum tyme neere the end ther ys simpli quiet weepinge or angrie recriminaciouns or silent attemptes to withstanden the payne. Haue ye nat seyn sometyme a pale face? Nat until ye see the Fellow at hys last! And yet it doth staye within the boundes of charitee, for yt is all done wyth the approval of the Archbishop.

- *Unto what may be the Emblazing of the Fellow compared?*

Ye must experience yt to yive credence that swich a thing maye exist. Imagine the best hanginge ye haue evir seen. Nowe, get out yower awesome deeth abacus and multiplye the entertaynment value of that hanginge by the power of X. That is just how good a real emblazinge kan be. Certes, sum folk call it cruel and saye that swich thinges sholde nevir happen in Engelonde. Ich saye to them: crye me a river, moonbattes, next yeere ye shall all be Fellowes!

Flaymes, creativitee, massyve amountes of cash, moore balm than a Lombard could sniff, and the eradicacioun of an heretic: that ys felaweshep Ich kan get behinde. See yow at Blazing Fellow, freendes!

—Th. F

(Thys content is approved by the Lords Appellant. In facte, Bolingbroke lykes this so much he ys makinge notes for a future statute. *Impriblogtur*).

September 12, 2008

If It Ain't Bolin'broke

A most noble and wikked auuesome column by Henry "S-Collar" Bolingbroke

WASSSSSSSSSSUP Churlez? Hypermasculinized loue to ech and everie oon of yow! 'Tis I, Henri Bolingbroke, coming right at yow lyk an arrowe to an Anglo-Saxones eye. This is my column of awesome content on this blog.

You see, the othir Lords Appellant want to make sure that we connect with yow, the peple. Thinges haue been getting a litel shakie. Sure, everichone did loue us when we seyde that we wolde correct the realme, but now the fikkle and untrewe peple do complayne that we misappropriate revenues and care moore for ower vainglorie than for Engelonde. Which is lyk a total load of cow-wasshe, for all of ower expenses aren necessarie. The obstacle course in my bakke-yard is crucial for militarie planninge. Thos Frensshe citie walles are nat going to scale themselues. The fact that yt also maketh an awesome paint-balle course is biyond the poynt. But lo swich moanes and lamentynge ye the peple do make. It peyneth me soore, I kan tell you. Heavy is the head that weareth the awesome.

So Tommy "The Swan" and Dick "Mauvais Cheval" askid me to wryte a blogge to connect wyth yow, the peple, and especiallie the younger voteres who reden of thes blogges and do worshippe at the parrisshe of St. Boyngboyng. And eek the othir lordes thoughte that my experience crusadinge ayeinst the paganes in Prusse wolde make me appealinge. I am a CRUSADE HERO, people. CRUSADE HERO. That just soundeth so good whan my scrybe types it out.

So as ye kan see, this is just a litel space for me to kynd of unwind about the day. And I unwind lyk a snake, baby, full of venom and anecdotes. Whan I askid Thomas Favent yf I could have a column on the blog he made a trewely good argument about focus and needing the proper talent and nat being sure if I had the experience to get the pacing right, and thanne I made a trewely good argument about my ceasinge from hitting hym on the head wyth a mace.

Peple, man. Everyichon hath an opinoun, ye know? I am going to yive yow sum of myne heere, and if ye agree nat, wel, peraventure I will imprisoun yow for months. HA. JUST JESTINGE. (OR MAYBE NAT?)

I saw *Roland, Ganelon, Saragossa* last week-end. I haue nat liked the othir filmes by Woodye Alanus but this oon was prettie good. I wisshe ther had been moore three-way battle scenes. I am eek prettie y-psychede about *Tantum of Solaas* even thogh it soundeth lyk the name of a papal bull.

Oh, and about the "S-Collar" thing, myn nick-name? The world hath been askinge. Yt standeth nat nat for "scoler." I did nat do verye well in school. In fact, had nat Dame Plagiarism been at hand, Sir Graduacioun nevir wolde haue arryved, for the Sistren de Keg were alwey in my chambre. But swich is the lyf. Ye need nat to knowe of lettrure and clerklie thinges whan ye be a CRUSADE HERO.

No, I am ylcept "S-Collar" by cause of my awesome neckwear, the which is all made out of pure white gold figures of the lettre S linkid togedir. Many folk asken: what doth the "s" stand for? It standeth for: stronge sexie superior seigneur standinge ovir yower sorrie ass as ye sobbe for yower lyf.

I haue been keepinge up my trayninge for the Supreme Joustinge Championship. I am werkinge out III or IV houres a daye and hitting the listes as much as I kan. I am born to kick asse and take names, except I am a slow writer and thus the number of asses kikked doth exceed names taken. Swich is the life. CRUSADE HERO, cherles.

This fat weeird guy keepeth hanging out with little Hal. I am a litel worried about this but my wife Mary sayd whatevir. 'Tis nat lyk the kid will ever be kyng any day (unless I depose Richard). HA. JUST JESTINGE. TO SAY AS MUCH WOLDE BE TREASOUN! (OR MAYBE NAT?)

My wyf just got her forehead done. That thing is so effing big now. It is lyk almost a spanne brood. HOTT! Whan I marryed her she was named Mary de Bohun and if ye know what I mean I haue been thinking about doinge a litel Bohuninge tonight. SMACK! CRUSADE HERO!

Ye knowe, I had VI minstrels when I fought the pagans at the Siege of Vilnius and thei still koud nat keep up wyth a real-tyme song about how much ass I was kikkinge. I bring the legendarye mode. I am the legendarye mode.

Let us see. What else? O, stop yower bullmerde about Chaucer and Kyng Richard. Kyng Richard will retourne whan it is good for the realm. I and the othir lords appellant are loial to the Crown of Engelonde and the Kyng who beareth yt. I haue no intencioun to evir taak the crown from Richard. I haue too much CRUSADING to do first. That stuff is moore awesome than watching "visages of death" while simultaneously receivinge a high-fyve at a combinacioun Farthingbakke & III Portales Doun showe. SMACK! BAM!

Okay, this hath made me thynk about Engelonde and kikking asse. I am getting some squirez and goynge to the bakke-yard to play peynt-balle. I will have Thomas put this onlyne.

I hope yow enjoy this. Or else ye shal perssihe (J/K LOL ROFL)

—Henry "S-Collar" Bolingbroke

★ ★ ★

THE BOOK OF THE FEERE AND SENTENCE OF THE WAYE TOWARD LAS VEGAS IN AMERIQUE
Geoffrey "LeVostreGC" Chaucer

June 2008–May 2009

Peraventure some of yow haue wondered what did happen when My Lord Kyng Richard and Ich did escape from Engelonde, driven far off by the Appellants, and did fynde ower way to the citee of Las Vegas. Thogh awey from my blog, Ich made sum thing of a smal diary of the trip yn a litel "Good Daye, Kitten" notebook, for methoughte that some oon koud of ower queste make a road movye or buddy filme yn tymes to come.

Heere beginneth the Booke of the Feere and Sentence.

I

My Lord Kyng Richard and Ich were in a shippe somewhere up the river from Bristol on the margine of the Great Occian Sea when the balm began to taken hoold. Me remembreth that I seyde sum maner of speche as "Ich feele daswed, peraventure we sholde telle the mariners oure des-tinacioun..." And anon ther was a gret noyse upon us and a great din, and the hevenes were fulle of what semed large egles, flying and plunging and shrillinge around the mastes and sailes of ower ship, the which was proceedinge wyth gret speed yn to the Occian.

Kyng Richard was relaxinge yn his travel-throne upon the decke, having applyed Rhenish wyne to his foreheed bettir to catche the bracinge breeze of the see. He askede: "What aileth thee, Geoffrey?" Yet Ich kepte mum. Mesemede bettir to seye no thyng of the egles. My Kyng wolde see them soon ynough, for he had deeper sniffed of the balm than Ich. So Ich muttered sum thyng about the gret puissance and wisdam of my Lord the Kyng and he did nod and smyle and sniff of moore balm.

Yt was yet ere pryme, and we hadde a greet and long crossinge wyth many leagues of travel bifor us. Oonly a fewe Norsemen, we knewe, had crossed the Occian See, and thei are crazy folk who basicallye shut down Europe for lyk two centuryes. Normal folk wolde long remember a daye when ye lose yower eye in single combat wyth yower uncle bycause he made yow drinke from a cup made out of yower brotheres skull; Norsemen just call it Tuesday. And yet tough as Norsemen we shal be, for my Lord the Kyng hath yt in his mynde to seen the gret citee of Las Vegas, the which Marco Polo and John Mandeville have descrived in their writinges, and the which lieth yn the foreyn contree of Amerique.

Thynges in Engelonde are on the edgie syde. The Lords Appellant, mainlye Kyng Richardes Uncles and Cousin, have seisid power for themselves. Sufficeth nat tyme and space heere to lament the deethes and persecutions thei haue poured doun upon the Kynges loyal subjectes. Ywis, the "Brat Pack" ys no moore: Michael de la Pole hath fled yn to exile, of his honoures ystripped, and Robert de Vere also (for whom Reims Launcerona soore sigheth). The Bishop Alexander Neville did lose hys honours also, and Justice Tresilian and Nichol Brembre were put to deeth. Yt ys as good a tyme as eny for a trip.

My lord the Kyng hath taken at his wille the good barge *Maudelayne*, the which ys commaundid by a Shipman, a good felawe who hath been y-tanned to a crisp by the sonne. My Lord the Kyng hath broghte CCC poundes of silver in coynes, and eek muchel silver plate, and hath filled the hoolde of the shippe with spycez and fyne deyntees and manye intoxicatinge substaunces, so that the shippe ytself doth seem a clerkes ensaumple ayeinst gluttonie: we have II monethes supplye of birddes to ete, larkes lapped in sugar, stewes of rabbit and swete custadis, and eek XX gret tunnes of wyne whit and red, and gret spycez of Inde for to make a man keep wacche al nyght, or feel joye, or be pusshid adoun by sadnesse. We have also a hogshead of Tequila, a hogshead of Rum, several barrels of beere from Flaundres, and XII gret vessels of crystal ful of balm. Thys had al been assemblid the night bifor by the purveyors of the Kyng, who dide knokke on the doores of merchauntz of Londoun and take the goodes for my Lordes use. Peraventure we have moore than necessitee doth demaunde, but when Kyng Richard doth devyse the provisiouns for a journey, he tendeth to pusshe yt as harde as he kan.

Yt ys the balm that doth worrye me. The gret balm of the Oryent hath many straunge effectes, and ther ys no soule moore reccheles and redeless than a kyng in the verye middle of a balm-sniffinge bynge. Ywis, Aethelred had loved the stuff. My Lord Kyng Richard had insisted that Ich sniffe of yt but an hour bifor, and Ich did succumb to *primus inter pares* pressure and thus took the weird oyntement up to myn nostrils. And then, as Ich stood upon the bordes of the shippe, and as the coost of Engelonde did vanisshe ynto the greye fog of the see, Ich gan to see gret egles and smal horned demons and al maner thyng, so that methought, "Ich bet this is what it is like to be William Langland on an average daye."

But Richard semed nat to suffir the visiouns of the balme. It did but set hys herte at ease, and also make hym have gret joye to touchen soft materials. He sat on hys throne, ypsrinkled wyth wyne, and sang a ditee concerninge the importuance of nat givinge up belief, the whyle he fumblid wyth a bit of velvet.

So Ich merely pulled my litel woolen hatte around my heede, and drewe the wynde of the sea thurgh my nostrils, and listened to the mariners as thei moved the ropes. Ywis, once Ich had lyved on the shippe of the Drede Pyrate Robertson, and so Ich get nat sea-sikke. Ich tryede nat to freke out.

For this is serious bisynesse, good rederes. A kyng on the run wyth his trustie Clerk of Werkes. A hoolde full of fyne spycez and dangerous balm. An Engelonde full of testy nobles wyth execucioners at the redy. The gret Occian Sea, which knoweth neyther map nor lodestone, and under which lurketh the Leviathan. And dayes and dayes of sailinge ahead of us. By Seynt Brendans boat! Ich shal be of good chiere. Be this the longest, straungest journey that man shal evir know, yet may the devil take me if Ich do nat stay stedfast by myne owene trewe Kyng.

II

Curse that Shipman! Aftir a night of drinkinge deep wyth the mariners, My Lord the Kyng and Ich did retyre to oure cabins to slepe.

And in the morning we were aloon upon a smal lyf rafte. The greye waves of the Occian did fiersely shake the boat, and the wyndes blew withouten mercy.

"Geoffrey," seyde My Lord the Kyng, "What meneth this?"

"Peraventure, My Trespuissant Lord Rightwys Kyng of Engelonde, did this Shipman hayle from Dertemouth?"

He did. A curs upon the haste of ower leavinge and the foryetfulnesse of my brayne. Ich had herde of this Shipman, a man al oute of Cristen charitee who did drawe wyn from the barrels of merchauntz whan thei slept upon hys ship. Apparentlye, the greet richesse of My Lord the Kyng had proved too temptinge a catch, and he had taken the goodes and left us on a smal lyf-rafte.

"By Good Seynte Edward! We shal dye heere!" Richard began to cryen and shoute to the sea, but oonly the gulles herde. Ywis, yt was a depressinge scene that made me undirstond exactly why the Anglo-Saxons were so bummed out about seafaringe.

"Yet peraventure we shal live," quod Ich, "For trewely, thogh we be on a ship al stereless, withouten map or oar or even an astrolabe, yet God in his gret goodenesse mayhap shal keepe us from drenchynge yn the see. For sikerly he kept safe Jonas in the mawe of the gret fisshe, and eek the Hebraik peple he kept safe whan they passid thurgh the sea. Have ye nat rede of my tale of Custaunce and the rudderless boat?"

"Thy tale of Custaunce sucketh Geoffrey. Yt is my leeste favourite of al of the tales that thou hast shown me yn draft. Thou hast managid to tak the most boring partes of hagiographie and romaunce and blend them togedir. Ich bet that yower tale of Custaunce and an undergraduate syllabus shal but rarelye come togedir."

Ich was a litel let doun, and pulled myn woolen hatte about me. But herkneth! Then Ich did see that ther was a bundel of thinges, y-covered by a blanket, yn the corner of the raft. My Lord the Kyng and Ich did unwynde the bundel to see that ther was sum breed and cheese and bottlid watir, and eek the XII gret vessels ful of balme. Even the crazie piratical Shipman knewe that balm was dirty and dangerous stuff.

"Food!" Ich seyde, "Thonked be God that is eterne on lyve!"

"Swyve the food," Kyng Richard seyde, "Thonkede be God for this good balm. Knowstow how much thys stuff ys worth?"

My Lord the Kyng was ful wel plesed to have the balm. Meseemed that even if he were to die upon the sea, he wolde be ful of bliss thus havinge good balm to sniffe.

Yet no balm for me. Yisterdayes visouns had been rathir freakye. Methoght that the see ytself was full of horrour ynogh as it was, and Ich neded no three-headed eagles or litel demon squirrels crawling up my legges to make this situacioun yet more scarie. So Ich stayed away from the balme, even whan Kyng Richard tryed to force it upon me.

O my Kyng! O wanhope and despeir, for the derknesse of the sea and the coldnesse of the wyndes, and the wylde waves that tossed our tiny ship! Why did I thus follow swich a sovereign, swich a Kyng ful of wilfulnesse, who was swich a bad judge of advisors and had swich a weaknesse for balm? Yt is the verye gift of the Goddess Natura to me, that the only folk whom I follow are the ones who are woode, the ones who are woode to lyven, woode to speken, woode to fynde salvacioun, desirynge of al thinges at the same tyme, the ones who nevir seye their *paternoster* or abyde by eny wel-known and prudent sentence from the *Distichs* of Catoun, but rathir burne, burne, burne, as do the merveilous explosif boxes of China, shootinge fyre lyk dragons across the sterres and in the middle ye kan see the litel flayme of a blewe light and al the folk watchinge say "Huzzah."

The dayes do blend togedir lyk different versiouns of *Piers Plowman*. On sum dayes, my Lord the Kyng commandeth the waves to bryng us to Amerique wyth the swiftnesse of falcons. On othir dayes, he sitteth yn derke depressioun and calleth out to hys missinge freendes. On othir dayes, yt pleseth hym to commaunde me to pleye endless games of tictactoe. And this nighte, as the waves of a storme toss us, he standeth upon the syde of the raft wyth greet majestee and cryeth: "Behold, lyk Aeneas we travel the waves to brynge our rule to alien landes, lyk Brutus who fared so wel over the Frensshe flod."

III

Derknesse covered myn eyen whan I oped them, and ther was a gret russhinge noyse, and sum thyng semed different upon the litel raft. So feble were my spiritz and so weak my limbes that Ich koud scarcely move to look about, but then lyk a thondir-dint Ich realized what was uppe. The raft was nat moving. The raft was on land.

For many dayes we had drifted, ful of dreemes and shoutinges, and mesemed we had lyved then in the contree of Morpheus, the god of sleep, neyther alyve ne dead. But nowe hopefulnesse dyd move me, and Ich stumblid onto a bank coverid wyth blakke rokkes.

"Geoffrey," quod Kyng Richard as he opened hys eyes, "Have we come to Amerique?"

"Certes, My Kyng, we have crossed the sea."

My lord the Kyng took the last of the balm and then we went on ower waye. The air was moyst and hot and smelled of manye folk crowded togedir. We cam to a grete high-way full of light, upon which manye cars did russhe and beepen their hornes. And so we crossid yt and came to a place of derke streetes and many large buildinges the which semed to be fortresses.

"God and Seynt Edmund be praisid," seyde My Lord the Kyng, "We have crossid the sea and come to the holy citee of Las Vegas. The book of John Mandeveille seyth that the citadel of the citee of Vegas is ful of straunge and magic light, the werke of tregetoures and necromancers. Let us searchen for the light."

Thanne bigan we to walk, and we saw ahead of us the gret light of many tall toweres ycovered wyth burning lights in all the coloures of Iris the goddes of the rainbowe. And ther was the pypyng of musique and the beeping of cars and eek a greate smelle of pizza.

"*Vivat* Las Vegas!" cryed Kyng Richard, as he steppid yn to the greate yerd ful of light.

And yet Las Vegas (for we knewe no bettir) was in muchel disarray. Al maner of folk did russhen and pusshen at us. And thei did crye wyth loud voyces. And sum did hoolde signes and shoute thynges. And a man tryed to get us to paye hym to pose in a photographe wyth a boa constrictor. And an othir was playinge the lute while nakid. The clamour and the noyse were lyk the roaring of manye animals.

"Alas," seyde Kyng Richard to me, "Beth ther a realme in thys world that shal nat falle? For the citee of Vegas hath been overtaken by riot-ers. Thys is werse than the yeere 1381, whan all those stinkie churles did marche upon Londoun. Yet ther are moore folk heere thanne evir did ryse duringe that terribil tyme, and thes folk seem ful of moore wrath. And eek thei are dressid moore poorly, thogh ower royal self wolde scarce have thoghte that possibil. Yet feere nat, Geoffrey, we are Kyng of England, and a Kyng is a Kyng no mattir wher he standeth, and the anonyntng of God yiveth us great might and puissance to dryve off thes churles and protect the good citee of Las Vegas."

He took a sniff of balm and clambered onto a fence wyth sum awkwardnesse.

"Herkneth, ye churles! Ich knowe yt is nat easy to accept that feudalism doth nat really exist at the same tyme that ye are makinge a transicioun ynto a capitalism that technicallye doth nat really apply to yower situacioun eyther. But behead nat the chancellor of this gret realme, and destroy nat whatevir ys the equivalent of the Savoy palace in this citee."

A crowd of churles did gather. Thogh they hearde My Lord the Kynges wordes, mesemed thei respected hym nat, for thei took sum picturez and also made litel japes.

"Ye shal have no captain but me," quod the Kyng, "Ywis, but follow me to the feeldes outside the citee, and ye maye have whatevir smal concessiouns that ower royal person may graunt wythout undermining the *status quo*."

Gentil rederes, Ich must saye that methoght Kyng Richard ful of gret eloquence, and yet whan he hoppid off the fence, the crowd of churles followid him nat. Indeed, the only folk who followid hym were two serjeants yn blue uniformes.

"What are you up to?"

"We are Richard, King of England, come to save the citee of Last Vegas."

"You have a long way to go buddy; this is Times Square. In New York City. On the other side of the country."

"Ywis, serjeant," quod the Kyng, wonderly y-pissed, "indeed the end of tymes shal come ful squarely yf ye kepe no ordir among thes cherles who riot yn yower streetes."

"Look buddy, the only rioting going on is your little performance piece here. What are you, an actor?"

"Yis," Ich pyped uppe, "We are wandering playeres from Old York Citee. Thys good man heere was perfominge the Fence-makeres Pageant of the Freake-out of Herod upon the Fence of Galilee."

"Well you need a permit. Get one or get out."

Kyng Richard was a litel ful of ire bycause Ich had called hym "man" and nat "kyng," but he realised that my counsel was good and my trickerie was of gret necessitee in that situacioun. We were ful wel bummed that swich a grete journee across the sea had broghte us nat to Las Vegas. Thogh the Shipman (Curse hys name! Ich shal make hym telle a tale wyth incorrect pronouns!) had taken ower sylver and plate, yet Kyng

Richard had hys undergarment made of perles, from which he plucked oon to paye for ower night at a grete hotel nearbye.

Ich wryte thys as Kyng Richard slumbereth yn a fyne bedde and Ich watche a filme of accioun on the paye-per-voir. The falafel of which I ate ys nat a peaceful guest in my stomach, and eek my brayne is ful of muchel wo, for ther is no thyng lyk the wrath of a disappointed Kyng. Paraventure Ich shal take anothir perle from Kyng Richardes skivvies with which to paye for a moyst and corny ale from the over-pryced minibar.

IV

The next daye Richard did nat want to get out of bedde. He watered hys Scandinavian space-foam pillow wyth salt teeres.

"For Goddes sake," seyde he, "Let us reclyne upon thys double bed and tell sad storyes of the travel delayes of Kynges. How sum have been rerouted, sum put in insufficient roomes, some arrived far too late to enjoy the joust, sum unable to sleep by cause of loude nearby wildfowl. Yet no Kyng hath been so sorely vexed as us."

And thanne my Kyng did cryen ful moore loudely than bifor.

"The moost sorweful thyng of al ys that the balm hath run out. O Geoffrey, if thou be a trewe and feythful liege unto me, go fynde me balm, and stint nat of thy queste until it be founde."

Ich lefte the inn and sighed soore. For what knewe Ich of the purchasyng of balm? Alas, Ich was yn a barbre nacioun, in which smal children mocked me for my litel woolen hatte, and fewe men semed to speke in propre wyse, and yet Ich hadde to fynde a valuable substaunce of questionable legalitee often solde by shiftie merchauntz.

Whan the goinge getteth tough, Chaucer sitteth doun for a litel bit. Yn a tavern, Ich plonkid myn elyvvsh rear on a bar stoole and put my chin in myn handes.

"What do you need, bub?" seyd the Hoost.

"Sum thyng to gladden the herte of a man, and to yive the spirit of vigour to a mannes limbes, and, to seye sooth, good Hoost, sum thyng that may help rectifie thys drasty daye, for Ich have been up but II houres and alreadie Ich have been tasked wyth an impossibil queste to fynde balm."

"Here, have a coffee."

Preysed be God for the smal thinges of solaas in the derkest of tymes, for thys liquor of coffee was moost rich and plesaunt, and did fill my limbes wyth lightnesse and my soule with joye. Certes, yt must have been designed by elves or other spirits that knowe muchel of gladnesse. Yf folk of my nacioun did drynke of coffee in the morning instead of wyne or ale, we wolde probablye have al redy inventid the newspapir and the novel.

"Did ye just saye balm?" came a voys, deep and musicale wyth a smal German accent.

A man in the robes of a lerned clerke did stand next to me. His hayre was lyk unto the crest of a phoenix.

"Buyeth this man balm?" seyd anothir, also in the robe of a clerk, who spoke thurgh hys nose wyth a smal and high voys.

"Yes, good sires, Ich seeke balm. Knowe ye of a balm-seller?"

"Wherefore buye ye balm?"

"To revyve my Kyng. Ywis, to rayse hym up again."

"Thou art caught, foul minion of Sathanas," seyde the tall man, "Thou art a witch, and we schal confirm it thrugh testinge and triale."

"What? How? Ich nam nat a witch ne never have Ich ne been."

"Do nat quintuple-negative me, foul necromancer," seyde the taller man, "O churl wyth the litel woolen hatte, thou shalt wisshe that thou had nevir spoken of balm, for thou art nowe in the grasp of the grete hunteres of wicches and writeres of the *Malleus Maleficarum (or, Witch-Hunting for Dullards)*: Heinrich Kramer and Giraldus Sprengfeld."

V

A crowd had gadred in a local park, for Ich was tyed to a stake, and Kramer and Sprengfeldes stout and bald servaunt Constans had piled strawe, stikkes, and wood for to burn me. As he did so, he kepte soore compleynynge about al moost everything.

But now my trial did begin. Kramer and Sprengfeld stood upon a wooden platform, both holdinge copyes of a large book. Behynde them was displayed a baner, the which seyde, "*The Malleus Maleficarum (or, Witch-Hunting for Dullards)*, cominge thys fall."

"Good lordes and ladyes of the Uppre West Syde," seyde Kramer in a loud voys, "The Devyl worketh many thinges in this world thurgh the power of wicches. Yet feare nat, for among yow are two greate inquisitores who haue togedir y-writ a book about nothyng but the destruccion of wicches. Ywis, the *Malleus Maleficarum* shal telle yow of why wicches are permitted to exist, what maner of evil they cause, and eek how thei shal be found and tryid. Nevir bifor has slightly outdated scholastic thoghte been so expertlye combyned with hearsaye and quotations from Augustine in order to persecute thos who are different! Todaye ye shal receyve a demonstraccioun. For, in the verye herte of ower neighborhoud, we have found a wicche who did seeke to rayse a Kyng from the dead wyth the magicale power of balm. Children of God and loyal citizens, bifor yow standeth a moost wretched man, exiled from the loue of God and held in the twysted embrace of the Feend. Bihold! We shal question hym, correct hym, bryng hym momentarlye bakke in to the lovinge armes of the felaweshep of Cristendom, and then burn hym yn to ashes. Constans, distribute the marshmallowes."

"Man," seyde Sprengfeld to me, "Thou stondest accusid of the cryme of wicchecraft. What saystow to this?"

"Ich did nat plan to animate the dead. That is nat the kynd of thyng that Ich do. Ask any oon. Rede of my blog: yt beth one hundred per cent necromancie free."

"And yet thou seydst unto us that thou wolde rayse thy Kyng."

"Ich meant metaphoricallye to rayse hym, for he was lyinge doun in hys bed wyth despeir."

"Depart nat from the literal meaninge with Kramer and Sprengfeld," seyde Constans, "for the lettre slayeth and thei like yt that waye."

At this poynt, Ich was ful nervous, and the falafel from yesternight helped nat the horribel groaning in the pitte of my stomach. Ich lookid out at the crowd and saw a face. Yt was My Lord, lookinge rathir confusid.

"But my Kyng liveth! He ys there! There ys my Kyng!"

"You mean you did nat just speke of raisynge the dead? You actually *did* it? That is so muchel werse," cryed Sprengfeld, "Constans, seyze that walkinge cadaver."

Kyng Richard did look prettye zombieriffique. Hys eyes were derke y-circled from weepynge and hys face was full pale from the thikke SPF LX base he habituallye wore ("Wilton Diptych White").

Constans, soorely complaynyng about yet moore thinges, grabbed my Lord the Kyng and tyed hym up next to me.

"Good morrow, Geoffrey."

"Good morrow, My Lord."

"Now," seyd Kramer, "We have both the wicche and the horribel result of hys foule magique. Good *frater* Sprengfeld, lat us proceed. We must use the method of scholastique stand-up. *Quaestio:* what is the deale wyth animated corpses?'

"The deale wyth animated corpses," seyde Sprengfeld, "ys diviyded up into fower parts. The first ys the case of corpses the which are imbued wyth the spiritz of demons. The secound ys the case of corpses that are animated by the acciouns of demons, swich as when Simon Magus made a dead dog move (gross). The thridde ys when the corpse was nat trewely dead but the wicche believeth yt to be animated thurgh magique. The fourthe is that sum tyme the wicche ys able to fille many a corpse wyth vital spirit and have them moove and hoold conversacioun with each other, as in the caas of Florida."

"By Seynte Agnes," seyde Kyng Richard, "Yif ye dare burn us, Inquisitores, then burn us alreadye. Ower royal eares kan nat beare to hear thys man go on and on about minutia. Ich suppose ye shal speke next of airplane peanuts."

"*Questio:* what ys the deale wyth airplane peanuts?" quod Sprengfeld, who had flippid to anothir page in the *Malleus Maleficarum*, "The deale wyth airplane peanuts ys divyded into four parts, the fourthe of which ys divyded into two opiniouns. The first part ys that airplane peanuts are devised by wicches to make mennes mouths saltye and thus receptif to the drinkinge of wyne and the doynge of the accioun of lecherye that endangereth soules. The second ys that wicches depryve airplane peanuts of all flavour and moysture and maken them a greate torture and payne for Cristen folk who eete of them. The thridde ys that wicches use enchantid airplane peanuts to flye about at nighte, thogh they do but thynke they flye for yt is all an illusion of the devil. The fourth part ys that the foil of airplane peanuts ys difficult to open, and concerninge thys ther are two opiniouns. The first ys that the difficultee ys a blessinge of God the which maketh men to avoyde the cursid peanuts, the second ys that the difficultee of opening the foyle ys a foule doinge of the wicches who trye to get us to jostle the person next to us wyth ower elbows as we open the peanuts and thus cause rancour and dissension among the good Cristen folk upon the plane."

"That ys yt!" seyde Kyng Richard, "Burn us nowe! Ich have pledged myself bodye and soule to the devil who did appeare in the forme of a marmoset. Ich have anonynted my body wyth the oile of airplane peanuts to flye wyth the Feend. Ich have doon al thes thinges, yif it will get yow to stop talkinge and just burn me!"

Constans turnid to us wyth hys torch, "Goddes bones, they make thes thinges so hot. I knowe it ys a torch, but why doth yt have to be so hot?"

"Lordes and ladyes," seyde Kramer, "the great thinge about the *Malleus Maleficarum* ys that yt ys a book about burning wicches that actuallye burneth wicches. Ye kan use the extra papir in the back for kindlinge and the bakke cover ys made out of blessid, quick-burning spruce."

Ich have to telle yow, of alle the wayes Ich thoghte that the thread of my lyf wolde be cutte (plague, bad blancmange, Bolingbroke, fallinge off of a dirt byke), thys was by far the most unusual. Ich soore missid my Philippa and my sones, and my litel hous in Kente.

Ther was a gret cryinge and screaminge. Methoghte at first that it was me, lamentinge my fate, but yt was actuallye cominge from a woman wrappid in white clothes yn the crowd.

Kramer, Sprengfeld, and Constans went up to the woman, who cryed and wept wondir soore.

Ich felt the bondes of the ropes beinge cut, and a yonge, gentil mayde wyth a knyfe, square glasses, and a cardigan did free me and my Lord the Kyng.

"Hurry up," she seyde, "Let's get out of here while they're distracted."

"Wayt," quod Ich, "Who is that woman? And who are yow?"

"That's Professor Kempe. I'm her TA, Hope."

VI

Fortuna hath smiled upon us. Thogh Fortuna ys rathir legendarilye untrustworthie, yet Ich am glad that she ys nat sticking it to us even moore right nowe.

Ich forgat that myn olde freende, Margerye Kempe, did teech in a universitee in the barbre nacioun of Amerique. She had been passinge by that morwenynge to get a bagel, and had seen the ruckus. Whan she and her

TA had us y-rescued, she broghte us all to her apartement for tea. The oonly flavour she had was "Bittre Sorwe For Yower Sinnes Zinger" but yt still tastid sweet yn the compayne of freendes.

Yt was good to see Margerye. She did saye that her department did nat end up givinge her credit for the two bookes of her lyf by cause they were written bifor she cam to the universitee. So she ys werkinge upon an introductorie textbook of critical theory, the which yiveth her muchel opportunitee to wepen and wailen.

"For oft," she seyde, "This povre creature thinketh upon deconscruxion and suffreth peynes soore."

We toold Margery of ower queste, and she loaned us her car, sayinge that erthely thinges do passe as a shadow upon the wall but nat to mess up the peynt job.

We startid out that aftirnoon, leavynge the citee thurgh manye a bridge and tunnel. Kyng Richard drove verye faste, and Ich fiddlid wyth the map. Bifor we knew yt, we were yn to the forest and wilderness of the land. Ich was ful of gret joye, and we did laughen much and listen to the songes of the radio. Yet whan the first gladnesse of our escape had passid, Kyng Richardes herte chaunged, and his mood, and he bigan to frowne and loure and sigh soore for balm.

We stoppid for dinner in Hautdesert, Ohio, yn front of a tavern full of much noyse of talkinge and dauncing.

Ich just wantid sum roast meat and bread, but Kyng Richard was al hyped up about fyndinge sum balm. My Lord the Kyng saw a straunge man sittinge at the bar and bicam verye excitede, for it semed that this was the maner felawe the which wolde selle and buye balm on a regular basis. This man had small glasses, and his hayre and beard were lyk a gret busshe, al of green. And hys clothes, the which appearid to be a vest and sum jeans, were al of green.

"He lookes lyk he ys half woodwose," quod Ich, "Ich wolde nat truste hym. Peraventure we shal get yn trouble wyth the Inquisitors ayein. This realme semeth to have moore inquisitors than yower average place."

But the tyme for counsel had passed, for Kyng Richard was alreadye talkinge to the man.

The green man was hight Bertilak Marx, and he was a poet and a wanderer. He seyde he was cleped a "Smyte" poet, by cause he was smitten wyth the worlde and also oft smytten on the heed by serjeants of lawe and inquisitors who approved nat of the crazie stuntes he pulled.

Oonly a fewe houres later, we sat yn Bertilak Marxes apartment. Hys wyf broghte us cans of fizzed watir which Ich did lerne was the Ameriqan versioun of beere. Bertilak promised us that hys balm hookup wolde come soon, and in the meantyme he lerned al of Kyng Richard that he mighte.

"Well boys, we must, yes, yes, at once, we must get some balm for this poor exiled King. But now at this exact moment you must hear some of my poetry. I have one that I think is going to be your thing, man. But before you hear it, you've got to do something?"

"What ys that?"

"Cut off my head and sleep with my wife."

Kyng Richard and Ich looked at each othir.

"Hey man, I'm just kidding. Here's the poem. It's kind of this massive protest thing about what society has done to our pronunciation over the last several hundred years."

And in hys elvyssh voys he read hys poem, the which startid sum thyng lyk this:

Vowel

I saw the longest vowels of my generation
shifting, moving hysterically back and forth,
dragging themselves through different parts of the mouth
and occasionally becoming dipthongs.
oddly pronounced sounds losing the ancient logic of spelling
and seeming to have extra letters that crazy orthography can't get
    right…

The which poem went on for lenger than Ich koud palate yt.

Ich wryte this from a bunk bed yn Bertilakes gest room. Hys wyf was kynde of givinge me the eye bifor Ich went to sleep. Ich feele verye uncomfortable wyth the culture of thes Smyte poets and their almoost heretickal ideas about personal expressioun, yet Kyng Richard ys very happy, the which is good to see, and of course he managid to get sum balm. Bertilak hath agreed to go on the road wyth us tomorrow.

VII

The next daye we got yn to Margery Kempes car: myself, my Kyng, and crazy Bertilak Marx spoutynge hys Smyte poetry. We were full of greet delight, for we knew we were performinge the sole gentil functioun of ower tyme: to move forward.

Ower pilgrimage took us on the many roades of Amerique, in the hot daye thurgh the great feeldes, and yn the sweetenese of the Ameriqan night. Kyng Richard and Bertilak Marx did stop at many a club of jazz and blues and manye a joynt of hooch and juke-boxes, and got yn to moore aventurez than kan be in any tail-ryme romance ywrit. All that road rolling bifor us, many tymes lenger than the road from Londoun to Caunterburye-wards.

Bertilak did speke much of Auld Auroch Grant, a freend of hys who was full of greet wisdam and elvyssh lore. Bertilak spent much tyme on the payphonez wyth a map and a notepad, chattinge wyth folk wyth unusual names and assayinge whethir he koud fynd Auld Auroch. "Can't go cross this country without seeing Auld Auroch Grant."

Yt was determined that Auld Auroch had settlid in a large manor hous yn the suburbes of New Orleans, so we directed Margery Kempes car there. We found a verye oold hous. Yt was night whan we did arryve, and we koud see no othir folk.

We got out of the car and Bertilak russhed wyth joye to the front doore and knokked, "Auroch. I got a wacky poet and the King of England here."

"I am not sure what you are talking about," seyde a voys from within the hous, "But if you are looking for the superannuated drug fiend who holds title to this place, he has gone on vacation and left me to guard his ramshackle but rather comfortable abode."

Ther did emerge from the shadowes of the door a great Gargantua of a man, wyth a funnye wide-brimmed strawe hat and a gret busshie beard. He was drinkinge deepe of a can of soda, and whanne he finished he let forth a loude belch.

"Hey man, we've traveled a real long way. Why don't you let us crash here a little?" implored Bertilak.

"What a laughable and importunate suggestion," seyde the large man, "I can see you have no sense of epistemology or cartography and are totally lacking in sense. You ruffians would probably try to rifle through my belongings in the night."

"O Fortuna," Ich seyde, "How faste yower smyle turneth ynto a frown."

"Did you just mention Fortuna, from the divine Boethius's ineffable *Consolation of Philosophy?*"

"Certes, Ich did," quod Ich, "For Ich have translatid that moost wonderful werke ynto the Englisshe tonge."

"Well that changes this situation by a considerable amount. I had no idea that I was speaking to such distinguished exponents of medieval culture. Please come in. I shall prepare both soda and a repast for all."

We did lerne that the mannes name was Francis Duffy and he was born in the town of New Orleans. He spoke of hys great love of hys mother and hys hatred of modern tymes, the which Ich thoghte a litel over the toppe. It semeth he ys a good felawe, al be that yt pleseth hym muchel to heare hymself talk.

VIII

And yet whanne we woke the next daye, Bertilak, Francis, and Margery Kempes car had al evanisshed, presumablie togedir.

We discovered a smal bille ytacked to the doore:

Mad-Boy King and his Portly Porter,

If I tried to explain you wouldn't get it. But Frank needs out of here in a big way. I felt this strong spiritual calling from him. It took all night to convince him, but I'm going to bring him to New York. He'll be all right there. There's no time like the present, so I took your car. I know you cats can handle anything. Stay smitten.

B. M.

"Cursed be thes Poetes of Smyte," quod Kyng Richard with muchel ire, "Their use of their freendes ys moore fre than their verse. Verily, they seeme to be lyk the outlawes under the greenwode shawe, or the peasantes who start collectif agricultural enterprises. They plese us nat. O, Geoffrey, we are half wey to ower destinacioun, and yet we have lost ower transport and eek ower guyde. How may we cross this extremelie large realme wythout an automobile?"

Ich did telle Kyng Richard what Ich had lerned of buses, the which are large vehicles y-stayned wyth many a beverage and sauce, that cram themselves ful of peple and traverse the realm. Thogh Kyng Richard did gretely wrinkle hys nose at this idea, yt semed the best waye to get from heere to ther, and so we went to a bus stop.

At the bus stop upon a bench was a large man wyth greet and wyde handes. His fingres were lyk unto iron, wyth gret spurres of bone and large nayles. He was dressid in a nyce white suit and heeld a contayner of meed on hys barm.

"Go to that etayn-lyk man and ask hym when the next bus will go," quod Kyng Richard, "The look of hym pleseth us nat."

Ich did approache the man and sitte next hym on the bench. The large man addressid me yn a maner of speche that semed curiouslye oold and regionale.

"Deere freend my nama is Grendel, Grendel Gombe. Ich have heere sum mead. Of mead woldest thou drinke? My modor seyde oft that lyf ys much lyk a botel of meed: ye never knowe whethir it will blear yower senses until ye hunger for blood and slaughter good warriors in the derke. But modor ay seyde 'Grendelkin ys as Grendelkin doth.'"

"Bless yow, Mayster Grendel Gombe, no merci. Mead yiveth me a bit of a headache. May I aske yow about the bus schedule?"

"Ye have nyce shoon," seyde Grendel, "My modor alwey toold me that ye koud knowe how a man will taste by lookinge at hys shoon."

Richard grasped me by the shoulder and marched me awey from the bus-stop and Grendel Gombe, "We shal nat take the bus. That character mesemeth verye dangerous, and yif we sit ther wyth hym, Ich have a feelinge he shal first narrate hys lyf storye and then kille and eat us. Lat us fynde sum other maner of passage to Vegas."

And so, seeinge that gret peril stood on every syde and al othir varietees of travel had been exhaustid, we choose that moost wrecchid, miserable, and dolorous waye, that woful path ful of peynes smerte and inconveny-ences loong: air travel.

The verray miserie and discord bigan when we got to the airport. We stood in a gret lyne of folk, weepinge and wailinge and chatteringe. Many a wom-man held an infant that did scream wyth loude voys the whole tyme, and eek manye grumpie men wyth large suitcases did pusshe their suitcases about and make a maner lourynge chiere. The whole thyng was ful wel depressinge.

Aftir this lyne, we reached a great gate over which was ywrit "Abandon all shoes, ye who entir heere." A gret number of sergeants wyth walkie talkies and bad attitudes did wandir about and telle folk to strippen of their clothes and their shoes and eek to put their oyntementz and fluides yn to smal bagges.

"Take off your hat," seyde oon.

"What maner woodnesse spekestow to us, knave?" quod Kyng Richard, who did glower hys best glower at the serjeant. Yt must have been frustratinge for My Lord the Kyng, for, back in Engelond, a glower lyk that from hym wolde have resultid in several fyne Cheshire arrowes intersectinge wyth a mannes sternum.

"Your hat. You've got to take it off." The serjeant poked at Kyng Richardes crown, and thanne he lookid at me, "And yours, too."

"Comfort yowerself, my trespuissant Lord," Ich did roune ynto Richardes ear, "For thys man knoweth yow nat. Thys shal be the last tyme that ye shal be forced to take off yower crown. Do it for the sake of convenyence, for otherwyse we may nat catch ower flight to Vegas, the which connecteth thurgh Dallas and the Worthie Fort."

Wyth muchel sadnesse, Kyng Richard put hys crowne upon the litel gray belt, and he wacchid yt wyth eyen almoost brimming wyth teeres as yt did slyde along.

Whan he walkid thurgh the gate, ther was a buzzinge noyse. A serjeant wavid a stick around Kyng Richard that did beep whan it approachid the place wher hys legges meete.

"He hath underwear made out of perles and silver," Ich explainid.

"Is that a religious thing?"

"Ye koud saye so. He has a real thing for perles."

Whan we had passid thurgh securitee, Ich boghte a magazine and Kyng Richard bought an eye-pilwe ful of swoote herbes and a *De Casibus* Tragedy (Volume II: Nero), and thanne Ich saw an internet kiosk.

"My sovereyn Lord, may Ich have a perle with which to chekke the internet? It hath been many monthes syn Ich updatid my blogg."

"Geoffrey, thou hast sworn a sacred oath to keep ower doynges secret. And Ich knowe thou kanst nat stay away from blabberinge on upon the internet. Woldstow have me on celebritee sytes y-mocked? 'Kyng Richard has boat, car stolen; is forced to remove hys royal crowne yn order to pass yn to a smal grey gate'? Nay Geoffrey, 'tis best to keep thee and the internet far asunder. The internet ys a cryppling addictioun, just lyk ale-coholism or factional politics."

Thys was a bit muchel coming from a man who koud basicallye found and organize a Balm-Feendes guild as well as wryte a self-help book on pearl addictioun. Whan he went to the privee, Ich got on the internet and there Ich found that my blog has been taken ovir by the Lords Apellant. Noon of my passwordes werked, nat even from Litel Lowyses account, and the blog ytself ys full of twaddle from Thomas Favent, Henri Bolingbrokes aye-man.

And thus Ich was much provokid and aggreved whan the folk gan boarden the plane. Ich rolled myn eyen whan a large man heeld up the lyne whilst trying to fill the overhead compartement wyth a suitcase the syze of a smal peasant cottage. Ich grucched and grumbled as Ich got ynto my seat.

"What beth the deale, Geoffrey?" quod Kyng Richard as we buckled ower seat-beltes, "Ower royal persone ys supposid to be the wrothful and occasionally despitous oon. Thou art meant to be the jocound and congenial companion. Be of better cheer."

Yt was wisdom, as it thinkede me, to maken vertu of necessitee, even yf necessitee involved being packed lyk salt herring yn to a stinkye and flimsy vehicle. Ich wolde see the greet cloudes of the skye, and peraventure biyonde them Ich wolde viewe the mocioun of the spheeres.

Ich waxed merry. The fayre men and wommen of the plane did a kynde of daunce, in which they moved the seat beltes about and waved their armes as certayn wordes were spoken. Yt was sum maner of ritual, for the folk of the plane lookid awey yn to their magazines or video playeres so as nat to disrupt the holinesse of the proceedinges. Paraventure the folke of Amerique do believe that their wondirful air playnes flye oonly thurgh the power of daunce.

Ich got up, so fillid Ich was wyth wondir and wyth felaweshep.

"Good folk. Ye goon to Vegas, God yow speede. The blackjack tabel quyte yow youre mede! Ich have a plan to do yow myrthe. This is the poynt, that ech of yow, to shorte with youre weye, in this viage shal telle tales tweye bifor the beverage servyce and aftirward he shal tellen othere two. How soundeth thys to yow?"

"I'm sorry, sir," seyde an attendaunt of the playne, "The Federal Aviation Administration has policies restricting tale telling contests on domestic flights. Please sit down and enjoy the in-flight movie instead."

IX

And came we thus to Vegas The lightes of Vegas looked wonder faire from the windowes of the playne, and Kyng Richard seemed finallye to been at pees, and yet he nas nat yn as good a mood as methoughte was fittinge for swich a joyous conclusioun to ower wanderinges. We who had endured the perils of the sea and faced the peril of inquisitores and goon across the roades of Amerique had finallye come to Vegas; the peple who walkid in derknesse have nowe seen a grete neon light.

At the airport, Kyng Richard came out of the privee holdinge the last thredes of hys perle briefes. "We shal nowe spend thes alle, good Geoffrey." We found transportacioun, and Ich tryed nat to thinke about my trespuissant Lord going commando. Ich pityed the cash exchange guy who handled the perles nat knowinge how close they had been to the "privee council."

Yn the cab ryde, Kyng Richard had me read to hym from Mandevilles descripcioun of Las Vegas and we decyded that we wolde staye at the casino of the Blemmyae, the which are peple of Vegas who have no head upon their shouldres but rathir have their face on the front of their chest where otherwyse a collar wolde be.

We chekkid yn to ower hotel room, the which was the fancyest place Ich did ever staye. Even whanne Ich was hoosted by the Visconti, they did nat putte me up in digges lyk this. Ther was a privee balcony wyth a pool yn the shape of a kidney, and a sette of televisoun wyth a screen so big that figurez on yt appeared of actual syze. Ther was a giant arrangement of botels of liquor ylit by many colours that did rotate, and eek ther was a giant bed yn the shape of a herte. Kyng Rychard had the Blemmyae chaunge the sheetes so that it was white. Ther was no hat racke, howevir, and the mirrours were rather lowe honge for yt was a room designed by Blemmyae.

We purchasid suits of liveree from a Lombard marchaunt. My Lord the Kyng did look the verray prince yn his suit of cloth-of-gold, sylver, white silk, and perles. And eek Ich got a prettye snazzie litel whyte blazer .

"Al thogh for al my regne Ich have pusshed thee yn to relatively boringe bureaucratic taskes," quod Richard to me, "Thou hast alwey been my favorite, Geoffrey. Thogh ther be several poetes writinge yn the Englissh vernacular, we do firmly declare that thou shalt be the best remembred. Treat us wel yn yower verses, Geoffrey. Nowe, lat us goon upon ower last real night on the town."

The Kinges note of finalitee did sore trouble me. Ich wondrid if the *De Casibus* tragedie he read upon the playne was too much of a downer. Ich purposyd to dissolve somewhat the cloudes of sorwe and hevinesse from my sovereyne.

O gentil folk, that was a night to remember, al be that Ich kan scarce remember yt. O the gret joyes of Vegas! The wondirs, selcouthes, and ferlies of that citee of great magique!

We dined upon straunge crustaceans and sundrie shelled thinges at the buffet of the Blemmyae. And eek thogh the sight of a Blemmye shoving a lobster yn to hys collarbone ys rathir disturbinge, Ich just looked down. Ther was muchel melted butter and al was delicious to the taste.

We sawe al the sytes and shewes of Vegas: Sigurd and Ragnar and their trained dragons were most merveilous. Thos men love their dragones. And eek we saw the greet performer Tristram Shindig, who belteth out many a tune and driveth the women of the audience yn to a frenzie as greet as that of the bacchantes of oold. He sang of hys moost revered and we known songes ("She ys a demoiselle, whoa, whoa, whoa") and eek also toold manye long metanovelistique digressiouns about the condiciouns of his birthe, lyf, and opiniouns.

Kyng Richard and Ich went to the high rolleres room of the Blemmyae casino, and did playe of poker and blackjack and the slotted machynes. We drank of manye a martini. Thogh Kyng Richard did seye sum thing of the mutabilitee of Fortuna whan he lookid at the roulette table, natheles he kept in a good mood.

The night turnid yn to daye, and Chaunticleer bigan to crowe. Kyng Richard and Ich were hoolding on to ech otheres shouldres and drunk as a mous, stumbling towardes ower room, whan we ran yn to a man yn a liveree moore fyne and rich than that of Kyng Richard. The man was tall, wyth hayre dark lyk a raven, and dressid al in white and goold and perles.

"What man artow?" quod Kyng Richard, "That goost about yn swich splendor yn ynsult to the majestee of ower kingshippe? Knowstow nat that there are swich things as sumptuary lawes, the which prevent noon but kynges from wearinge the moost precious thinges?"

"I am the King, man."

Kyng Richard as fiers as a leon glowered upon thys man, wyth ful despitous herte.

"Churl. King thou art nat. We are Kyng of Engelond, and al the Kyng thys toun kan hoold. Thou art no thyng but a hound, a dogge. Of what realme art thou Kyng and who made thee?"

"Gee Mister, I didn't mean to offend you. The people made me king. They call me king."

Back yn the hotel room, Kyng Richard was gripped fullye by sorwe and disese: "O Geoffrey, my peple call me nat Kyng. Syn that we crossid the Occian, no word hath come to me to ask for my royal aid and counsel. The peple of Engelond do love the litel lordes that have taken my governance and power, swich as that fat crazie Gloucester and that muscle-bound Bolingbroke."

Kyng Richard continued to sobbe and Ich got hym some tissuez, and then he askid me to leave. Ich wryte thys from the lobbye wyth blearye eyes. Ich must fynde sum place to sleep.

X

And yet sleep did Ich nat. Yf Ich knewe of the daye that awaitid me, Ich wolde have slept, even yf it had to be on the floor of the lobbye. But nay, Ich decyded to have sum of the magical liquor of coffee, and Ich went back yn to the casino.

Ther, Ich sat at a table of poker wyth a motleye crewe of gambleres, the kynde who are still readye to search for the favour of Fortuna whan yt ys almost Pryme. Ther was a woman of the Blemmyae wyth a lowe cut dresse (so that she coud see), a man wyth a large hatte and a larger moustache, a poorly shaven manne yn a bathrobe wyth a white russyan known oonly as "The Gome," and eek a greyinge but beautiful cynocephala who had oones been a model for margin illustraciouns.

"Hey," quod The Gome, "Ye used to be in marginal illustraciouns. Ye used to be big."

"Ich am yet big," quod the cynocephala, "Yt ys the margins that got smal."

The game startid wel at first, for Ich remembrid the counsel Kyng Richard had yiven me earlier ("Geoffrey, it bihoveth thee to knowe whan to keep yower cardes, and knowe whanne to cast them awey; eek thou must knowe whan to pace esily away and when to russhe awey wyth gret speede.") But soon, whether yt was the gret disorientacioun causid by the departure of the martinis from my brayne, or the effects of the coffee, or the madnesse and enthusiasme of the felaweshep at my table, Ich was playinge lyk a foole. Ich wagered al the coyne Ich did possess, and at the last Ich had to bet the litel gold cuffe-linkes that Philippa had yiven me for ower anniversarie. O Fortuna! Lyk the moon thou art ever chaunging, and lyk a badlye designed bicycle seat thou art a payne in the butt.

Ich had lost every thyng, and went wyth gret sorwe to my room.

As Ich entered the elevator, Ich bumped shouldres wyth a large man. Methoghte Ich had seen hys crewe-cut and hys crazed expressioun many a tyme bifor, thogh hys clothynge was straunge.

"What man was that?" methoghte as the elevator (rathir low-ceilinged) ascendid.

Yet the wanderinges of my imaginacioun were stopped lyk a hippye in an airport by what Ich did witnesse yn the room.

My Kyng laye yn the gret whirlpool tubbe, the whiche he had made yn to a maner of green bog wyth the ayde of sum bath saltes. He hadde the stereo from the room blaringe at the top volume, and he had founde balm, for an empty contayner of yt laye by the syde of the tubbe. As Ich entered the room, he brandished a large sword.

"Thou must help me to my end, Geoffrey," quod Kyng Richard.

"Savinge yower majestee, what the heck art thou talkinge about?"

"Ich came to Las Vegas to slaye myself, Geoffrey. That ys the secret. Ich broghte thee by cause thou art a poet and thus able to undirstond swich thinges. Thou kanst record my endinge yn thys greet citee of merveils, aftir a nyght in which Ich have comported mynself oones moore lyk a kyng. Ich thoghte of bringinge Gower, but hys octosyllabiques are moore appropriate for a sea shantye than for the deeth of a roial prince. Ich have nevir toold thee, Geoffrey, but thyn iambic pentameter ys pretty awesome. Peraventure oon daye my story shal be toold in yt, eyther by thee or by sum oothir worthy poet. Ich wisshe for thee to throwe the stereo yn to the bathtubbe and end ower royal lyf."

"My King, lat us nat jump too quicklie to slaye owerselves. Lat us just fynde sum breakfast. Where ys the menu of room servyce?"

"No mattir where! Of breakfast no man speke! Lat us talke of graves, of wormes, and of bookes that in the future shal be ywrit concerninge ower poore style of governance. Lat us choose executores and talk of willes—and yet nat so, for what can we bequeath save the flashie clothes we bought in Vegas? Ower land, ower lyves, and all are Bolingbrokes, and no thyng can we call ower own but…"

"Bolingbroke!"

"Yis Geoffrey, Bolingbroke. The beefye man wyth bad table manners who hath taken my kyngdom. Rubstow yt yn?"

"Yt was Bolingbroke. Ich sawe Henry Bolingbroke yn the lobbye, thogh he was dressid sumwhat yn the maner of a busynesseman of Amerique. O Richard, thou sayst Ich am a poet. Thogh Ich am paraventure nat worthy of that great name, yet Ich have the knowlech and the instinctes of a makere of tales, and Ich knowe yn myn herte roote that thy tale endeth nat yn a bathtub. Ryse up, mighty Kyng, and rouse yowerself as did yower fadir, the greet Prince Noir, and yower Grandfathir, who defeated the Frensshe wyth swich power that no one in Paris spoke the subjunctif for yeeres. Yower enemye ys heere, yn thys hotel. If Bolingbroke ys thy problem, then thou sholdest solve hym."

Kyng Richard roos up from the watir, and Ich averted my eyes so as nat to witnesse his roial bisynesse.

"Thou spekest trewely, Geoffrey, and lyk a trewe knight. Lat us fynde thys Bolingbroke and take back my kingdom."

At my counsel, we dressid in disguises. We had large false feet and custom pantes broght up, and eek berets, and thus put on the countenance of visitinge film-makeres from the land of the Sciapods, the which are a folk who have but oon leg. Wyth gret resolucioun, we hoppid out of the elevator and did look for Bolingbroke. Around the corneres of the machynes of slotte did we seeke hym, and eek throgh the steaminge passages of the buffet we hoppid.

We founde hym wyth a gret route of oothir folk yn a ballroom. At first, Ich worryed that Bolingbroke had broghte wyth hym a gret force of men at armes, yet thes were nat men at armes. Bolingbroke satte around a table wyth several oothir men. The table was covered wyth bookes and smal shreddes of parchement, and eek several dyce the which were reallye verye intricately maad yn the shape of Platonic solids.

Richard and Ich lookid at ech oothir, noddid, and stealthily hoppid towardes the table, losing owerselves yn the crowd, which fortunately had several real Sciapods yn yt.

"Okaye, so who gooth to the PTA meetinge?"

"Harvey schall," seyde Bolingbroke, "And we shal also bringe Susan, Dwayne, and Mary."

"Verye well," the man who was doynge moost of the spekynge seemed to be a monk of sum sort, for he bore a tonsure, and also had large eye-glasses. He peered at a large stakke of notes and eek a foldid sheet yn front of hym ylabeled "Suburbs and Schedules Game Maysteres Screen."

Ich lookid at the sheet of papir yn front of Henry Bolingbroke:

Character Name:
Harvey Johnson
Character Occupacioun:
Mid-Level Management
Mediocritee X
Fitnesse XII
Memory XIV
Putting Up With Stuff XIX
Entitlement XV
Tax Code Knowledge XIX
Glibness XX
Pre-Existing Condiciouns? None
Character Advantages:
Expert PDA User (+V to schedulinge rolls)
Suffers Fools Gladly (+II to meeting efficiencye)
Character Disadvantages:
Distraccioun: III children (VII, IX, XII) (−V to all focus rolls)
Bad Haircut (−II persuasioun)

"Okaye," seyde the man behinde the game maysteres screen, "Ye arryve at the PTA meetinge. The principale biginneth to suggest that the fund-rayser for thys yeare shal have the theme of 'A Little Night Music.'"

"Harvey shal speke up," seyde Bolingbroke, and he putte on hys best Ameriqan accent, "'Dr. Williams, I think that 'A Night to Remember' is a better theme, since not everyone might get the reference. I'd personally be willing to serve on the decoration committee as well.'"

"Make yower 'convynce school administratour' roll."

The dyce clatterid.

"A XX! Whoohoo!"

"A criticale successe. The principale taketh yower suggestioun to herte."

Suddenly ther was a gret brightnesse and a gret flashinge.

"We have yow now, Bolingbroke," seyde Kyng Richard, who had just snapped several photographes of Bolingbroke dressid in hys businessman costume and fully ywrappid-up yn a game of "Suburbs and Schedules" at a Las Vegas role-playinge game convencioun.

"Wherefore snapstow picturez, Sciapod?"

"Ich nam nat no Sciapod," seyde Richard, triumphantlye throwinge off hys fake large foot, "We are the royal majestee of Engelonde, and we have just taken picturez of thee, Bolingbroke, engaged yn ful muchel nerdlinesse. How shal thys playe wyth thy manye followeres who thinke of thee as a cold-blooded killinge machyne and emblem of chivalrie?"

"Shewe them nat," cryede Bolingbroke wyth gret wrathfulnesse, "Be ye kyng or no, Ich shal crusshe that camera."

"Nay, Ich have alredy uploaded thes photos to Twinkler, and Geoffrey shal poost them to a blog."

"But Richard, taak pitye upon me. Ever synce my youthe, Ich have felt constrayned by the ideales of chivalrique masculinitee. Ich have longid to escape yn to a magicale world of storyes, in which I lyved as an Ameriqan business professional negotiatinge the demaundes of raisynge a family, contributinge to the communitye, and attainynge success yn my career."

"Ye kan do that yn Engelonde too, ye knowe," Ich seyde, and thoghte of Philippa, Lowys, and Thomas.

"Kyng Richard, grant me yower mercy."

"Nay, Bolingbroke, that Ich shal nat. For I am myself constrayned, and moore than thee, and yet thou tookst yt upon thyself to destroye al my games and joyes."

Kyng Richard threw hys handes across the table, throwing the scrappes of parchement and litel dyce in al direcciouns.

"And moreover, Bolingbroke, thy outward face sheweth no thyng of thy inward thoghtes, and thou hast an armee of men who bileve yn the strengthe and violence thou seme to adore. So yt ys a fittinge punisshment that thy role playinge game habit be exposid, unless thou kan come to termes."

"What termes?"

"We do planne to present a papir at kalamazoo, but bifor that, we shal clayme ower royal majoritee and take the realme back yn to ower handes.

Thou and thy covyne of flunkies shal make no attempt to stop us. Thou must swere nowe, Bolingbroke, that thou shalt nat stand in ower waye as we winne back ower crowne. And eek thou shal give Geoffrey hys blog bakke."

Bolingbroke knelt and swoore, upon payne of beynge strukke by leprosye, that he schold nevir bitray Kyng Rychard ayein, and Kyng Richard and Ich did leave the hotel wyth muchel joye.

Lo, yt semeth that manye thinges kan be curid by a trip to Las Vegas, and eek yt semeth that Amerique ys a place ful of muchel blisse and blunder. And thus Ich ende myn account, gentil rederes, for Ich did get backe my passwordes todaye and shal bigin agein wyth my poostes of blog. And eek my herte lighteneth, for soon aftir the feest of Kalamazoo Ich shal see Philippa and my hoom agein.

*   *   *

THE RETURN
Geoffrey "LeVostreGC" Chaucer

Whan that May with hir dayes longe had coom, Ich did oones again fynde access to my blog, aftir the many aventurez of which ye have rede above.

May 6, 2009

Yawp!

What a long, straunge trip yt hath been. Tyme sufficeth me nat to tellen yow of the wonderes of Las Vegas, and of the grete egles and swich that Ich sawe whanne Ich did sailen wyth my lord Kynge Richard from Bristol to Vegas-ward, and of the serious mead collecioun that a man can get whan he sette hym out to fynde a serious mead collecioun, and of the grete feere and sentence that did posses us.

The Lords Appellant aren all crookes and berers of false-tidinges, and Thomas Favent ys the maner of man that gooth to Blazinge Fellow and yet hath nat tyme to visit his grand-dame. The re-brandinge of my blog plesid me nat, and so Ich haue taken it y-back. Fight the powere, sistren and brethren.

Ich wryte this pooste of blog from a "Tavern of Halydaye" in Grand Rapids in the realme of Michigan, wherat Kynge Richard and mynselfe haue ordrid "Steppe Brethren" on the "on demaunde" (the which narratif dealeth wyth two Tartar warlord brothirs on the steppes). A-morwe, we get back yn to the car and dryve to that place of which Sir John Maundeville whilom descrived yn his book: Kalamazoo.

May 10, 2009
Exhaustid

The feeste of Kalamazu wyth its revel and jolitee did make Las Vegas look lyk an anchorhold on the moon on a Sunday. Kyng Richard ys still slepyng and hath commanded me to fecchen hym sum elixir rich yn electrolytes. Me repenteth soorely the muchel drynkyge and litel sleepinge. And eek myn dauncing at the gret revel on Saturdaye was a litel iffy. So jocound Ich was that Ich did the *slyde electrique* and now feel sumdeel embarassid. Philippa shal nevir let me lyve it doun. Myn litel woolen hat was nigh lost. O the wondirs of Kalamazu!

Ich shal wryte moore of the feeste latir, but nowe myn eyen do ache. Ich am goinge to pikke up sum thyng for thys headache.

Le Vostre

GC

June 15, 2009
Nickel and Groted

My gentil rederes,

Ich haue had but litel tyme for poosts of blog syn Ich have come home. For home ys where the herte ys, and also where the time-consuming family mattirs lie in wait.

Philippa hath been mightily y-freaked at me for the tyme that Ich spent in Vegas. And alas, Ich haue lerned that fals is the man who seyd that al thing that happeth in Vegas doth remayne in Vegas; rathir, thos thynges that hap in Vegas aren revisited seven-fold upon eny sely man who thinketh to kepe them undir cover. Ich speke nat of harlotrie, for Ich nam so nat lyk that, but let me telle yow Ich haue nat in my possessioun the goold cuffe-linkes the which Philippa did yive unto me for ower last anniversarie. Let us just saye that the table of poker knoweth wher thei might be. Methinketh the redy applicacioun of some diamondes and a trip to Fiji wolde remedye the situacioun, but my finances are so bleak that Ich wolde rather read *The Mayor of Casterbridge* than look at my chekke-book.

Litel Lowys groweth moore un-litel everich daye, and now—by Saynt Abelardes misfortune!—he prepareth for the course of universitee. This somer he hath an internship y-taken, and in the fall he shall enter Oxenforde as a geologie major. "But wherefore geologie, my swete son?" Ich askid hym. And he seyde to me, "No astrolabes."

Every daie Lowys petitioneth me for money for clothes, bookes, swete herbes to applyen to his shouldres and nekke, and licorice and cetewale to chewe for to sweeten hys breathe. Ich do suspecte that *amor* hath kikked my sone in the shins at the same tyme that college hath hym by the nekke-bone, and temperance cometh nat to hys aid in the tag-team. Yet swich is my love for hym that Ich fayne wolde yeve hym al that he wolde aske, but my finances are so bleak that Ich wolde rather wear a "Burn Me I'm a Lollard" t-shirte at Blazinge Fellow than look at my chekke-book.

And al of this procedeth from the economic downturn causid by the brief rule of the Lords Appellant, who did maken everything go at VIs and VIIs.

And eek my job descripcioun hath chaungid, or, rathir, expandid. Biforn, whan Ich was the Clerke of the Kinges Werkes, Ich did sum light administracioun of building projectes and got to travel (bandits notwithstondinge). And yet now ther nys no money to paye eny crafter or artisan, and King Richard hath been zealous with the lay-offes. So Ich have had to make up for the bad economie by also bicoming an amateur mason, carpenter, plumbre, tiler, dyer, weaver, and eyebrow-plucker (ask nat about the last oon). Many yeeres yn the custoumes hous made me nat a jakke of all trades, and Ich haue no idea how to redesign Westminster Halle wyth oonly my litel woolen hat, an abacus, and a knowledge of Frensshe and Italyan verse forms. Helas! *To yow, the Economye, and to noon othir wight, complayne Ich, for that ye be so swyved!*

Ther is sum talk of outsourcing minting to the gold-digginge ants of Ceylon, thogh the commons of parliament may oppose yt.

Ich praye that yow fare better than I. Until next tyme I remayne

Le Vostre

GC

September 10, 2009

Chaucer Sparkleth in the Sonne

Somer ys ygoon-out, singe "ah wel" at a resonable volume.

The world is chaungid overal, and al diminisheth and groweth scarce. The economique downturne hath growne into moore of an economique downfal. My Lord Kyng Richard hath—wyth peraventure a bit too much enthusiasme—made "deep cuttes" yn spendinge on the realme. He hath reducid the system of writs to two: a writ of "brybe" and a writ of "no brybe." And eek he hath declarid that al royal statutes shal not be copyed on to parchement and read in the town square by sheriffs but rathir proclaimed on Peeper.

This use of Peeper for broadcastinge the lawes of Engelond may save parchement and moneye, but it hath causid sum confusion bycause My Lord the Kynge knoweth not much about hys Y-Phone. Exempli gratia, here are the Statute Peepys of August:

@fishmongers_guild lower your pryces on halibut
@laborers calme down or els
@terentusresenourr I love yow. leave the woman with the weirde name and be my industrial gaveston
@the_realm ignore the last tweete
@the_realm seriousli, ignore it or suffir payne of deeth for tresoun

Along wyth the economie, the lawes of the realm, and the privacie of Kyng Richardes crusshes, it semeth that myn happynesse ytself hath taken a downturne. Synce Ich did from Vegas-ward return, withouten my anniversarie cuff-links, my deere wyf Philippa hath removid the pleasure of her compaigyne from me. Ywis, whanevir Ich seeke to speke swete thinges to her, she semeth moore offendid than Margery Kempe at a Johneson and Johneson focus group ("no moore teeres"). Whan Ich do pull mynself bedwards, she doth litel but murmur a "hullo" and continue to rede of hir teenage sparklie vampire love storie, *Vespers*. Thys oon tyme, Ich startid to singe unto her and she seyde, "Geoff, thou art Clemence of Barking Up the Wronge Tree."

What to do? A fortnight ago, Ich did haue sum beeres wyth Tommy Vsk and he had sum ideas.

By the waye, let not the haterez convince yow otherwyse, gentil rederes, for the Uskster liveth yet. Yt is trewe that Dr. Hwaet did replace hym wyth a Cybermonk that knewe only how to walk and recite basic liturgical formulae, the which was beheadid wyth muchel effort and sum sparkes and crackles. It took XXX blowes of the swerd to sever the Cybermonk's metal nekke. Vsk now traveleth wyth Dr. Hwaet and hys companioun Wat Tyler thurghout a multiverse designed by a Welshman. Fantastik!

So Dr. Hwaet came by in the TOWAERDES and dropped the Usk-dogg off for a while. Usk and I were in the garage havinge sum Molessone longenekkes and I toold hym of Philippa's coldnesse. And he seyd, "If she to thee ne do no daliaunce, thou shouldest considir hanging out moore wyth thy man-freendes." He spak muchel to me of fisshing and eek of football and eek of a restaurant yclept "Owls" in which the comely serving wenches do dress lyke Athena and haue fayr foreheads (at leest a spanne broad). And then he gave me a book.

Aftir he leeft, Ich did reede of the book, the which is yclept *The Bromance of the Rose*. It ys writen by Judd De Poitou, and featureth a Dreamer (Seth Rojean) that entereth the fayre garden of the lord of pleasure. Yn this garden, the Dreamer looketh depe ynto the fountain of Narcissus, and in yts cristal watirs he seeth a fayre and delicaat Rose. The Rose ys also a woman bycause this ys an allegorie and allegories are lyk that. The man falleth in love.

So the Dreamer loveth the Rose, but a numbir of evil allegorical figures appeare to nip the relaciounship in the bud. Daungier, Ful Schedule, Incompatible Musique Tastes, Office Gossip, and Uninformed Gender-Based Assumpciouns al rear their allegoricallye ugly heades. The Rose rejecteth the Dreamer and thus he ys in the dogge-house (yt is an allegorie so he actuallie ys in ther wyth the dogg).

At thys poynt in *The Bromance of the Rose*, the Rose pretty much disappeareth. The Dreamer doth seek the advice of Freend. The Freend taketh the dreamer to hys "man cave" and ther thei playen of electrique guitars and the Freend convinceth the dreamer that the Rose ys an inadequate substitute for male companie. The Rose ys forgotten, and the two men go to "Owls" and also Vegas and playen of pool and foozball and joustinge and chevissaunce. It was lyk the average afternoon at Henri Bolingbrokes house, but quieter and wyth fewer beheadinges.

Ich did stop readinge whan the Dreamer and the Freend went to the Russhe concert. Ich take but litel joie from prog rock, and Kevin de Smythe did thys maner of thing so much bettir backe yn the dayes of Good King Edward. Ich wente up to bedde and sadlie closid my eyes, while Philippa burned our beste candles readinge of teenage sparklie vampyres. She was already on to the next oon, *Compline*.

Tommy Vsk, for al of hys travel thurgh tyme and space, had whiffed on the adyvce front. So Ich went back to basiques and chekked out a copye of *The Art of Post-Courtlye Love*. Yt did suggest that "A man sholde knowe those thinges that plese hys wyf."

The oonly thyng that semeth to plese Philippa thes dayes are thos large bookes of teenage sparklie vampyre romaunce, so Ich decyded to reade oon of them. And knowe ye what, lordinges? Yt was actuallie pretty decent.

Sure, the prose kynd of maketh *Dives et Pauper* look lyk Nabokov, but the storie pulleth me yn. Yt maketh me feele lyk Ich am XVtene agayne and "Just Lyk Hevene" hath come upon the radio. Once a goth, alweys a goth (Ich am talkinge to you, Spain).

In this fyne book of sparklie vampyres, Bella Cygne moveth from Essex to Yorkshyre to lyve with her fathir, who ys a sheriff and escheator. At a scole ful of recentlie coyned stereotypes, she witnesseth the fayre skyn and fashion-sprede slow-mocioun hotenesse of the Cu Chulainn clan, the which have all eaten long ago of the magical Irisshe Salmon of Really Good Hair (oon byte of this magical salmon and ye shal have good hair for evir). Aftir Bella doth see the hottest of the clan, Edmund, stop a wagon wyth hys bare handes, fight off twentie churles, and brood so much he did make Angel look lyk Mister Rogeres, she doth realise that the Cu Chulainns are vampyres. But they are good vampyres, who drinke wyne. Ther is considerablie moore sexual tensioun than in *Piers Plowman*.

Yt is reallie very good. Ich did reade al of *Vespers,* right through to *Compline* and Ich have just startid *Matins*. This ys absolutelie the beste teenage sparklie vampyre love storye Ich haue evir reade. And the moore wondirful thing ys that Philippa hath seen me readinge and suggestid that we visit Yorkshyre together. Yt ys amazinge how much good a well-placid "It pleseth me to watch yow sleepe; Ich fynde it fascinatinge" can do.

Thys is a bandwagon upon which Ich wolde lyke to leap. Ich am thinkinge that Ich shal add a litel sparkle to that *Tales of Canterburye* projecte Ich have been werkinge on for several yeeres nowe. Ich am now writing the recentlye-renamed Wyf of Bathory's Prologue.

"Experience, though noon auctoritee / Were in thys world, were right enough for me / To knowe not to date a werewolf..."

CONTRIBUTORS

Brantley L. Bryant is Assistant Professor of English at Sonoma State University.

Geoffrey "LeVostreGC" Chaucer blogs at houseoffame.blogspot.com and is working on a forthcoming poem, a collection of the "tales" of a group of pilgrims on the way to Canterbury.

Jeffrey Jerome Cohen is Professor of English and Director of the Medieval and Early Modern Studies Institute at the George Washington University. He is the author of *Hybridity, Identity and Monstrosity in Medieval Britain*, *Medieval Identity Machines*, and *Of Giants*. He blogs at In the Middle (www.inthemedievalmiddle.com).

John Gower is an illustrious poet worthy of the laurel wreath who has acquitted himself admirably in England's three languages. He does not blog and never will. He deserves both a book of his own and better treatment in this one.

Robert W. Hanning retired in 2006 after forty-five years of teaching in Columbia University's Department of English and Comparative Literature. At some point early in his career he discovered the importance and many uses of humor: as a shield against institutional frustration and despair; as a useful pedagogic tool; and above all as a potent expression of the joy he derives from studying literature (especially medieval literature) and from his many friendships with colleagues and former students. His book *Serious Play: Desire and Authority in the Poetry of Ovid, Chaucer, and Ariosto* will be published by Columbia University Press in 2010.

Bonnie Wheeler is director of the Medieval Studies Program at Southern Methodist University, founding and executive editor of the journal *Arthuriana*, and series editor of both The New Middle Ages and Studies in Arthurian and Courtly Cultures (New York: Palgrave Macmillan). Wheeler has edited and coedited twelve books, most recently *The Collected Correspondence of Abelard and Heloise* (2009). The author of several essays on Arthurian literature, Chaucer, and medieval romance, Wheeler often appears as a TV talking head. She has written and recorded two sets of lectures for The Teaching Company. She has just finished a term as president of the Council of Editors of Learned Journals. She is completing the late historian Mary Martin McLaughlin's biography, *Heloise and the Paraclete*.

INDEX OF BLOG POSTS

Index Postorum Bloggi de Galfrido Chaucer qui in hoc libro continentur
Or, an Index of Postes of the Blogg of Geoffrey Chaucer In This Booke Contayned

Supplyed by a Sub-Sub Librarian.

Playced in the order in which they appearen yn thys volume.

Continued

Index   Continued

Continued

Index   Continued